WE ALL LIVE DOWNSTREAM

writings about mountaintop removal

EDITED BY

Jason Howard

MOTES
BOOKS

WE ALL LIVE DOWNSTREAM
Writings about Mountaintop Removal

edited by
Jason Howard

© 2009
All Rights Reserved.

ISBN 978-1-934894-07-1
ANTHOLOGY

Book design
EK LARKEN & JASON HOWARD

Front cover design
SILAS HOUSE

Cover photos used with permission
CHEYENNE HOUSE *(creek)*, SILAS HOUSE *(faucet)*

A percentage of profit from sales of this anthology will be contributed to efforts dedicated to ending mountaintop removal coal mining in Appalachia.

Visit these online sources for images and more information about this issue:
WWW.ILOVEMOUNTAINS.ORG
WWW.KFTC.ORG
WWW.MOUNTAINJUSTICESUMMER.ORG

MOTES BOOKS

LOUISVILLE, KENTUCKY

www.MOTESBOOKS.COM

Dedication

For the creeks I know and love – Dorton Branch and Straight Creek –
and for my grandparents, who lived on their banks:
Ethel Coots Howard (1922-2005)
Betty Mae Garrison (1930-1979)
Frank & Norma Jean Garrison
Myrtle Sumpter Moore

– JKH

Contents

LAND

PEOPLE

WATER

HERITAGE

Preface

I am very proud to be a Kentuckian. Of all the many things my Creator has seen fit for me to have accomplished, there is one simple fact that brings me the most honor and the greatest sense of self, and that is that I am an Eastern Kentuckian, a proud hillbilly who traces my family back at least eight generations in our beloved mountains – Martin County, Lawrence County and, eventually, Boyd County.

There is no better home than Kentucky. We have a deeply ingrained, almost mystical, sense of place – a sense of belonging that defines us. And it is our love of our special place, and the catastrophe it faces, that moves us to do what we must: speak truth to power.

Sitting here in my home in Tennessee, I am not far from the mountains as the crow flies, but in many ways, I am a million miles away. In the mountains, we still live with enduring poverty, a frustrating lack of opportunity, poor health, education far below national averages, an addiction epidemic, and more.

There's not a doubt that there is a crisis in Eastern Kentucky. Crises are systemic, and the system at the root of our 100-year-long crisis is the unchecked power of the coal companies. We've known it for a long time, and we've fought it for a long time. Every step for justice in the coalfields has been a long, drawn out, hard-won battle – too often bloody, too often lethal. No one has struggled against or suffered more from the coal companies' power than our coal miners and their families.

First, there was the desperate struggle to unionize, to improve working conditions in the coal mines and the unconscionable living conditions in the coal camps.   Then, miners and their families courageously led the fight to improve mine safety and to prevent that slow death known as black lung. Next, the coal companies fought against the surface mining laws in the 1960s and 1970s and the protections they promised for the residents of the mountains. The companies fought the severance tax and the unmined mineral tax. And finally, the companies fought Kentuckians for the Commonwealth over those diabolical broad form deeds.

And in each of these epic struggles, the coal companies sounded panicked alarms. They assured us that each reform, each step toward dignity, empowerment and safety for miners and their families, or each new law to protect the mountains, would signal the death of the coal industry.

However, their cries of swift and inevitable doom were patently false; the coal companies are bigger and badder than ever, with hundreds of millions in profits hightailing it out of the mountains every year. The same is true not only in Kentucky but in West Virginia and the other coal-producing states of Appalachia; let's not forget our brothers and sisters there.

The coal industry is thriving. What's dying is our mountains. And they are dying so fast, so shockingly fast.

In September, I made my favorite journey — my journey home to Eastern Kentucky. The trip is always meaningful and special, but this one was life changing. It was deeply marred by my visit to mountaintop removal coal mining sites. Oh, I had read the books: *Lost Mountain, Moving Mountains, Missing Mountains.* I had read the lawsuits and judge's decisions (some of which were overturned by the man now serving as our Chief Justice, John Roberts), articles and history books and historical fiction, too. But nothing, absolutely nothing, could have prepared me for the trauma of seeing mountaintop removal coal mining for myself. I flew over barren moonscapes where the only thing growing is invasive, non-native grasses. Where once were our ancient, verdant hills and the most biodiverse forests in North America, I saw nothingness.

On the ground, visiting with families in Grapevine, I heard the harrowing stories I had read about: busted unions and miners; lack of ability to collectively bargain for better wages, benefits and conditions; intimidation and bullying at all levels; chronic health problems not only in miners but in the whole community; arsenic levels in drinking water 100 times higher than is safe; mothers putting Mountain Dew in sippy cups while they bathe their babies to prevent their children from drinking anything that comes from the tap, so poisonous is the water; children who paint water as black or red because they don't know creek water is supposed to run clear; collapsed and dry wells; choking dust, cracked foundations and windows; non-stop noise from blasting; overloaded coal trucks terrorizing already nominally safe roads; companies' small promises of mitigation and damage offset that either come not at all, or come too late.

And perhaps most maddening, I saw the coal companies' smoke and mirrors, bells and whistles, the double speak and sleight of hand that tries to convince Appalachia and America that this is actually good for us, that we need it, and that we're better off for it.

Let me be clear.

Mountaintop removal coal mining is a tragedy.

Mountaintop removal coal mining is a scourge on our people and on our land.

Mountaintop removal coal mining is devouring vast acreages of irreplaceable hardwood forests, filling our sacred hollows, burying precious headwater streams, and eliminating wildlife habitat.

And with its monstrous equipment and mechanization, it is also eliminating coal miners' jobs.

The fact is this and nothing less: mountaintop removal coal mining is killing our mountains, the very thing that has produced us, the source and repository of our utterly unique culture and heritage.

I have been taught it is abusive to point out a problem without highlighting a solution. And although the companies would have us believe there is no alternative for Appalachia's people and economy, and our nation's urgent need for energy independence but to blow up our mountains, do not believe them. There is a solution, one our president, Barack Obama, believes in and urges and for which he and Congress have designated hundreds of millions of dollars.

The solution is new power.

The solution is the green collar economy.

It is the future, and I say the future must come to Appalachia, and especially to Eastern Kentucky, and it must come now.

We are honest about our past. We are realistic about our present. And we are optimistic about our future.

Our miners and our coal have powered this country for 100 years. Half of the nation's electricity still comes from coal, 16percent of that coal from Kentucky. The price has been so much more than what folks see on their utility bills – the cost has been our environment, our pristine streams, our wildlife, our health and even our lives. It is only right that Appalachia be first in line for money from the stimulus package to create green collar jobs.

One of the many things I love about the green collar economy is that it puts to rest, once and for all, the archaic argument that we must choose between our environment and our economy. The truth is that has always been a false choice sponsored by big industry.

We can fight poverty and pollution at the same time.

We *must* fight poverty and pollution at the same time.

To do anything else is to slide backwards, and we are so over being backwards.

Let me clear, in case I haven't been. The definition of a green collar job is a family-supporting, career-track position that directly contributes to preserving or enhancing environmental quality. Those new power jobs are perfect for us because here in Appalachia, we love mountains, and we are due for the opportunity to provide something positive and healthy to ourselves and our environment, after a century of providing America with so much of her coal-fired energy.

To our politicians, I say stop spending our tax dollars to subsidize coal companies that are making millions. Instead, invest in our region's precious resources with new solutions like a solar panel factory located in the mountains. Invest in our workers by providing training in new energy job skills.

We live in America, a land of pioneers and innovators. The one thing that actually slows forward-thinking green entrepreneurs and employers is that at present they cannot find enough trained, green collar workers to do all the renewable energy and new power work they are creating. That's good news for our rural communities, which suffer from chronic lack of job opportunities – communities where coal companies have literally run off other industries to keep workers dependent on dirty coal jobs.

Green entrepreneurs, come on down! We need you in Appalachia, land of the fabled self-reliant, hard-working, creative folk who only want to be self-sufficient and provide for their families with an honest day's work.

Coal is a finite resource and a 19th Century fuel, and this, my friends, is the 21st Century. It is time and we are ready for new power, modern power like solar and wind to meet our energy needs. The green-collar, new-energy economy makes use of the fact that enough sunlight hits the surface of the earth in one hour to power our entire planet for a full year.

So how does that fancy fact impact coal miners and their families? One solar panel has 4,000 parts. Think of the jobs that would be created by a solar panel factory in Hazard, in Grundy, in Huntington. There is money for that type of job creation in the current stimulus bill, and coal miners – current and retired – should immediately be given the job training to build solar panels.

Let me tell you about another type of new power we are ready for here in Appalachia. People all over the region are standing up and stepping out for a more just economy and a safe, healthy environment. You are our most precious resource, our most powerful source of energy, and our best hope for a better future.

This morning in my prayer and meditation I was not all surprised that one of my readings was about Mahatma Gandhi, whose peaceful, nonviolent resistance to the British and brilliant civil disobedience joined by ordinary people is the perfect model for us as we ask the coal companies to leave. I'd like to share that reading with you:

> *"I claim to be an average man of less than average ability.*
> *I have not the shadow of a doubt that any man or woman*
> *can achieve what I have, if he or she would make the same effort*
> *and cultivate the same hope and faith."*
> –MAHATMA GANDHI

> *While most people think of ordinariness as a fault or limitation, Gandhi had discovered in it the very meaning of life – and of history. For him, it was not the famous or the rich or the powerful who would change the course of history. If the future is to differ from the past, he taught, if we are to leave a peaceful and healthy earth for our children, it will be the ordinary man and woman who do it: not by becoming extraordinary, but by discovering that our greatest strength lies not in how much we differ from each other but in how much – how very much – we are the same.*

> *This faith in the power of the individual formed the foundation for Gandhi's extremely compassionate view of the industrial era's large-scale problems, as well as of the smaller but no less urgent troubles we find in our own lives. One person can make a difference.* *

My fellow Americans: will you be that one person who makes a difference?

Call your representatives in Washington. Call your representatives in Frankfort, Charleston, Columbus, Richmond, Nashville. Tell them you want new power, and you want it now.

Educate and empower yourselves with the facts, share the good news with your friends and families, and let's bring the 21st Century new-energy economy to Appalachia.

And, don't forget, when your lawmakers do the right thing, thank them! Send them a jar of shucky beans, a homemade apple cake. Write them thank you notes, long petitions with grateful signatures. Phone their offices and leave kind messages. That is how we were raised, is it not?

Let them know you see and you acknowledge and you appreciate their progressive and position actions. And then, vote for them again, and vote for others who run on a progressive and positive platform.

And while you are at it, why not run for office yourself? I am serious.

We all believe in that better future. We love Appalachia; we love our families and communities, our streams and rivers, our forests and fields, our clean water and our precious air. And, of course, we love mountains.

ASHLEY JUDD, Tennessee & Kentucky

Based on a speech delivered on the Capitol steps at I LOVE MOUNTAINS DAY in Frankfort, Kentucky, 17 February 2009

SOURCE:

[*] Eknath Easwaran, *Words To Live By: A Daily Guide To Leading An Exceptional Life*, 4th ed. (Tomales: Nilgiri Press, 2005), 58.

Introduction

Water and mountains have shaped my life. Like many other Appalachian children, I grew up playing in the creek and climbing the mountains around my family's home in Eastern Kentucky. Our small holler even took its name from the creek than ran through it — Dorton Branch. During the summer months, I waded in its current, overturning rocks in search of crawdads. My friends and I would spend hours there catching minnows and planning our next fishing trip, often to the music of Dwight Yoakam and Patty Loveless that drifted from neighboring porches.

Once, just before Wednesday night church, I took a dare from a friend that I could swing across the creek on a grapevine. Halfway across, the vine snapped, dropping me into the water with a splash. Soaked to my waist, I sulked inside to a back pew, my shoes squishing with each step to the beat of "There Is Power In The Blood." My dad dealt with me later that night at home.

The creek wasn't always my friend, though. Each spring seemed to bring a flood and new lines of worry on my mother's face. A child of poverty, she and her family had often been forced out of their home by the floodwaters. Pain choked her voice as she recalled being roused by her grandmother in the middle of the night and led to their front porch, where she and her sister were lifted into a waiting rowboat. After the waters receded, they'd go back, salvage what they could and start over.

She told me this once just after a powerful flash flood had covered the road in front of our own house in 1990. "They hardly ever came like this," she noted. "They seem to get faster and stronger every year."

Statistics from the National Weather Service,[1] the United States Geological Survey[2] and the Office of Surface Mining[3] support my mother's observations, as do testimony from residents throughout the Appalachian coalfields.

"You can't blame this on God," wrote Denvir Mitchell, a witness to disastrous flooding in Logan County, West Virginia, in a letter to the Ohio Valley Environmental Coalition. "Blame it on who's doing it. Massey Coal and all of the other coal corporations."[4]

For decades, Big Coal has laid waste to Appalachia through mountaintop removal mining. Since 1985, more than 1,200 miles of streams have been impacted as a result of this devastation. Over 800 square miles of mountains have been destroyed. Each year, the explosive equivalent of 58 Hiroshima-sized atomic bombs is detonated by the coal industry in the region.

There's a saying in the anti-mountaintop removal movement that "what we do to the land, we do to the people." The residents of Appalachia are realizing this, and it's moving them to speak out. Their voices are joining with others from across the country.

They're echoing from the streets of Manhattan to the mountains of Georgia.

They're ringing from the plains of Illinois to the open ranges of Wyoming.

And now, at long last, they're being heard in the halls of Congress and in the White House.

Many of these protests are collected in this volume. They are the work of students, writers, artists and activists from 17 states. Some are from celebrated writers, others are being published for the first time.

There's the fifth grader who is determined to fight mountaintop removal until he's "laid in the ground." The high school student who knowingly sacrificed a lucrative college scholarship funded by the coal industry by decrying their abuse of the land in an essay. The bestselling novelist who confronts her own lackluster efforts at conservation.

Each piece – whether it is an essay, editorial, short story, poem or song – is an eloquent tribute to the land, people, water and heritage of Appalachia that mountaintop removal is destroying.

What I find particularly special about this anthology is that it establishes the younger writers as members of a national movement against a runaway industry. My hope is that their inclusion will be a first step in a lifetime of fighting for social justice in Appalachia and beyond, to be, as Bobby Kennedy once said, a "tiny ripple of hope [that will] build a current which can sweep down the mightiest walls of oppression and resistance."

Now that's a flood I'd like to see in my creek.

Jason Howard, Kentucky

Sources:

[1]David M. Gaffin and David G. Hotz. "A Precipitation and Flood Climatology with Synoptic Features of Heavy Rainfall across the Southern Appalachian Mountains" in *National Weather Digest*, September 2000, 3-15.

[2]Jeffrey B. Wiley and Freddie D. Brogan. "Comparison of Peak Discharges among Sites with and without Valley Fills for the July 8–9, 2001, Flood in the Headwaters of Clear Fork, Coal River Basin, Mountaintop Coal-Mining Region, Southern West Virginia" (Washington, D.C.: OSM, 2003), 10-11.

[3]U.S. Department of the Interior, "OSM Valley Fill Study: Samples Mine Valley Fill #1" (Washington: D.C.: OSM, 2000), 25.

[4]Denvir Mitchell. "A Heartfelt Letter From The Floodlands Tells It Like It Is." *Winds of Change*, July 2004.

I believe that we need to rethink our strategy of protest; we need to no longer show gruesome pictures of moonscape Appalachia or vent our frustrations on rickety picket signs. I believe that abstracting from normal protest strategy will let us make the boldest and freshest stand.

COOPER BURTON, Kentucky
High School Freshman

A "reclaimed" mountain is pieced together and topped with non-native grasses for erosion control ... the grasses, however, are not even eaten by deer or other wildlife native to the area.

FRANCES BUERKENS, Kentucky

LAND

We come and go, but the land is always here.
And the people who love it and understand it
are the people who own it – for a little while.

WILLA CATHER, *O Pioneers*

Scene of Destruction

As barren as Mars,
unnatural,
the mountain
decapitated
to get coal.

Isn't there a better
way?

Josh Bullard, Kentucky
Fifth grade

Kentucky's Underground Economy

When you fly over the Appalachians of Eastern Kentucky, you can see the gray scars on the mountains, pockmarks reaching far to the north and east that are the results of a kind of strip-mining called mountaintop removal. Most Kentuckians never see that part of the state because it is so isolated, and most people across the nation (which burns the premium coal from these mountains) don't know how costly their cheap electricity really is.

It could break your heart to know.

It takes just a dozen guys with giant D-9 bulldozers about a year to wreck a mountain. They dynamite it, then shove the shattered vegetation and topsoil (called spoil or overburden) down into the valleys, followed by chunks of bedrock.

Everything in this horrific pile dies. Even the streams are buried. Every rain is a flood. Slurry ponds spill black sludge. People living near mine sites hear the cacophony of dynamite, dozers and coal trucks 24-7. Their houses flood and crack. Their children come home from school sick, covered with coal dust. The well water is black.

There is a long history here of struggle against exploitation by coal companies. Now, in ever more dramatic circumstances, people are fighting to preserve their land, their homes, their communities, their cemeteries and their lives.

Appalachians love the mountains fiercely, yet mining is a way of life. Many don't want to protest the destruction of their mountains for fear the region will lose jobs. But nearly two-thirds of the mining jobs in Kentucky have been lost in the past 25 years because mountaintop mining is more efficient than deep mining.

The United States gets half its electricity from coal, and about a seventh of that comes from Kentucky. But coal money has not lifted Eastern Kentucky out of poverty. In fact, the strip-mined counties have the highest poverty rates in the state, not much improved from when President Johnson visited about 40 years ago and declared war on poverty. Eighty percent of the coal, more than $2 billion worth, leaves the state, much of the profit going to distant corporations.

The coal industry brags about reclaiming the land. It envisions factories and golf courses on flat land, and it will repeat this sunny song to anyone who will listen. But the true wealth of these flattened mountains can't be replaced.

It's a loss not only to Appalachia but to the entire nation. According to Erik Reece, in *Lost Mountain*, a new book about mountaintop mining, the Appalachians are one of a kind – there has never been a forest as diverse as this ancient mesophytic ecosystem. When the glaciers retreated, leaving a sort of strip-mined landscape, the unscathed Appalachian forests reseeded the continent. They remain the continent's seedbed, Mr. Reece says.

With mountaintop removal, the ancient forests won't come back in a hurry. The fertile topsoil, which took thousands of years to form, can't be recreated. The timber that might offer economically profitable, self-sustaining industry is flung aside, along with other valuable plants, animal species and minerals. Any miracle medicines the forests might yield will be gone. It's our Brazilian rainforest.

The 2006 economic outlook is bleak for the Kentucky mountains, where people's lives are secondary to coal profits, as they have been for more than a century. Eastern Kentuckians are forced to trade their heritage and their children's future for jobs now. And this ecological disaster promises to seriously harm us all if it continues at this pace.

BOBBIE ANN MASON, Kentucky

Originally published in The New York Times, *5 February 2006*

We Have Met the Enemy...

A country is made of mountains and street corners. A country is the relationship between the two.

New York City. The woman who lives across the street from me is ninety-two years old. Her huge black mutt, 105 in canine years, hangs out her third story window all day, watching people walk by. When fire trucks scream, when car alarms wail, when subways roar beneath and shake the building, he leans out the window, unfazed, panting, paws crossed.

His owner was born and raised in New York City, like her mother and her mother before her. She pays seventy-five dollars a month on a rent-controlled apartment. The neighborhood has changed around her from Polish to Puerto Rican to Gay. She has never been out of New York. She has never been to the Apollo or Central Park or the Metropolitan or Chinatown. Once she went to the Rockaways but she was glad to get back home. She lives in New York, some would say the greatest and most diverse city in the world, and stays within a twenty-block radius of her apartment. She is a small town, New York City woman, and she is not so different from the rest of us.

Human beings are, by our nature, even in this global world, localized.

June in Eastern Kentucky. Mountains rolling in strong black layers. Big leafy pawpaws. Sweet honeysuckle. A sign on a small white church: "Come pray with us, it's legal here." Birdcall. Wind-chimes. A lone trailer, painted sky blue, with a well-groomed lawn and pretty border of begonias. It sits at the edge of a field of leveled timbers. Splayed like murder victims. A yellow dog asleep in the road. Long legged. He stands slowly and ambles to safety when a car drives by. His tail, alert, his ears tipped back, listening to the cool green of woods. Studded with beech, hemlock, oak, dogwood. Swaying and cloaked in fog.

In New York, trees stand like oases in the pavement. At night, they glow under light streaming from windows, the aimed beams of cars. In New York, trees are never in darkness. Trees, the lungs of the city. Brave, stalwart, generous. Wherever there is a tree, the pavement is conquered and subverted. They remember the sky. They fight for space like the rest of us. They are city trees. A beauty more precious because it must withstand. The trees of New York bless us and keep us. In the endless swirl, a tiny sapling in shallow dirt surrounded by pavement: holy.

In Fall, the pagoda trees on the south side of my street change colors first. The north side trees stay green for another two weeks. City buildings and trees create their own seasons, their own timing and environment.

In Spring, I walk past the Limelight, church turned nightclub, and see two dwarf cherry trees, choked with old Christmas lights and tiny stapled fliers, shaking in the wind and pumping bass. They are flowering pink.

There is one tree in the old Jewish Cemetery locked between buildings on 21st Street. In winter, snow blankets the graveyard and stays untouched except for the small trident prints of sparrows. Once, I saw a pair of child-sized footprints leading from a grave to the blank brick wall of a nearby building. The footprints crossed over the shadow of the lone tree laying flat and bright on the snow, more like a reflection, a mirror image, than a shadow.

On 6th Avenue, where beautiful drag queens lean their taut bodies against fences and bet on pick-up basketball games, I see summer tomatoes sprouting in a cement planter. I see zucchini running along red and white bakery strings trained up a thin redbud trunk. Two yellow blooms in the crook of the tree, like a flower behind a woman's ear.

Here, in the city, we plant tomatoes, we plant zucchini, on the sidewalk. Someone may pick them before we do. But picking and eating is not the point. To grow them, here, is the point. We, too, believe in life.

The wonder of carbon, hydrogen, oxygen. That holy trinity. The same stuff of mountains, of rock, earth, water, air, stars, you and me.

At core, in our fibers, in our blood, we are the same. The beauty of difference is that life springs from it, from connection and recombination. The beauty of life is our fundamental sameness.

In the womb, bone and flesh develop simultaneously. There is no order, no hierarchy of one above the other. The city, the country, need each other. Must care for each other. Must rise up in protest for each other. Without each other, we could not define ourselves. Without each other, we could not exist.

City people know the sanctity of a tree, endangered by pavement, by people, by a parade of peeing dogs. That cool, slender shade.

What does it mean to cut down a tree that grows where it will, unlinear? What does it mean to destroy such wild growth? To kill a space, unplanned. The deep space of trees.

What does it mean to kill a mountain?

By three in the afternoon, Lena Sizemore's front porch in West Virginia used to be cast in the cool, rounded shade of Kayford Mountain. But now, when she sits on her front porch on Sunday, the sun strikes Lena in the eye because Kayford Mountain is gone.

A sloped, solid form swaying with trees. A mountain. Some 300 million years old. Giving life to millions. Ants, humans, fox, deer. For generations. A mountain.

It was part of Lena's perspective, her identity, her history. A part of her being.

It is gone. Removed by bulldozers and a coal company seeking the fastest, cheapest way to make money.

300 million years old. Gone. In less than a year.

In New York City, we know the sky in relation to the buildings that occupy it. We see geometrically. Framed slivers of blue. Hexagons of grey. There is no sky without building.

This is our perspective. Our identity.

Standing at the corner of 16th Street and 6th Avenue, I look south and see a gaping blue absence above the jagged hem of skyline. Two twin rectangular shapes: missing.

There is a hole in our profile. A wound of contour. Our mountain, erased.

The Twin Towers were burned and felled by Al Qaeda.

Kayford Mountain's mighty breathing bulk was removed by Massey Energy.

We are all defined by the space we live in.

We New Yorkers feel strongly about our favorite delis, where our faces and orders — but rarely our names — are known. We New Yorkers care about the corner of 14th and 8th, grieve when hot dog carts move and landmark graffiti is painted over. We chart the changing seasons by mannequins in shop windows: from sundress to wool hat. We are connected to our land, grey and unyielding though it may be. Pavement absorbs our 19 million footfalls, our gum. Pavement joins us. Blessed sidewalks, blessed slabs.

June in Eastern Kentucky. Winding roads without guardrails. Steep drop-offs. Light filters through branches, bouncing off leaves. Purple pods hang from redbud trees. Thunder, in the distance. The high clean notes of a redbird. Shushing wind in leaves. Here there is great beauty. And a litany of grief sung alongside the joy.

Clouds reflected in slurry ponds. Land scooped like ice cream. Groan of bulldozer. Rumble of coal truck. This is mountain country. And the mountain is gone.

In its place: bright neon grass, the sick joke of 'reclaimed land.' Thistles. Purple and leggy and stringy. Click of crickets. No bird call. Machine tracks. Stunted trees. Dried leaves and decimated bushes. Honeysuckle covered in dust.

It is a question of identity. From mountain to "site." From peaked to flat. Mountaintop removal is an attack on identity, on shape, a violence of the deepest kind.

I meet a woman whose thirteen-year-old daughter was killed by an illegally overloaded coal truck. She holds up a photograph of a child with bright, eager eyes and says, "She was a good girl."

I meet a man with a tiny Cherokee arrowhead dangling from his neck; he closes his gnarled fingers around it and says, "Found it in my family's graveyard before it was bulldozed."

I meet a woman whose power flickers in and out, a poison disco in counterpoint to the blasts from the mountaintop removal site above her house. She says, with a bitter, mirthless laugh, "I have just enough time to reset the clocks before the power goes out again."

It is a global world, but what of the domestic? How are we connected to each other? By what we give? What we take? What we defend?

The Appalachian Mountains run from Maine to Northern Alabama. They connect us.

When there is a disaster in New York, we get noticed as a city. When someone levels our landscape, it makes international news.

Mountaintop removal is a national disaster. It is terrorism. The lives taken, the thousands of miles of land and stream ravaged. The stolen sense of safety. The irrevocable loss. It is the rape of a place, a people, by an industry that acts with filthy remorseless impunity and politicians snug in their pockets.

Mr. Don Blankenship, CEO of Massey Energy, I'm calling you Osama Bin Laden. What you've done to the mountains and their people is an attack on the fabric of this country. I stood on the pile of the Twin Towers, sifting for bodies. I stood on that mountain that men like you made and handed out gasmasks and oranges to firemen with burning, stricken eyes. I know what I'm talking about.

New Yorkers are connected to Eastern Kentucky. We use the labor and resources that the Appalachian Mountains yield to run our dishwashers, our twenty-four hour laundromats, to keep the bulbs of Times Square burning bright. Most of us live in spaces smaller than trailers, fifty times as expensive, surrounded by nothing but brick. The city that never sleeps. Alive, running, lit, available, open. Using, taking, burning, wasting, roaring.

We are not self-sufficient. We go to the supermarket and buy a tomato, not considering where it has come from – the miles traveled, gas used – for us to eat an avocado in January, a papaya in March. What cool patch of dirt, what water, what bent back and picking hands.

A coal miner dies in West Virginia, and in New York, I flick on my computer, my television. We take no responsibility for energy, for where it comes from, for who digs it out of the mountain, the desert, the sea. We take no responsibility for the mountain, the desert, the sea. A little unthinking motion of finger and wrist. The light turns on.

I grew up in the 1980s, in the Cold War, the enemy so far away. There was a simplicity in that kind of danger. But the threat to the world is no longer as simple as a button pushed, a faceless missile. Mutually Assured Destruction has a much sleeker cloak, and we wrap it around ourselves, each of us. Human damage is our aggregate hunger, greed, modernity. We are all accountable for our way of life – our plastic bags, running water, revving engines – that threaten the planet, the ozone, the Arctic and sea levels. We are all responsible for the human force and gnawing hunger that gives this generation, this era, its sense of the world coming to an end. The threat is more than a stranger holding a finger poised over a button. The threat is us.

And we have control over that greatest of threats: ourselves.

Legendary Speaker of the House, Tip O'Neill, famously said: "All politics is local." He understood that the concerns of small towns and big cities must simultaneously determine the actions of Washington, D.C. He understood the need for the local here and the local there to unite and rise up, together.

Mountaintop removal is something we can control. It is something we can stop. No matter where we live, skyscraper or mountain, it is something we can fight. It is an attack, it is war, it is violence of the deepest kind. The towers fell in on themselves. The mountain is gone. We must reach out to each other. We must save ourselves. There is no other way.

NEELA VASWANI, New York

Who Owns Appalachia?

Chorus   Who owns Appalachia,
       What's happened down through time?
       Those not born and raised here
       Claim what's long been yours and mine

The Creek and Cherokee,
Choctaw and Shawnee
When Native nations roamed
These mountains were their home

The Scottish and Irish,
Welsh and English
Made these mountains home
And claimed them for their own

Repeat Chorus

Coal companies bought her,
Stripped her and logged her
Turned her water foul
And blew her mountains down

Repeat Chorus

These hills hold my soul
King Coal owns my land
Oil barrens own King Coal
It's time we take our stand

SUE MASSEK, *Kentucky*

Puny

The clouds up here are big and chunky and they hover over you, like they could steal your breath quicker than you could call bull. They spread and spread and spread until your eyes get tired of looking for the end of them.

My legs brought me out here and then up here. My heart couldn't have done it. It was shot. My head was shot, too, from trying to switch into somebody that Granddaddy wouldn't want to take riding out to the farm in his El Camino.

Granddaddy did end up taking me for a ride, though. He brought me out here to this big, mean landscape. And then he left me at the foot of the mountains, which are the worst, most torn-apart looking volcanoes you could ever lay your eyes on, constantly fuming clouds and coal dust, and spewing out their insides.

As soon as he got me out here to the end of the world, he ditched me. I wish I could say he had been doing something important when the ground turned in two and he dropped off this earth. But he was just standing at the gas stop down by Sunny Creek Baptist, staring at the price of gas going up, smoking and swearing, when his heart came out of his chest.

There was a woman who wanted to take me home. But her mouth made me think of a cave or a tobacco leaf and I had had enough of both for one lifetime.

My legs road-runnered me up the nearest hillside past the trumpet vine flowers that I never knew I wanted to see, that I never knew I'd want to lay by Granddaddy's fat dead body, by his worn-out sticker.

My legs kept taking me up to this point were I could see how everything in the world pointed up, pointed towards the place where maybe Mama was and where maybe Granddaddy would get through to after he did his time in purgatory. It felt good to see that everything else was reaching up, too, wanting as bad as me to be up there with Mama.

In a lot of directions they were treating those mountains bad, blowing them to the moon and back, but when I squinted my eyes just so and looked in the other direction, the land was so big. There was a set of gold colored trees that made me feel warm. That big land made you feel like just a puny popcorn kernel waiting to be popped. It felt good to be cradled like that, by that warmth that wouldn't make you pop until you were ready to pop.

I would've turned off every single light bulb in Granddaddy's house if it would've kept them from tearing down those mountains that made you feel so safe. And so small.

Lucy Flood, Idaho & Kentucky

My Beloved, Lost But Not Forgotten

As I sit here, my thoughts turn to all those who have loved and lost. The tears fall silently down my cheeks, falling as the rain fell down a once beautiful mountain slope. No one hears the pain as they fall, but the grief is there nevertheless. A pain so deep it will be felt by my seed many years in the future; long after my body has returned unto the mountain soil. What! Are you speaking of love and romance, you say? Yes, of love and romance no man can hope to match with mere physical touch. A spiritual love of the land and place in which the mountaineers feel to the soul and beyond time.

I fell in love with the mountains at the ripe old age of fifteen and three-quarters. That was an important time for me. A time of awakening, a time of learning and grasping what life really means. I can still remember standing on an old rugged back porch and thinking, "Ah! These may not be the largest mountains in the world, but their closeness to me makes me feel strangely safe and loved." I had come home without ever being here before; I had come to a realization of God's love and a gentle breeze kissed my face, and I was entranced by the sheer beauty of God's magical land, Appalachia. The word slips off my tongue as if an endearment so sacred one whispers it to the air so it is carried to the land, the stream and mountain nearby.

Not wishing to disturb the scene before me, I tiptoed close to the big oak near the stream and watched a doe and a young fawn quenching their thirst. The slightest movement from me drew the deer back into the thicket, but not before I saw the buck, proud and strong on the edge of the woods with a watchful eye in my direction.

Awesome, this new land I had ventured into. Wonderfully, protective of its own and yet gently inviting me to be a part of all that the land entailed. As the wind caressed my hair, I felt free, unencumbered by the cares of youth and the decisions awaiting me in the future. I had never known such joy; laughter sprang up within me that I could not have predicted and did not try to restrain. I laughed out loud, a bountiful laugh to the flowers and the trees surrounding me. The echoes of my laughter returned to me in answer to my happiness, lovingly receiving my emotional expression of adoration. I could be myself here: unafraid, somehow stronger just by standing next to my newly discovered love. A love of a lifetime is what every young woman longs for, and I had found mine in the land and the people here in the foothills of West Virginia.

For 19 years, I lived as one with my beloved: my land my family and my Appalachian way of life. Then came the time I would come to call growth! I was no longer a young woman just flourishing in the light of my beloved; I had to become a warrior fighting for the land and people that had given me so much through the years. I had the strength with so many gathering with me in the fight. Surely, the Appalachians could stop this invasion to our hearts and peace of mind, but not so. It was not meant to be. My beloved was trodden down and murdered a little at a time. Piece by piece the aliens came and destroyed my beloved. Raping and replacing with a mere morsel of what we once had. How could anyone wish to tear away its essence, its beauty? Ripped away are hardwoods, medicines and streams, leaving a void in the heart just as a lover's departure.

So final, so certain has the death of my beloved become reality, my soul cries out, "Come back, come back! Oh, return to me, my majestic one, my strong and upright one. Whisper once more your secrets to me. Tell again how my ancestors once walked for miles in the snow to their one-room schoolhouses, of the streams full of water and life flowing through our lives, void of pipes and slurry. Oh, beloved! Leave me not. I will miss you greatly and will mourn with all those who have loved and lost you."

Still my tears fall silently. No sound is made to stop them.

PATRICIA BRAGG, *West Virginia*

Gone

Millions of years
in forming,
once plentiful,
beautiful,
lively
and joyful.

Animals and trees were
everywhere, then somebody decided
that coal is worth more
than our heritage
and the ancient and biologically
diverse Appalachian Mountains.

Deer, rabbits, squirrels
are murdered
with bulldozers and explosives. Destroyed
within moments.

The plants and animals the coal companies bring in
aren't always native –
with predators gone, they become a nuisance, threaten
the natives to the area.

Now the beauty is gone.

And all we have left of our mountains
are memories of how they
used to be, the worries
of how they will be, and
a hope that we can
change before it's too late.

JUSTIN KENNADY, *Kentucky*
Fifth grade

Apathy

My mind wanders a gossamer hill
through ghost thoughts of what might-have-been
but never will, reality – the ho-hum dream drum
day-to-day existence beats the pattern for my feet
that roam the humming of the street light speeding
in my head, blinds me from the truth that lies
beyond the Bluegrass alibis where
mountains used to stand for
something but now
don't stand at all.

DONNA MCCLANAHAN, Kentucky

A Mountaintop Experience

When God created heaven and earth, he looked at his handiwork and declared it "good." Each act of creation received this word of divine satisfaction. As time passed, only one part of God's creation became the subject of disappointment and anger – ourselves. But after the destruction of the Flood, God declared he would not repeat this act. As Christians, we believe that God even took human form in order to redeem us. The apostle Paul believed that redemption extended to the whole of creation. ("The creation itself will be set free from its bondage to decay..." – *Romans 8:21*)

Throughout time God has shown his continued love for creation. But God seems to have a special love for mountains. Time and again, when God wants to meet Man, he chooses mountains. Abraham was asked to sacrifice Isaac on a mountain. Moses was called to receive the Ten Commandments upon a mountain, and God showed him the Promised Land from a mountain. Jesus preached his greatest sermon upon a mountain. Monks in medieval England and Ireland saw mountains as "thin places," places where it is especially easy to pray and communicate with God. *Psalm 68* even speaks of God having a mountain for his abode.

As a beloved part of creation, mountains themselves have been seen as participating in praising and thanking God. In the Psalms and elsewhere, the mountains and hills are described as skipping for joy. If we may speak to God from atop a mountain, the mountains themselves also sing praise to their Creator in their own special language.

Mountains have also given us enduring spiritual metaphors. Paul, in his first letter to the Corinthians, speaks of a faith that can move mountains (*I Cor. 13:2*), though he goes on to add that without love, such faith is meaningless. Paul here is speaking of faith so strong it can accomplish the impossible. Moving mountains was meant to stay just that – impossible.

What then can we say about mountaintop removal? First we must acknowledge that man has indeed developed the capability to move mountains. We have that capability – but should we exercise it? Clearly God did not mean that we should, for to literally move a mountain makes the metaphor meaningless.

But mountaintop removal does far more spiritual damage than the destruction of language. The Appalachian Mountains, according to geologists, are among the oldest in the world. This means they are among the first mountains God created. The beautiful Appalachian Mountains are a balm to the soul. Their destruction speaks of the soul's sickness.

If God loves mountains so much, and scripture is clear that he does, how must we grieve him when we destroy them? When scripture bids us look up to the hills, from whence comes our help, how may we when those hills are gone? Where is hope or comfort then, when the signs of hope given by God, the mountains, have been leveled?

Psalm 24 tells us that the earth, and the fullness thereof, belongs to the Lord. Woe on us if we continue to destroy what is the Lord's. But the woe, the shame, is for more than just disobeying God. When we destroy the beautiful, the sacred mountains, we reject God's gift. It is a gift near to the heart of God. To destroy the mountains is to spit in the face of God. It must break his heart.

DENISE GIARDINA, *West Virginia*

Sweet Marie

Marie, it's hard to see you
Give yourself away like that
Even though I am one of those
Who chooses to take

No it ain't right, but what's done is done

Chorus   There'll be no riots in the streets
                No one to scream your name
                'Cause you have always been there
                And you will remain, Marie?

Marie, the trees have stopped growin'
And the water's turning black
They might call it love but they want you for something
You'll eventually lack

I hear the sound of steel slowin' steel
As the platform comes in view
They're takin' you away
On that evenin' train

Repeat Chorus

Oh, Sweet Marie
Oh, Sweet Marie

BEN SOLLEE & DANIEL MARTIN MOORE, *Kentucky*

Moving Mountains

Not since the glaciers pushed toward these ridgelines a million years ago have the Appalachian Mountains been as threatened as they are today. But the coal-extraction process decimating this landscape, known as mountaintop removal, has generated little press beyond the region. The problem, in many ways, is one of perspective. From interstates and lowlands, where most communities are clustered, one simply doesn't see what is happening up there. Only from the air can you fully grasp the magnitude of the devastation. If you were to board, say, a small prop plane at Zeb Mountain, Tennessee, and follow the spine of the Appalachian Mountains up through Kentucky, Virginia and West Virginia, you would be struck not by the beauty of a densely forested range older than the Himalayas, but rather by inescapable images of ecological violence. Near Pine Mountain, Kentucky, you'd see an unfolding series of staggered green hills quickly give way to a wide expanse of gray plateaus pocked with dark craters and huge black ponds filled with a toxic byproduct called coal slurry. The desolation stretches like a long scar up the Kentucky-Virginia line, before eating its way across southern West Virginia.

Central Appalachia provides much of the country's coal, second only to Wyoming's Powder River Basin. In the United States, 100 tons of coal are extracted every two seconds. Around 70 percent of that coal comes from strip mines, and over the last 20 years, an increasing amount comes from mountaintop removal sites. In the name of corporate expedience, coal companies have turned from excavation to simply blasting away the tops of the mountains. To achieve this, they use the same mixture of ammonium nitrate and diesel fuel that Timothy McVeigh employed to level the Murrow Building in Oklahoma City – except each detonation is 10 times as powerful, and thousands of blasts go off each day across central Appalachia. Hundreds of feet of forest, topsoil, and sandstone – the coal industry calls all of this "overburden – are unearthed so bulldozers and front-end loaders can more easily extract the thin seams of rich, bituminous coal that stretch in horizontal layers throughout these mountains. Almost everything that isn't coal is pushed down into the valleys below. As a result, 6,700 "valley fills" were approved in central Appalachia between 1985 and 2001. The Environmental Protection

Agency estimates that over 700 miles of healthy streams have been completely buried by mountaintop removal and thousands more have been damaged. Where there once flowed a highly braided system of headwater streams, now a vast circuitry of haul roads winds through the rubble. From the air, it looks like someone had tried to plot a highway system on the moon.

Serious coal mining has been going on in Appalachia since the turn of the 20th Century. But from the time World War II veterans climbed down from tanks and up onto bulldozers, the extractive industries in America have grown more mechanized and more destructive. Ironically, here in Kentucky where I live, coal-related employment has dropped 60 percent in the last 15 years; it takes very few men to run a strip mine operation, with giant machines doing most of the clearcutting, excavating, loading, and bulldozing of rubble. And all strip mining – from the most basic truck mine to mountaintop removal – results in deforestation, flooding, mudslides and the fouling of headwater streams.

Alongside this ecological devastation lies an even more ominous human dimension: an Eastern Kentucky University study found that children in Letcher County, Kentucky, suffer from an alarmingly high rate of nausea, diarrhea, vomiting and shortness of breath—symptoms of something called blue baby syndrome – that can all be traced back to sedimentation and dissolved minerals that have drained from mine sites into nearby streams. Long-term effects may include liver, kidney and spleen failure, bone damage and cancers of the digestive track. Erica Urias, who lives on Island Creek in Grapevine, Kentucky, told me she has to bathe her two-year-old daughter in contaminated water because of the mining around her home. In McRoberts, Kentucky, the problem is flooding. In 1998, Tampa Energy Company (TECO) started blasting along the ridgetops above McRoberts. Homes shook and foundations cracked. Then TECO sheared off all of the vegetation at the head of Chopping Block Hollow and replaced it with the compacted rubble of a valley fill. In a region prone to flash floods, nothing was left to hold back the rain; this once forested watershed had been turned into an enormous funnel. In 2002, three so-called "hundred-year floods" happened in 10 days. Between the blasting and the flooding, the people of McRoberts have been nearly flushed out of their homes,

Consider the story of Debra and Granville Burke. First the

blasting above their house wrecked its foundation. Then the floods came. Four times, they wiped out the Burkes' garden, which the family depended on to get through the winter. Finally, on Christmas morning 2002, Debra Burke took her life. In a letter published in a local paper, her husband wrote: "She left eight letters describing how she loved us all but that our burdens were just getting too much to bear. She had begged for TECO to at least replace our garden, but they just turned their back on her. I look back now and think of all the things I wish I had done differently so that she might still be with us, but mostly I wish that TECO had never started mining above our home."

In the language of economics, Debra Burke's death was an externality – a cost that simply isn't factored into the price Americans pay for coal. And that is precisely the problem. Last year, American power plants burned over a billion tons of coal, accounting for over 50 percent of this country's electricity use. In Kentucky, 80 percent of the harvested coal is sold and shipped to 22 other states. Yet it is the people of Appalachia who pay the highest price for the rest of the country's cheap energy – through contaminated water, flooding, cracked foundations and wells, bronchial problems related to breathing coal dust, and roads that have been torn up and turned deadly by speeding coal trucks. Why should large cities like Phoenix and Detroit get the coal but be held accountable for none of the environmental consequences of its extraction? And why is a Tampa-based energy company – or Peabody Coal in St. Louis, or Massey Energy in Richmond, Virginia – allowed to destroy communities throughout Appalachia? As my friend and teacher the late Guy Davenport once wrote, "Distance negates responsibility."

The specific injustice that had drawn together a group of activists calling themselves the Mountain Justice Summer Movement, was the violent death of three-year-old Jeremy Davidson. At 2:30 in the morning on August 30, 2004, a bulldozer, operating without a permit above the Davidsons' home, dislodged a thousand-pound boulder from a mountaintop removal site in the town of Appalachia, Virginia. The boulder rolled 200 feet down the mountain before it crushed to death the sleeping child.

But Davidson's death is hardly an isolated incident. In West Virginia, 14 people drowned in the last three years because of floods and mudslides caused by mountaintop removal, and in Kentucky,

50 people have been killed and over 500 injured in the last five years by coal trucks, almost all of which were illegally overloaded.

On the third of July, I drove across 10,000 acres of boulder-strewn wasteland that used to be Kayford Mountain, West Virginia – one of the most hideous mountaintop removal sites I've seen. But right in the middle of the destruction, rising like a last gasp, is a small knoll of untouched forest. Larry Gibson's family has lived on Kayford Mountain for 200 years. And most of his relatives are buried in the family cemetery, where almost every day Gibson has to clear away debris known as "flyrock" from the nearby blasting.

Last year, Kenneth Cane, the great-grandson of Crazy Horse, came to this cemetery. Surrounded by Gibson and his kin, Cane led a prayer vigil. Then he turned to Gibson, put a hand on his shoulder, and said, "How does it feel to lose your land?"

"What was I going to say to him?" Gibson asked me, sitting at the kitchen table of his small, two-room cabin beneath a single, solar-powered fluorescent bulb. Certainly an Oglala Lakota heir would know something about having mountains stolen away by men in search of valuable minerals.

A short, muscular man, Gibson is easily given to emotion when he starts talking about his homeplace – both what remains of it and what has been destroyed. Forty seams of coal lie beneath his 50 acres. Gibson could be a millionaire many times over, but because he refuses to sell, he has been shot at and run off his own road. One of his dogs was shot and another hanged. A month after my visit, someone sabotaged his solar panels. In 2000 Gibson walked out onto his porch one day to find two men dressed in camouflage, approaching with gas cans. They backed away and drove off, but not before they set fire to an empty cabin that belongs to one of Gibson's cousins. This much at least can be said for the West Virginia coal industry: it has perfected the art of intimidation.

Gibson knows he isn't safe. "This land is worth $450 million," he told me, "so what kind of chances do I have?" But he hasn't backed down. He travels the country telling his story and has been arrested repeatedly for various acts of civil disobedience. When Gibson talks to student groups, he asks them, "What do you hold so dear that you don't have a price on it? And when somebody comes to take it, what will you do? For me, it's this mountain and the memories I had here as a kid. It was a hard life, but here I was equal to everybody. I didn't

WE ALL LIVE DOWNSTREAM

know I was poor until I went to the city and people told me I was. Here I was rich."

Just down the mountain from Larry Gibson's home, in the town of Rock Creek, stands the Marsh Fork Elementary School. Back in 2004, Ed Wiley, a 47-year-old West Virginian who spent years working on strip mines, was called by the school to come pick up his granddaughter Kayla because she was sick. "She had a real bad color to her," Wiley told me. The next day the school called again because Kayla was ill, and the day after that. Wiley started flipping through the sign-out book and found that 15 to 20 students went home sick every day because of asthma problems, severe headaches, blisters in their mouths, constant runny noses and nausea. In May 2005, when Mountain Justice volunteers started going door-to-door in an effort to identify citizens' concerns and possibly locate cancer clusters, West Virginia activist Bo Webb found that 80 percent of parents said their children came home from school with a variety of illnesses. The school, a small brick building, sits almost directly beneath a Massey Energy subsidiary's processing plant where coal is washed and stored. Coal dust settles like pollen over the playground. Nearly three billion gallons of coal slurry, which contains extremely high levels of mercury, cadmium, and nickel, are stored behind a 385-foot-high earthen dam right above the school.

In 1972, a similar coal impoundment dam collapsed at Buffalo Creek, West Virginia, killing 125 people. Two hundred and eighty children attend the Marsh Fork Elementary School. It is unnerving to imagine what damage a minor earthquake, a heavy flash flood, or a structural failure might do to this small community. And according to documents that longtime activist Judy Bonds obtained under the Freedom of Information Act, the pond is leaking into the creek and groundwater around the school. Students often cannot drink from the water fountains. And when they return from recess, their tennis shoes are covered with black coal dust.

Massey responded to complaints about the plant by applying for a permit to enlarge it, with a new silo to be built even closer to the school. It was this callousness that led to the first major Mountain Justice direct action on the last day of May. About a hundred out-of-state activists, alongside another hundred local citizens, gathered at the school and marched next door to the Massey plant.

Inez Gallimore, an 82-year-old woman whose granddaughter

attended the elementary school, walked up to the security guard and asked for the plant superintendent to come down and accept a copy of the group's demands that Massey shut down the plant. When the superintendent refused, Gallimore sat down in the middle of the road, blocking trucks from entering or leaving the facility. When police came to arrest her, they had to help Gallimore to her feet, but not before TV cameras recorded her calling Massey Energy a "terrorist organization."

Three other protesters took the woman's place and were arrested. Three more followed.

In the end, the media coverage at the Marsh Fork rally prompted West Virginia governor Joe Manchin to promise he would put together an investigative team to look into the citizens' concerns. But seven days after that promise, on June 30, Massey received its permit to expand the plant.

The history of resource exploitation in Appalachia, like the history of racial oppression in the South, follows a sinister logic – keep people poor and scared so that they remain powerless. In the 19th Century, mountain families were actually doing fairly well farming rich bottomlands. But populations grew, farms were subdivided, and then northern coal and steel companies started buying up much of the land, hungry for the resources that lay below. By the time the railroads reached headwater hollows like McRoberts, Kentucky, men had little choice but to sell their labor cheaply, live in company towns, and shop in overpriced company stores. "Though he might revert on occasion to his ancestral agriculture," wrote coal field historian Harry Caudill, "he would never again free himself from dependence upon his new overlords." In nearly every county across central Appalachia, King Coal had gained control of the economy, the local government and the land.

In the decades that followed, less obvious tactics kept Harlan County one of the poorest places in Appalachia. Activist Teri Blanton, whose father and brother were Harlan County miners, has spent many years trying to understand the patterns of oppression that hold the Harlan County high school graduation rate at 59 percent and the median household income at $18,665. "We were fueling the whole United States with coal," she said of the last hundred years in Eastern Kentucky. "And yet our pay was lousy, our education was lousy and they destroyed our environment. As long as you have a polluted community, no other industry is going to locate there. Did they keep us uneducated because it was easier to control us then? Did they keep other industries out because then they can keep our wages low? Was it all by design?" Whether one detects motive or not, this much is clear – 41 years after Lyndon Johnson stood on a miner's porch in adjacent Martin County and announced his War on Poverty, the poverty rate in central and southern Appalachia stands at 30 percent, right where it did in 1964. What's more, maps generated by the Appalachian Regional Commission show that the poorest counties – those colored deep red for "distressed – are those that have seen the most severe strip mining and the most intense mountaintop removal.

There is a galling irony in the fact that the Fourteenth Amendment, which was designed to protect the civil liberties of recently freed African slaves, was later interpreted in such a way as to give corporations like Massey all of the rights of "legal persons," while requiring little of the accountability that we expect of individuals. Because coal companies are not individuals, they often operate without the moral compass that would prevent a person from contaminating a neighbor's well, poisoning the town's drinking water or covering the local school with coal dust. This situation is compounded by federal officials who often appear more loyal to corporations than to citizens. Consider the case of Jack Spadaro, a whistleblower who was forced out of his job at the U.S. Department of Labor's Mine Safety and Health Administration (MSHA) precisely because he tried to do his job – protect the public from mining disasters.

When the Buffalo Creek dam in West Virginia broke in 1972, Spadaro, a young mining engineer at the time, was brought in to investigate. He found that the flood could have been prevented by better dam construction, and he spent the next 30 years of his career at MSHA investigating impoundment dams. So when a 300-million-gallon slurry pond collapsed in Martin County, Kentucky, in 2000, causing one of the worst environmental disasters this side of the Mississippi, Spadaro was again named to the investigating team. What he found was that Massey had known for 10 years that the pond was going to break. Spadaro wanted to charge Massey with criminal negligence. There was only one problem. Elaine Chao, Spadaro's boss at the Department of Labor, is also Kentucky Republican Senator

Mitch McConnell's wife; and it is McConnell, more than anyone else in the Senate, who advocates that corporations are persons that, as such, can contribute as much money as they want to electoral campaigns. It turns out that Massey had donated $100,000 to a campaign committee headed by McConnell. Not surprisingly, Spadaro got nowhere with his charges. Instead, someone changed the lock on his office door and he was placed on administrative leave.

Spadaro's story seems to validate what many coalfield residents have been contending for years – that the very agencies that should be regulating corporations are instead ignoring the law, breaking the law and at times even rewriting the law in their favor, as when deputy secretary of the Department of the Interior (and former coal lobbyist) Stephen Griles instructed his staff to rewrite a key provision of the Clean Water Act to reclassify all waste associated with strip mining as merely benign "fill material." A federal judge rejected that change, arguing that "only the United States Congress can rewrite the Act to allow fills with no purpose or use but the deposit of waste," but the change was upheld in 2003 by the U.S. 4th Circuit Court – on which sat John Roberts, now Chief Justice of the Supreme Court.

On July 8, I was standing in Richmond, Virginia's, Monroe Park, next to a pretty girl with pierced lips and colorful yarn braided into her blond hair, as Mountain Justice activists prepared to march ten blocks to the headquarters of Massey Energy to demand the closure of the prep plant behind Marsh Fork Elementary School.

Short, gray-haired Judy Bonds stepped to the mike and told the crowd, "I'm honored to be here with you. We're an endangered species, we hillbillies. Massey Energy is terrorizing us in Appalachia. Little old ladies in their seventies can't even sit on their porches. They have to cut their grass wearing respirators. That's how these people have to live. The coal companies are the real terrorists in America. And we're going to expose them for the murdering, lying thieves that they are."

With that, the marchers started down Franklin Avenue, behind a long banner stretching across the street that read: INDUSTRIAL CAPITALISM KILLS OUR LAND AND PEOPLE. They marched on past blooming crepe myrtle trees and exclusive clubs. Then they hung a right, and suddenly we were all standing in front of a granite-and-concrete monolith that had been cordoned off with yellow tape.

Don Blankenship is the CEO of Massey, a man that many feel has dubious access to the Bush administration. Records show that from 2000 to 2004, whenever MSHA assistant secretary David Lauriski weakened a mine safety standard, it usually followed a meeting with Blankenship.

The stated goal of the Richmond march was to get Blankenship to personally accept Mountain Justice's demand that Massey shut down the prep plant next to the Marsh Fork Elementary School. Of course, everyone knew that wasn't going to happen.

On April 9, 1963, snarling police dogs pinned a black protester to the ground on a Birmingham, Alabama, street. *The New York Times* was there to report it. Martin Luther King Jr. and the Southern Christian Leadership Conference were ecstatic. "We've got a movement, we've got a movement!" one member exclaimed. "They brought out the dogs." Without the arrests in Birmingham, and the press that followed, John Kennedy would not have pushed for the Civil Rights Act, and without daily attempts to register black voters in Selma, and the violence that followed, Lyndon Johnson would have dragged his feet for years on the Voting Rights Act. King and the SCLC knew they needed numbers and they needed confrontation. They needed Bull Connor's dogs and Selma sheriff James Clark's police batons coming down on the heads of older African Americans. They needed to call out, for all to see, the men who enforced brutal oppression every day in the South.

In their own way, Mountain Justice activists worked hard to expose the injustice spreading across the coal fields of Appalachia. Through nonviolent actions and demonstrations, they attempted to show the nation how coal companies break the law with a pathological consistency and operate with little regard for the human consequences of their actions. But on the national stage, Mountain Justice Summer couldn't compete with high gas prices and a foreign war, even though it is precisely that war over oil that is driving coal demands higher and laying mountains lower faster. That plus the fact that U.S. energy consumption increased 42 percent over the last 30 years. Urban affluence and this country's short-sighted energy policy are making Appalachia a poorer place – poorer in beauty, poorer in health, poorer in resources, and poorer in spirit.

"This wouldn't go on in New England," Jack Spadaro told me last July, up at Larry Gibson's place. It wouldn't go on in California, nor Florida, nor along the East Coast. After the '60s, America and the mainstream media seemed to lose interest in the problems of Appalachia. Though the Martin County slurry pond disaster was 20 times larger than the Exxon Valdez spill, the New York Times ignored it for months. But the seeming invisibility of the people in Appalachia does not make their plight any less real.

That the civil rights movement happened so recently in our country's history can seem dumbfounding, but not to the people who still live in the shadow of oppression. Those who live in the path of the coal industry – beneath sheared-off mountains, amid unnatural, treeless landscapes, drinking poisoned water and breathing dirty air – are fighting their own civil rights battle. And, as in the past, justice may be slow coming to the mountains of Appalachia. But justice delayed could mean the ruin of a place that has sacrificed much for this nation, and has received next to nothing in return.

ERIK REECE, *Kentucky*

Originally published in ORION Magazine, January/February 2006

The Awakening

Safe
The scarlet salamander slept
Under
The silent shining snow
Till
Spring's sweet sun
Touched
Her frozen bed.
On
Melting ice
She
Slithered skyward
To
Search for home,
But
The squirrel
The oak
The laurel
The snake
The brook
The fox
The deer
The sparrow
The mole
The hare
The shrew
And
The Mountain
Were
Gone.

EARL HAMNER, California

Oh Good Old Mountain

Oh good old mountain,
oh good old friend,
will I ever see your smiling
face again?

Your hat has been blasted off your head,
your smile has been blown away
and it is only now that I noticed
you're growing smaller day by day.

The animals
are suffering
with each poisoned
breath they take.

The clouds in the sky
surround you no more.
The trees are all but gone
and what is this all for?

Oh good old mountain,
oh good old friend,
maybe if we try
we can make your pain end.

ANNA LEIDECKER, Kentucky
Fourth Grade

Richland Balsam Epitaph

High in the Blue Ridge stands a graveyard, one of many on these mountaintops, eerie aeries where the dead stand erect, monuments to themselves. Richland Balsam does not sound dead or dying. Words *rich* and *land* and *balsam* ring full and heavy with sap and life: verdant, aromatic, green words. But only ghosts abide here now, ghosts of greenness, straight and sharp as needles, rising from the mountain, accusing the sky. Hollow white bones deny the sun with silvery glint. Falling corpses lean together, cry and tremble above decaying brothers. Richland Balsam mourns.

Before death, light lived here, thousands of feet above sea level, a sacred cathedral, hushed and quiet and cool. Sunlight filtered gently through evergreen mesh and tended earth swollen soft and full with blessings of rain. Mosses, lichens, ferns, shrubs – so many living things thrived beneath the sheltering canopy of Red Spruce and Fraser Fir. Inviolable and pristine, it seemed. Perhaps then, as now, merely a dream: secluded haven for fragile things.

Then the killers came, invisible, insidious, launched by millions unaware of their power to ravage, in a war instigated by ignorance and waged by apathy. Now acid rains, and where nature reigns, one law exists: survival of the fittest. This holocaust appears irreversible.

A few years back, some friends and I followed the Blue Ridge Parkway from Boone to Cherokee, North Carolina. Although I'm a native North Carolinian, it was my first real trip on the Parkway, and I wanted to see it all, every mountain, tree, leaf and hawk. One friend, a botanist, raved about the incredible beauty of a particular trail on top of a mountain called Richland Balsam (short for Richland Mountain of the Balsams). At 6,410 feet, it's the highest peak in the Great Balsam Range separating Haywood and Jackson Counties.

"You won't believe how lovely it is," my friend told me. "It's so green and perfect and pure, shadowy and cool. It's like stepping into a fairyland, a magical place."

At milepost 431.4, however, the fairyland is gone. The 1.5 mile nature trail still loops around the top of the mountain, and it is still a beautiful place, but now it winds through weeds and the rotting remains of Red Spruce (*Picea rubens Sargent*) and Fraser Fir (*Abies fraseri [Pursh] Poiret*). Defenders of Wildlife lists this type of forest as the second most endangered ecosystem in the United States. My friend told me that, although there is no concrete proof, scientists believe acid rain is responsible. It weakens the trees' resistance to the aphids which literally suck the life from them.

"But there must be some way to reverse this, to save these trees, this habitat," I said.

"No, there's really nothing anyone can do. All of these trees are dying now, and that means the fragile plant, animal, and microbial life that can only exist in their shelter will die too."

Later, excited by a mini-nursery of spruce seedlings apparently flourishing beneath a huge tree, I asked, "But won't these grow and replace the dead trees?"

"That tree is dying and, without its protection, the seedlings will die too. This forest may never grow back, and even if it does, it probably won't be in our lifetime."

In the silence that followed, the wind pushed pale dead trunks against one another and, as they moaned, I felt a raging inside myself at the needless loss of this small forest, or any part of the environment that humankind has damaged or killed.

I cannot accept feeling helpless. The only way to cope with my anger and sorrow is to do something. Whether or not Richland Balsam is lost, I must do something. I'm not a scientist, a leader, a crusader or a reformer. The steps I take are small, but important to my peace of mind. Everyone can recycle, conserve and protect, and there are numerous resources available to tell you how to do these things.

The point is to do them. Every day. For the rest of your life. I've been as guilty as anyone of forgetfulness, laziness or blatant indifference, but Richland Balsam changed my attitude. I saw one real result of apathy, and realized my responsibility. It's like voting. You may think, "What good can one individual do?" But the combination of every individual effort amounts to an incredibly powerful force that may just keep what's left of this planet, our habitat, alive.

Writer Robert McKee says, "Storytelling is the most powerful way to put ideas into the world today." I believe that has always been the case and always will be. So, as a writer, there's something else I can do. I can tell the stories of places like this in our Appalachian mountains, places that are dying or disappearing at a terrifying rate.

Mountains that are being destroyed for an 18-inch seam of coal.

Communities that live with blasting and flooding and dust from overloaded coal trucks on their roads.

I can tell the stories of the people who live there, too. I can put the idea into the world that they are part of our history and our future, and that they are worth protecting.

PAMELA DUNCAN, North Carolina

Unnatural Disaster

Coal Education Development and Resource (CEDAR) Scholarship
Committee
P.O. Box 1375
Pikeville, KY 41502

Dear CEDAR Scholarship Committee Members:

I am fully aware that the writing prompt for this scholarship instructs
the writer to "convince the audience that coal is beneficial and that
it impacts lives in a positive way." In order to sufficiently prepare my
article, I researched several websites for the purpose of furthering
my knowledge about the coal industry. The main website on which
I found my preliminary information (http://www.coaleducation.org)
could not stop praising the form of mining known as mountaintop
removal.

I have a slight problem with this.

All around my family's land, mountains have been completely
destroyed due to this process. While I recognize that mountaintop
removal is much easier and more efficient than underground mining,
I do not have to like it. As I found more and more information
suggesting that mountaintop removal will be the economic savior of
the Appalachians, I became appalled. I do not see why people derive
pleasure from taking away our natural beauty.

I tried to think of ways I could work around the mountaintop
removal issue and still praise the benefits of coal. I was going to focus
my paper on underground mining, but could not find anything good
to say about it, either. You see, underground mining recently ruined
the entirety of my family's property. A company robbed the pillars
of an old mine underneath our hills and our house, which caused
irreparable damage. I could not bring myself to lie just to receive a
scholarship.

I had already signed the paper saying I would participate in the scholarship contest, and I could not back out of that. Therefore, I decided to write an article about coal using my own opinions and views. I know that I have completely disregarded the writing prompt and basically have no chance of receiving the CEDAR Scholarship, but I am okay with that because I was honest with myself. I hope someone receives it who sincerely deserves it. Thank you for this opportunity.

Sincerely,
Jessica Boggs

~

Almost 130 years ago, the first broadform deeds began to be signed in Eastern Kentucky. Unsuspecting farmers signed away the mineral rights to their property to enterprising local entrepreneurs, never knowing they had signed a death certificate for their land. In the late-19th and early-20th centuries, the only form of mining conceivable to these people took place in the dark underground mines that were just beginning to take shape in the region at that time. Coal was picked by hand and hauled out with the help of mules. Mountaintop removal and strip mining, and the machines that helped create them, weren't even thoughts on the mental horizon of coal company bosses. Broadform deeds were just unneeded pieces of paper kept in a file somewhere up north; only Xs scratched on a dotted line in exchange for a few pieces of gold.

Then came the 1950s and 1960s. Instead of having to tunnel far into the earth to get their much-needed coal, companies could now use a handful of men and newfangled bulldozers and dynamite to blast away hundreds of feet of mountains, exposing money in the form of shiny black rocks. Broadform deeds now became invaluable to the mining industry due to the fact that most of these deeds included clauses that allowed mining companies to access minerals in any way possible. With a roar of an engine, callous dozer operators rolled their machinery over mountains that had been family land for hundreds of years. Trees were uprooted, hillsides torn off and the lives of entire families ruined. Despite numerous laws having been proposed and put into action, the tragedy of mountaintop removal has only gotten worse over the past 50 years.

As you drive through Eastern Kentucky, it is hard not to notice the huge chunks of mountains that appear to be missing, as if some awful disaster had ravaged their crests and contours. Instead of lush vegetation and rich scenery, these mountains have become scalded, seared versions of themselves – harsh dirt and scattered patches of brown grass roll slowly over the landscape, as if the Midwestern plains have been picked up and dumped onto the Appalachians.

Apparently, the federal Surface Mining Control and Reclamation Act of 1977 (SMCRA) can be interpreted loosely or ignored altogether. This legislation states "reclaimed land must be as useful as the land was before mining." While this is a nice idea, it seems that coal companies see it just as that – an idea. They have no consideration for those of us who believe that most of the usefulness of a mountain stems from the tiny detail that it is, in fact, a mountain and not a slightly sloping patch of dirt.

Of course, the mining industry has all sorts of rebuttals for this argument. They speak of the wonderful economic opportunities awaiting the poor hillbillies – the business parks waiting to be built, the shopping centers full of big box stores ready to be inundated with SSI checks, the lovely baseball fields and walking tracks poised to be appreciated by the youth of the county.

But do they think about the jobs they take away from their own workers? Instead of several hundred men hard at work deep inside the mountain, five or six park their pickups on top, pack diesel fuel and blasting caps into a hole and wait for the boom. The Environmental Protection Agency has said that even though the amount of coal produced is still high, these new methods of removing coal have lowered the need for miners.

Mountaintop removal has been lauded for its easy creation of flat land in the steep Eastern Kentucky mountains. These plateaus are supposed to serve as a giant beacon of light, calling new businesses to the region, but no one seems to realize that companies do not want to root in the back of a hollow. The flat land is touted as easily accessible, but the majority of strip jobs I have ever seen require a four-wheel drive vehicle and a lot of courage to visit. In my county, mining roads wind up mountains, through many tight, gravel-covered switchbacks, and lead to chopped off peaks at the confluence of several hollows. I cannot imagine a Wal-Mart Supercenter moving in at the head of Beetree Branch, a curvy one-lane road that ends up at a secluded, abandoned strip mine.

There are also the environmental ramifications to consider. In addition to the blatant elimination of land, mountaintop removal creates valley fills, loose dirt packed into the hole from which the coal was removed and where the mountain used to be. These valley fills are usually not strong enough to support large structures, creating potential problems for the new businesses built on them.

Valley fills also eradicate mountain streams. Bill Caylor, the current president of the Kentucky Coal Association, has often rebutted this, saying, "Ninety-five percent of the 'streams' that are covered with fill material are actually intermittent or ephemeral streams – those that basically flow only in connection with a rainfall event."

So what?

Even if the mountain is gone, the rain is still going to fall. Without the ditches, streambeds and gullies to flow into, the rain will attack the fill dirt. Valley fills are not known to respond well to rain, especially the harsh downpours typical of Eastern Kentucky in the spring and summer. Flash flooding occurs, creating horrendous mudslides that have covered roads, houses and stores in many areas of this region.

Perhaps if "foreigners" – faraway faces speaking with clipped northern accents – didn't own so many of our local mining companies, the pace of mountaintop removal would be slowed. It is very hard to live in the mountains and not love them, to not feel a sense of self and kinship when surrounded by these solid masses that have stood for millions of years.

People with no connection to the mountains cannot fathom why it hurts to see hills collapse. They do not have the years of family history with these mountains; their third-great-grandfather did not pick out *this* piece of land or build his family's first cabin out of trees from *that* ridge. It is easy for them to pick up the phone and tell a manager 500 miles away to uncover the Whitesburg 15 seam. They do not have to watch the destruction. They do not have to watch their grandparents' memories go up in a cloud of rock dust.

I cannot deny that coal mining has played an important role in my family. In the 1970s and 1980s, my grandfather owned and operated several small mines on our property. He stripped several benches on the mountain, but never conducted any form of mountaintop removal. It is partially due to the revenue from these mines that my family can live comfortably today. However, there is a large difference between removing a portion of the side of a mountain and completely flattening it. Though I am grateful to the role that coal mining has played in my family history, I still cannot condone mountaintop removal.

Several miles outside of Appalachia, Virginia, there is a spot on the map that the *Virginia Atlas & Gazetteer* lists as Roaring Fork. It is in this former community that my great-great grandfather, Joseph Boggs, was born and raised. Even though most of the families who once resided there had moved by the 1950s, the valley and mountains were still full of life. I have a picture of Roaring Fork that was taken in the late '50s. In it, a small cabin sits in the middle of a field, surrounded by green mountains. Fifty years later, everything is gone. Those mountains have been replaced by sheer dirt cliffs, *No Trespassing* signs and red gates held shut with a string of Masterlocks. While not stolen with a broad form deed, this land was bought by a coal company at a tax auction and destroyed. Joseph's parents, who were buried on the land, now lie in an unmarked grave in a cemetery across the county.

Bill Caylor has said in reference to mountaintop removal as a whole, "Once reclaimed, it's hard to tell that mining has ever occurred there, unless someone locally told you. It *still* will look like a mountain. What's left is flatter."

He must be kidding himself. If he has ever seen land like Roaring Fork, there is no way he could have made that statement. When a mountain is taken from being a source of life to a place of death, it is not just flatter. It is a ruination of lives, of memories, of the earth.

It is heartbreak of the highest order.

JESSICA BOGGS, Kentucky
College Sophomore

[Editor's Note: Jessica Boggs is recipient of the 2009 MOTESBOOKS YOUNG ACTIVIST AWARD.]

Reasons For Hope

April 1997, I rounded the curve into Blair, West Virginia, and found a horrible sight. A dragline sat on the edge of a chopped off mountain, while all around were burnt shells of houses. Arch Coal was operating one of the largest mountaintop removal mines above this historic town, while its land company was buying out residents to keep them from complaining.

Much has changed in the nearly dozen years since my first visit. The mine at Blair became the center of a landmark lawsuit over valley fills, and the mine remained idle for a decade. Only this year did the mine win all approvals to expand, but lawyers quickly won yet another slowdown. The movement against mountaintop removal has grown exponentially. Unfortunately, in West Virginia, mountaintop mining has continued, even expanded. Whether or when it is halted under the Obama administration remains to be seen. However, the constant legal and citizen pressure has forced improved mining practices.

So as we are inspired by a new President with the audacity to hope, I find a number of hopeful developments in the coalfields, most of all in the economy and culture of the coalfields so treasured by Patricia Bragg. Trish, as her friends know her, is the heroine of my book, *Moving Mountains; how one woman and her community won justice from big coal.* And it is her county of Mingo, at the very southern tip of West Virginia, where much progress is being made toward a post-coal economy.

The original lawsuit over valley fills, which began in 1998 and bears Trish's name (*Bragg v. Robertson*) roused West Virginia leaders to face hard facts about the future. Less than 40 years of surface coal remain on the mountains in the state (130 years of coal are still underground), according to the Energy Information Administration. Settlement of portions of the Bragg case also encouraged restoration of the mountains after mining, replanting native hardwoods. On those mountains that remain flattened, real economic development— rather than a few schools and buildings—has been encouraged.

The Mingo County Redevelopment Authority, led by Terry Sammons who had grown up in the county before eventually graduating from Harvard Law School, made a master plan for all existing and prospective mountaintop mines. Soon all the other coal-producing counties also created master development plans.

For decades, the best paying jobs in southern West Virginia were in mines or with related industries. Schools and government have been the next largest employers. Sammons and other business leaders have worked to bring other types of businesses as replacement for expiring coal-related jobs. Since 1998, jobs created by post-mining land use jumped from 1 percent of the total labor force to 17 percent. By 2018, jobs at these post-mine sites are expected to exceed coal-mining jobs. A 650-acre industrial park on a former Arch Coal surface mine houses one of the largest wood flooring plants in the east, owned by a division of Mohawk Industries. A coal company built Twisted Gun golf course. Active mountaintop mines are building 15 miles of the future King Coal Highway interstate, which will provide sites and access to new industry, including a new airport. The most recent project is controversial among environmentalists. The authority has won backing for a coal-to-liquids plant to make diesel, which can be used by mining machines. Biomass (plants and wood waste) would be mixed with coal, as well, reducing the plant's CO_2 footprint.

Southern West Virginia has become one of the nation's leading destinations for ATV riders, with thousands visitors every year. Though not directly related to changes in mining practices, the Hatfield-McCoy trails were the brainchild of the late Leff Moore, whose ancestor built the locks and dam to float the very first coal down Coal River and out to the rest of the country. When Moore saw the popularity of ATVs on Bureau of Land Management land out west, he wondered why that couldn't happen in West Virginia. After years of negotiations with tight-fisted land companies, which own most of the mined land in the state, Moore's dream will soon encompass nine counties with nearly 2,000 miles of trails.

As someone who first installed solar hot water and a wind generator in 1986, I'm particularly enthused about talk of solar and wind energy on the mountains and in the community. A new citizens group in Mingo County is looking at enticing a solar or wind factory to the area. Activists along Coal River in Boone County assert that wind generators on their mountain would produce more energy than mining the coal. Trish, herself, is looking into an inexpensive solar hot water heater. She and I talked about how wonderful it would be if a local business could start up, installing hot water systems.

Tens of thousands of acres of mined land could be transformed into fuel factories. These mines were reclaimed before the Bragg case forced state regulators to tighten up post mining regulations. Many of the mines had been allowed to replant only sparse grasses. Now Jeff Skousen, a West Virginia University soil sciences professor who has studied how to reclaim mines for two decades, has won a grant to study whether switchgrass can be grown on this land. That grass can be turned into cellulosic ethanol, the next wave of ethanol that does not take away from the food stream by using corn. Skousen does face difficulties: land at mines from the 1980s and 1990s was compacted to prevent runoff, and few nutrients were restored.

I chose to focus on Trish in my book because her own life is a shining example of what the coalfield people she so loves can accomplish. In the midst of bitter struggles and lawsuits to bring better mining practices, Trish managed to go to college; first to the local community college, then to West Virginia State University, nearly two hours from her home. Struggling through serious illness, she graduated summa cum laude with a degree in psychology, then went on to a full-time job. Trish doesn't like to be singled out because many others struggled against out-of-control mining as well. But she does want people, especially Appalachian women, to realize they can fight for what they believe in – and triumph.

As I think of the improving future of the coalfields, I remember a brief encounter at Trish's 50th birthday party on August 9, 2008. A man in his early 20s joined several dozen of Trish's family and friends. He sat on a couch, giving his baby daughter a bottle. When he mentioned he had to leave for his job as a mine guard, Trish's neighbor, Mike Carter, a miner and school board member, asked about his job, which paid $10 an hour. "You need to go to college," Mike told the young man. "Start taking a class."

You can have a better future, young man, as can everyone in the coalfields. Just have the audacity to hope.

PENNY LOEB, West Virginia

Old–Time Preachin' on a Scripture Taken from a Tree

A mind unhitched to a heart? – Shuckies!
if a mind don't drag a heart behind it

like a pony cart, I say, what kind
of mind is that, but wandered off,

and not just astray, a-lost! That heart
is like a tree cut from its roots –

a sip of freedom, spiked with the gall
of death, a breathing in without

the chance to let it go. That's what
a theory is, my friends, 'taint real,

it's rootless and unrooted in time,
and also meaning. Yes, to mean

means not just now, but all the way
to yonder. A good idea is good

because it begs a spell to reach.
Now, a tree will not deny its roots

and roots will not betray the ground
they're woven to, and none of it

will say there's no such thing as sun
or wind or rain. – That makes a heap

of hearts hitched-up to trees. Now ask
yourself which is more free, a tree

or you, and which of the two gives freely?
By grabbies, what's true for trees is true

for mountains, rivers, birds – gracious!
This is where you're livin' and everything

you love is here! Now ain't that
a pleasant breeze, and ain't that

a lovely rustle in the leaves?
To hear it is to hear ourselves

belonging where we live, and blessed.
But let's not think together we

have found this perty thing; let's know
it is the other way around:

we're found and made and rooted here,
and bound to being where we're bound.

I hope we're going to the heart,
I hope we're tied up in that glory.

O, recall that hilltop sermon and all
those blessings flowing from it for

the meek and poor, them other folks
half-whipped. If you can see where such

a river winds right down to you –
you salt and pepper of this earth –

then look up and pinch your eyes to see
just where that river got its start:

you'd best believe that mount is real
and where we always are forever.

Let us think about that with our hearts,
beating in amen time. Amen.

MAURICE MANNING, Kentucky & Indiana

As the Mountains Fall

As the mountains fall
Their dust spread far and wide
We watch with heavy hearts
And disbelieving eyes
The building blocks of life
Scattered all around
We can't put them back
But we can hold our ground
Bleeding, we watched them die
But we're not letting go
If just to save a life
That's all we need to know
Holding on
Holding tight
With our hearts
And words
We fight
So we're not letting go
Though it may cost us much
We'll keep pushing hard
'Cause that's all we've got

ERIN STAPLETON, Tennessee
High School Freshman

What's So Bad About Coal?

Dear Editor,

Tonya Amburgey posed the question "What's so bad about promoting the coal industry?" in her column "Not Much To Say" on May 21ˢᵗ. Does she even know what she's saying?

Coal has always been, and always will be, both a blessing and a curse for Appalachia and its people. More often than not, it comes as a curse and rains down plague upon the people that call these mountains home.

Amburgey points out that mountaintop removal mining "seems to be the most visible and most misunderstood form of mining." I think she's slightly mistaken. Mountaintop removal *is* the most visible form of mining, but the only thing misunderstood about it is that the coal industry thinks it can fool Appalachian people into believing that it's actually a good thing.

She states that mountaintop removal turns "unusable mountainsides" into "developed" land that can be used for tourism.

Who deemed these mountainsides – that have sustained an entire group of people for centuries – condemned and worthless?

Beyond that, who said that we have to flatten our mountains to bring in tourists?

Surely, tourists don't come to the mountains to see gaping scars cut out of them that are poorly masked by non-native grasses and no trees – because they don't grow where there is no soil.

Kentucky's coal counties may supply 91 percent of the state's electricity, but they remain in economic distress and the poorest in the state.

What's so bad about promoting the coal industry?

IVY BRASHEAR, Kentucky
College Junior

Leslie County
Sung to the melody of "Skibbereen"

O Daddy dear I often hear you talk of Leslie County
Her creeks and valleys green her mountains of wild bounty
They say it was a pretty place of honeysuckle smell
O why did you abandon it, the reason to me tell

O son I loved my native land with every bit of my pride
Till they took the mountaintop and all that we had died
You couldn't breathe the air to save ye life the water it was nasty
And that's the cruel reason why I left old Leslie County

O it's well I do remember that gray December day
The company man and the sheriff come to drag me rough away
I'd laid in front of the dozers to make them stop before me
And that's another reason why I left old Leslie County

Your mother too, God rest her soul, fell on the snowy ground
She fainted in her anguish having seen the mis'ry round
She never rose but died and went to the land of uncloudy day
She found a quiet grave my boy in dear old Leslie County

And you were only two year old and I hated to raise you elsewhere
But I had to take us to a place where good folks would give us care
I wrapped you up in my coat and fled in the night unseen
I heaved a sigh and said goodbye to dear old Leslie County

SILAS HOUSE, Kentucky

Midnight Madness

The Christmas-week spill of a billion gallons of toxic coal ash in East Tennessee was not only an unprecedented disaster but an appropriate symbol for eight years of gross environmental neglect and regression – eight years during which the energy industry literally and absolutely ruled America. The lava flow of poisonous gray sludge that crept across the landscape, eating fields and trees, at least three houses and a wide section of the Emory River, offered the media arresting front-page images from a region they habitually neglect. It coincided with the "midnight madness" of the departing Bush administration and its feeble EPA, who as a final flourish of obeisance to corporate masters gutted the stream buffer zone rule, for 25 years one of the few regulatory restraints on mountaintop removal mining. Tennessee's 300-acre coal ash spill, from a ruptured retention pond at a TVA power plant, bore no direct relation to mountaintop removal – except that the fate of the Emory River has been the fate of hundreds of miles of Appalachian streams where the mountains have been decapitated. And the spill bore a deadly family resemblance to another horror in Kentucky in 2000, when an artificial lake created by a mountaintop mine in Martin County released 300 million gallons of coal slurry, burying houses and yards and contaminating streams and drinking water. At that time the EPA, not yet emasculated by Bush appointments, called the Kentucky break one of the Southeast's worst environmental disasters.

December's newsphotos and video gave Americans a bitter visual taste of what the Appalachians have suffered for two decades. Of all the dirty tricks predatory corporations have played on this increasingly defenseless country to which they cling like bloated ticks, none is dirtier nor more apocalyptic in its consequences than mountaintop removal. American coal companies whose Final Solution turns Appalachian mountains into lifeless slag heaps set a standard for ruthless myopia and environmental destruction only the Russians and Chinese have ever challenged. Americans who have never seen a valley with a whole pulverized mountain pushed into it can't imagine the wasteland parts of Kentucky and West Virginia have become – more than 1,200 miles of streams buried under coal waste and rubble, 400 mountains destroyed, some million-and-a-half acres of land rendered uninhabitable by the end of the decade. Not merely the degradation of a classic American landscape, but the willful devastation of entire human and animal biosystems, of a native people and a way of life – a micro-civilization that seemed expendable to the usual businessmen with too much money who wanted more.

"I've reported on devastation around the world – from natural disasters such as Hurricane Katrina, to wars in Central America and the Middle East, to coastlines degraded by fish farming," John McQuaid writes in *Smithsonian*. "But in the sheer audacity of its destruction, mountaintop coal removal is the most shocking thing I've ever seen. Entering a mountaintop site is like crossing into a war zone."

The well-documented history of coal mining in Appalachia is full of the violence and intimidation that was necessary to keep miners and their communities subservient to the corporations. But over the years exploitation refined itself, evolving from armed goons, strikebreakers, beatings and killings to the strategic purchase of judges and politicians, the muzzling of key media, and deployment of the best flacks and lobbyists money can buy. And the best legislators. Leading the movement to roll back the administration's 11th-hour assaults on the environment – along with the stream buffer zone rule, Bush also targeted restrictions on oil drilling in the Utah canyonlands and uranium mining near the Grand Canyon – is Ron Wyden, a Democratic senator from Oregon. Where were the senators and congressmen who represent West Virginia and Kentucky, and Tennessee, where mountains crumble and rivers run gray? Look deep, deep in the pocket of Big Coal, where they've nested comfortably for generations. West Virginia's senior senator, Robert Byrd, became the improbable darling of Democratic liberals when he took an early stand against the war in Iraq, but as Big Coal's high commissioner in Washington he's no darling to environmentalists. Politicians like Byrd and Kentucky's reactionary Mitch McConnell justify bioregional catastrophe in the name of "jobs" and "the local economy," though study after study showed that jobs were short-term and devastation permanent (as a result of mechanized mountain-crushing, West Virginia has actually lost 50,000 jobs since 1978). Freed from reelection pressure, President Bush serviced his coal bosses even though a well-publicized poll showed two-thirds of the public in favor of stream protection and nearly 85 percent disturbed by the mountains' destruction. In the era of mountaintop removal, the coal companies' grip on the mountains has grown even tighter than in the time of clubs and guns.

Resistance seemed feeble and futile. Subservience to the coal industry is a habit than divides communities and individual families, often bitterly. But in spite of physical threats, police harassment, ostracism and media blackouts, a network of grassroots movements is spreading across the mountains, dedicated to fighting mountaintop removal and the hegemony of the coal barons. True community activists, beginning with no outside expertise or foundation money, they've made a welcome spectacle of their indignation and drawn the wrath of the coal combines with their efforts "to stir the emotions of the people," as West Virginia Coal Association president Bill Raney put it.

Mountain people have a history of fighting back, as any student of the bloody coal wars can attest. But "where's the outrage?" is the big question most troubled observers, native and foreign, have been asking about the United States of America. America's recent resistance to its corporate predators, including the overreaching ones who have just destroyed our housing and financial markets, our economy and our pension system, has been little more than anemic. During the depressions of the 1890s and the 1930s, whole neighborhoods rose up violently to oppose bank agents and policemen who were enforcing foreclosures. The only reaction to the foreclosures of 2008 was a rash of suicides among the newly homeless.

If something's truly rising in the Appalachians, it has implications that reach beyond the region and the critical struggle against mountaintop removal. If these underdogs should save a few mountains and win a few battles against Big Coal, maybe more Americans will recover their faith in the power of citizens' outrage and grassroots resistance. I always thought the best people were the ones who got lumps in their throats, as I did, when Joan Baez sang "The Ballad of Joe Hill": "…and smiling with his eyes, says Joe, what they can never kill, went on to organize." Joe Hill's ghost hasn't had much to smile about lately. I hope he has his eye on the hills of Kentucky.

HAL CROWTHER, North Carolina

The Time Is Now
based on "Wagon Wheel" by Bob Dylan and Ketch Secor

Headed out east to the land of the mines
Looked at the mountains and I saw no pines
Strolled through a field barefoot
And my feet turned black

I made it up the hill in about half an hour
Pickin' a bouquet of non-native flowers
From the reclaimed land
That's bare and empty and bland

They blast them up then mine them out
Ugliest thing I've ever seen there's no doubt
Hey hey they flatten the land
Well they flatten the land and take all the coal
Man, to me this is gettin' real old
Hey hey they flatten the land

I was going through a valley looked to the sky
Saw some flat mountains
And began to cry
All this has to stop somehow

Yeah, we're gonna put and end to this wait and see
Come on everybody come and sing with me
Yes we are going to stop this

It's time to end this
Yes the time is now
All of this is going to end somehow
Hey hey the time is now
I said hey hey the time is now
Yes I said hey hey the time is now

KATHLEEN SMITH, Kentucky
High School Sophomore

Global Sickness

Every spring – just as the weather is starting to warm when only hints of winter are left and the green shoots of trees are recapturing the landscape – my family and I step out to the front yard and visit our fruit trees, looking for the telltale buds that mean we will have pears, apples and paw-paw fruits in the summer. Nature is caught up in the hum of life, and everything is preparing for summer with fresh new growth and budding flowers that will one day supply the next generation of plants. Last year, however, all this young growth was murdered by a surprisingly late spring frost, and suddenly there were no pears, no apples, no paw-paws.

Trees with fresh green branches were distorted in shape, and still are a year later, because the new growth was killed off and left dead. The real loss was for the animals that profit yearly off of the nuts, fruits and grasses that should have been there. When I see starving deer, their ribs showing jagged against undernourished hides, I can't help but wonder how many people care – or even know – that this is happening, or why it has been occurring more and more frequently with each passing year.

Imagine you've been infected with a virus. The virus enters your body and steals your cells to make more copies of itself; it depends on the fact that it can spread and grow infinitely within you. Like an illness, it can be neglected and ignored, but this will not make it go away. If you feel too busy or unwilling to pay for a doctor, you will only become more and more ill over time, and the longer you wait, the harder it will be to fix the problem. Anyone who has ever been sick knows that there are only two possible outcomes: either the virus is fended off and destroyed, or it kills the host organism it has invaded.

Factories and big corporations are Earth's viruses. The majority of the population, especially those within these corporations, sit back and let it happen; as long as they can get something out of it and don't feel like they immediately have to do something about it or die, why spend or lose money over it? Why take the time or effort? Just like people sick with viruses, we do little about the destruction inflicted by our corporations until our lives are threatened. Coal companies and lumber concerns and toxin-belching factories have the mindset of a virus, believing they can expand forever on the surface of the earth while they dig, tear and poison it to death; on top of it all, they truly believe that if they stop or slow down, they will die — all or nothing. And just like a virus, they are wrong.

In the case of the earth, once these companies sufficiently destroy the thing they thrive off of, they will die with it; we all will. In the same way our bodies retaliate to sickness, the earth is sending us warnings about the battle it is fighting. These messages come in the form of floods, tornadoes and huge hurricanes, this odd change in climate that is far too hot or far too cold, or cold when it shouldn't be and vice versa. We have all the signs and symptoms, but we still don't see the big picture and we're running out of time.

Carbon emissions are the ever-popular thing to blame for global warming. But I don't think that's all there is to it. Stopping carbon emissions would probably help, but we have so much more to think about. When we destroy forests to make way for houses and pavement, or for things like mountaintop removal and coal mining, we are not only destroying habitats but also decreasing the amount of oxygen released into the air, depleting our own life force. Further, with an increase of pavement and lack of shady trees, it's no wonder the Earth is increasing in temperature every year. Think of how much heat tar and pavement absorb in the summer. The little things build.

One Christmas when I was eight, my dad took me out shopping and let me wander the store so I could buy my mom presents without his help. I picked up lots of little things, things that were small and inexpensive but that I thought she would like: jewelry, candles, a card, sweet-smelling soaps and other trinkets. When I came back, my total was over a hundred dollars. I felt so guilty, and it made me realize that those small things really do add up. Take a few examples: we cut down more trees, there's less oxygen in the air, carbon dioxide increases because the trees aren't there to use it. This changes the atmosphere and, eventually, our climate. The cause may be something we never hear about, such as gruesome amounts of methane gas polluting the air and producing even more greenhouse gases because of too many cows.

I am fortunate enough to live in the midst of evergreen pines and the glowing white trunks of sycamores. I feel most at home when I am sitting, meditating to the sounds of nature around me — birds, wind in the trees, bugs, the crashing of a squirrel through dead leaves. The trees, standing tall, most of them older than I am, make me feel safer. It pains me to imagine a world without this peaceful place of refuge from the technology and tumbling chaos of the day. It makes me confused, as well, to see that people can stand by and watch it happen and not care. Sometimes when I, or others, mention the devastation, we are shot down by the "logic" of a viral mindset that knows it can't be wrong because this is how it's always been, and this is what everyone else says, and we can't stop growing and expanding or we will die.

Coal mining, specifically the method of extraction called mountaintop removal, sums up in one fell swoop the major problems of various industries. Just this year I visited a coal community and saw firsthand a reclamation site. They call it reclaiming the land, but that's not what it is, because after the way they rape these mountains they cannot possibly be made habitable again. When a site is reclaimed the dirt and rock are pushed into piles, and chemical grass "seed" is sprayed on it to appear green from a distance. Even from that distance the sight made the knot in my stomach, there since the beginning of the trip, tighten until I shook. We stood in the unpredictable spurts of rain and wind, but that's not what made me want to get back into the truck and huddle around myself. I forced myself to see, really see, what was in front of me and what it meant, and though I'd learned about it and seen pictures, it was nothing like this reality, and nothing can compare to it.

When a coal company blows up the mountain, it commits all five of the major destructive acts by which corporations and factories are killing the earth: pollution of the air, pollution of the water, chopping down trees, tearing up the land, and adding to the carbon emissions and fuel crisis. They clear the land they are mining of all trees, these heavily forested areas, without even using them, just dumping them once they are out of the way. They then use explosives to get to the coal underneath, entirely destroying the once rich land. Since machinery has replaced manpower, they are adding to the carbon emissions as well by using the fuel for their digging tools and trucks. They are digging up coal, which in the long term is only going to run out and leave us in the dark without an alternative — in which case the company really will die. And finally, the coal is cleaned using chemicals that create a black slurry called sludge, consisting of poisons like arsenic, acids and coal dust, which they then dump into holes in the ground. From here the poisons leak into the underground water supply and often flood across the land so that toxins are released on people and into streams and soil for miles around. The mining industry, in this way, has effectively done absolutely everything it can to ensure its own death. In this way it resembles so many other industries.

Unfortunately it isn't just some weather change here and there that we have to worry about, but the things that come with this. Aside from hurricanes and floods, too much warmth at the wrong time of year can cause illnesses to spread more easily, or allow new ones to come into existence. I know people who really take care of themselves, eating right, exercising, sleeping well and taking vitamins daily. This year, one of my teachers who lives this careful, healthy life got bronchitis. Bronchitis is not the kind of illness that spreads easily, or from person to person contagiously. But this year she and others I know contracted it. This year, people are still getting colds even in late April, and haven't been able to completely alleviate the ones they came down with earlier in the year. The allergies in combination with unusually cold weather are making it easier to get sick.

Earth isn't the only one getting sick as a result of the corporate viruses, and if we don't find a way to change things soon, planet Earth won't be the only one on the brink of death.

MACKENZIE KIRCHNER-SMITH, Kentucky
High School Junior

Scream of the Butterfly

for Jim Morrison . . . When the Music's Over

What have they done to the earth?
What have they done to our fair sister?
Ravaged and plundered and ripped her and bit her.
—JM

Would you mourn,
my lizard king,
for this hollow mountain?

Cry for high walls,
strip jobs,
a crownless queen?

Before the storm,
earth stood in high heaps
around deep hollows.

Then tumbled boulders
filled her streams and
choked her screams.

The rape left her black
with diesel and fairy dust:
the fleeting promise of coal.

I covered my head with ash
and turned away.
I could not bear the scars
on my fair sister.

NEVA BRYAN, Virginia

Holy Ground

From the top of this mountain
You can see the world
The oak tree where we used to play
When Mother was a girl

The storehouse, the smokehouse,
The stripping room, the barn
The old log house where generations
Lived here on this farm

Chorus   This is holy ground – to me it's holy ground
And nothing but the hand of God
Shall ever tear it down
Take your dozers and your dynamite
And head on back to town
Get off my land 'cause where you stand is
Holy ground

To the top of this mountain
We've often had to climb
To get away, to kneel and pray
Among the rocks and pines

Our little family graveyard
It's a hard place to get to
But we are mountain people
So nowhere else would do

Repeat Chorus

Refrain   This is holy ground – to me it's holy ground
And nothing but the hand of God shall ever tear it down
I will shout it from the mountaintops
And all the hills around
Get off my land 'cause where you stand is holy ground

JESSIE LYNNE KELTNER, *Kentucky*

Hope In The Mountains

Yesterday was a great day for the people of Appalachia and for all of America. In a bold departure from Bush-era energy policy, the Obama administration suspended a coal company's permit to dump debris from its proposed mountaintop mining operation into a West Virginia valley and stream. In addition, the administration promised to carefully review upward of 200 such permits awaiting approval by the U.S. Army Corps of Engineers.

With yesterday's action, President Obama has signaled his intention to save this region. His moratorium on these permits will allow the administration to develop a sensible long-term approach to dealing with this catastrophic method of coal extraction.

I join hundreds of Appalachia's embattled communities in applauding this news. Having flown over the coalfields of Appalachia and walked her ridges, valleys and hollows, I know that this land cannot withstand more abuse. Mountaintop removal coal mining is the greatest environmental tragedy ever to befall our nation. This radical form of strip mining has already flattened the tops of 500 mountains, buried 2,000 miles of streams, devastated our country's oldest and most diverse temperate forests, and blighted landscapes famous for their history and beauty. Using giant earthmovers and millions of tons of explosives, coal moguls have eviscerated communities, destroyed homes, and uprooted and sickened families with coal and rock dust, and with blasting, flooding and poisoned water, all while providing far fewer jobs than does traditional underground mining.

The backlog of permit applications has been building since Appalachian groups won a federal injunction against the worst forms of mountaintop removal in March 2007. But the floodgates opened on Feb. 13 when the U.S. Court of Appeals for the 4th Circuit in Richmond overturned that injunction. Since then, the Corps has been working overtime to oblige impatient coal barons by quickly issuing the pending permits. Each such permit amounts to a death sentence for streams, mountains and communities. Taken together, these pending permits threatened to lay waste to nearly 60,000 acres of mountain landscape, destroy 400 valleys and bury more than 200 miles of streams.

The Corps already had issued a dozen permits before the

White House stepped in, and coal companies have begun destroying some of these sites. The bulldozers are poised for action on the rest. Typical of these is Ison Rock Ridge, a proposed 1,230-acre mine in southwest Virginia that would blow up several peaks and threaten a half-dozen communities, including the small town of Appalachia.

In a valiant effort to hold back destruction, the Appalachia Town Council, citing its responsibility for the "health, safety, welfare and properties" of its residents, recently passed an ordinance prohibiting coal mining within the town limits without approval from the council. But that ordinance lacks the power to override the Army Corps of Engineers' permit. And while the Obama administration order will reverse the Bush-era policies and stop the pillaging elsewhere, the town of Appalachia remains imperiled.

The White House should now enlarge its moratorium to commute Appalachia's death sentence by suspending the dozen permits already issued. The Environmental Protection Agency should then embark on a rulemaking effort to restore a critical part of the Clean Water Act that was weakened by industry henchmen recruited to powerful positions in the Bush administration. Former industry lobbyists working as agency heads and department deputies issued the so-called "fill rule" to remove 30-year-old laws barring coal companies from dumping mining waste into streams. This step cleared the way for mountaintop removal, which within a few years could flatten an area of the Appalachians the size of Delaware. This change must be reversed to restore the original intent of the Clean Water Act and prevent mining companies from using our streams and rivers as dumps.

The Obama administration's decision to suspend these permits and take a fresh look at mountaintop removal is consistent with Obama's commitment to science, justice and transparency in government and his respect for America's history and values. The people of Appalachia, Virginia, and the other towns across the coalfields have been praying that Barack Obama's promise of change will be kept. Thanks to yesterday's decision, hope, not mining waste, is filling the valleys and hollows of Appalachia.

ROBERT F. KENNEDY, Jr., New York

Can't Put It Back

(Wrecklamation Song)

You see the corpse laid out before you
You see the mountain's blood run black
Oh, she was killed as she lay sleeping
And they can never bring her back

For a long time the coal was hidden
The mountain's life surged through her veins
Then they tapped and drilled and blasted
Now she's gone, and who's to blame?

Chorus   But they say, "Hey, we're gonna put it back …
Gonna put it back just like we found it!"
Then they make a wreck and call it "reclamation"
Pick away the beauty and leave an open sore
Well, you boys know you can't put it back
You can't put it back just like you found it
There's a whole lot of sky where it used to be mountain
And there ain't no mountain where there was before

Now there is nothing that is casual
About the costs and casualties
It's hard to watch a mountain murdered
For she can't be buried, only grieved

And there is life out in these coalfields
That has been lost to those coal mines
Because it's mostly now a minefield
A money war – the killing kind

Repeat Chorus

You see them scrape away her essence
You see them take her bones & flesh
But you get used to bitter water
And you forget it once was fresh

They strip and gouge 'til they find riches
They simply can't believe their luck
They chop the top off of the mountain
And haul her heart away in trucks

Repeat Chorus

KATE LARKEN, *Kentucky*

I Care

Throughout my life, I have seen and done important things but there is one thing that beats all: trying to stop mountaintop removal.

My classmates and I have dedicated the whole year to assist in defeating the pollution of streams in Appalachia caused by mountaintop removal.

They're making flat land, but they're also taking away treasured ground. This matter has gone on long enough and that's why we're taking a stand for people who don't have a voice in what happens to them. Some are threatened by the coal companies if they try to speak out, criticizing the coal industry.

We don't care what people think of us or say to us. You want to know why? Because we believe in this cause. Believe me, this is going to be stopped. I don't care how and I don't care when, but the coal companies will be stopped. This is a matter that I'll believe in till I'm laid in the ground.

MARK REYNOLDS, Kentucky
Fifth grade

Larry Gibson, a trusty guide and lifetime advocate against mountaintop removal. He lives on the peak of Kayford Mountain (WV), dealing with earthquakes from blowing the mountain apart and fighting the Canary Coal Company.

FRANCES BUERKENS, Kentucky

PEOPLE

Change will not come if we wait for some other person or some other time. We are the ones we've been waiting for. We are the change that we seek.

BARACK OBAMA

Becoming Beauty Again

Sometimes when I am lost in the rolling gray sadness
of cities,

Sometimes driving in my automobile

on the wide dead rivers of interstate highways

I see a meadow, burnished grass,
a pond like a silver crown,
garlands of pear blossoms, a grape arbor
twining its small green hands

I see myself go to the great white switch
that keeps the refrigerator running and the saw
spinning and the light connecting its circuitry,
that keeps the factories pumping, the drillers
whetting appetites, the dozers and treecutters
grinding and growling and grating and greasing,
that doesn't forget the manufacturers of weapons

And in one volcanic motion, using both hands
and every nerve in my body,
I flip the big switch
off.

Off.
That quiet.
Loud stunning quiet.
Paralysis of storm quiet.
A quiet that doesn't last
yet a quiet forever come.

I will walk away from the switch
terrified out of my mind,
also mindlessly happy while
the eye of the storm passes over.

JANISSE RAY, *Georgia*

Even With Mountains, A Little Can Do A Lot

Down in East Tennessee, inside Anderson County and near Knoxville and Clinton, there is a little town called Norris. That is where I live. Although it is a very small town with a lot of woods and a big field right in the middle, things are beginning to grow. An asphalt plant might come in down the road, polluting and fouling the air. A Wal-Mart is being built nearby as well, which will probably shut down a lot of businesses.

Norris isn't too far away from the Appalachians, and sometimes my family goes up and hikes in the woods there. I love it. It's not only beautiful, it's quiet, peaceful and full of wonderful things such as animals and wildflowers and old, old trees. That is one of the things that strikes me when I go there. Everything is so old. Even Norris, the tiny town squashed in between big cities, gets bigger, but the mountain doesn't change. It just grows older and older.

Unless it gets destroyed by mountaintop removal. Then a wonderful place is lost to the world.

Mountaintop removal happens all over America. It is an extreme type of coal mining in which entire mountains are literally ripped apart. This new type of mining began in Appalachia in the 1970s; it occurs in Virginia, West Virginia and Kentucky, as well as Tennessee. It is destroying hundreds of miles of these places, polluting the waters of lakes and of rivers that flow all across the country, devastating habitats for millions of animals.

But mountaintop removal can be stopped, despite how hopeless it looks. Just like any other issue that looks too large to confront, when people come together they can do more than they could have hoped to do before, alone.

Why should we trouble ourselves with it? There are many reasons.

One is because mountaintop removal mining is causing serious issues with the environment. According to the Nature Conservancy, the mountain coal region – which is found in Tennessee, Kentucky, West Virginia and Virginia – contains some of the highest levels of biological diversity in the country. It is also where many U.S. cities are supplied with drinking water. As mountaintop removal pollutes the water in that area, it isn't as clean as it should naturally be.

Water isn't the only way mountaintop removal is negatively affecting the environment. More than seven percent of Appalachian forests were cut down and more than 1,200 miles of streams across the region were buried or polluted between 1985 and 2001. Mountaintop removal is also having a serious impact on fish, wildlife and bird species, as well as harming the neighboring communities.

The families who live near these sites are suffering. They face flooding, blasting and water pollution from sludge dams. Researchers at the University of Kentucky have concluded that floods are definitely increasing in places near mountaintop removal sites. Also, families are forced to live near continual blasting coming from the site. The impact of the blasting not only makes life much worse but also often cracks wells and foundations. Lastly, sludge dams caused by the mining process contaminate water that they use for drinking. It's not a place where many people would want to live.

There are over 300 million people in the United States. If everyone did something, we could make a big change for the better. If everyone works together, we can make it happen. If just one person can make a difference, as everyone says, then think about what we could do if everyone wanted to help.

What one person can do is spread the word. If people don't know about the problem, how can they fix it? Another thing one person could do is write to Congress. Letters add up if everyone writes. In 2007, for instance, the Clean Water Protection Act was introduced in the U.S. House of Representatives and is currently co-sponsored by many representatives because they've received thousands of letters from citizens.

A little can do a lot. Every person can make a difference. Scattered, we *might* do something; but together we *will* do it. We can change for the better!

GRAHAM MAREMA, *Tennessee*
Seventh grade

Mining on Wilson Creek? Not Ever

I am Beverly May and, along with the other members of the Floyd County Chapter of Kentuckians for the Commonwealth and many of my neighbors, I have brought the petition asking the Energy and Environment Cabinet to declare the Wilson Creek watershed, including Cedar Cliffs, unsuitable for surface mining.

I feel unspeakably grateful and blessed that I was raised and still live on Wilson Creek. Land on Wilson Creek has passed down to me through the family and I now own wooded hillsides on both sides of the watershed, a field with an orchard and garden, and a small spot by the road on which I recently built a house. My family also lives on Wilson Creek and many of my neighbors have been friends since childhood. Obviously, I have a lot at stake in this petition as do my neighbors.

Many families have called Wilson Creek home for five or more generations, creating a complex web of kinship and friendship, interdependence and respect that might be thought of as a unique human ecosystem. In our culture, it is difficult to compare human values to economic values. We can assign no dollar figure to the worth of living among good people in a place where it is possible to feel safe, known and valued. Who knows what a ton of neighborly goodwill is going for on the market this week? I do know it is infinitely more valuable than a ton of coal. My neighbors and I come before you because we cherish our community and the land, forests and streams it depends on and we know it is now endangered.

I would like to describe for the Energy and Environment Cabinet the petitioned area and why it meets Congress' criteria for designation as unsuitable for surface mining. The Wilson Creek watershed is home to 94 families whose houses are spread along the three miles of Wilson Creek and its main tributary, Big Creek. This is a heavily-populated, rural community that is growing. Several of the young people who grew up on Wilson Creek have built homes here in recent years and there are more young people who hope to build in the future. If the 94 homes on Wilson Creek were located on the edge of a city it would be called a subdivision and no state agency would knowingly allow loss of water supply, blasting, dust, road hazards or flooding. Surface mining, even when done strictly following the applicable state and federal regulations, creates a hazard to the community that would be unacceptable to the public in any other circumstances.

The threat of surface mining encroaching on a heavily populated area is precisely the sort of perilous situation Congress sought to prevent when it framed the 1977 Surface Mining Control and Reclamation Act (SMCRA) that was later adopted by the Commonwealth of Kentucky. In SMCRA, Congress authorized the regulatory agencies to designate areas unsuitable for coal mining when mining would "affect fragile, historic, renewable resources or natural systems resulting in substantial or significant damage to the protected values or resources." Congress further explained its intent in setting up the Lands Unsuitable for Mining designation by saying, "While coal surface mining may be an important and productive use of land, it also involves certain hazards and is but one of many alternative land uses. In some circumstances, therefore, coal surface mining should give way to competing uses of higher benefit."

My fellow petitioners and I believe it is a "higher benefit" to preserve the community of Wilson Creek and the watershed this community depends on. The framers of SMCRA could not have foreseen the day when mountaintop removal and vast area mines would go from being a rare exception to business as usual in Appalachia. The destructive impact of mining has vastly increased since 1977; consequently, use of the Lands Unsuitable provision should also increase to reasonably balance human and coal interests and to preserve places for people to live.

Of the "protected values and resources" Congress had in mind to protect through Lands Unsuitable for Mining designation, one of them was surely human life. That value is addressed in the first allegation of our petition, which is that Wilson Creek is already a flood-prone area and that further mining within the watershed will increase the likelihood of more severe flooding and, most ominously, flash flooding that can endanger lives and homes.

The Division of Permits has already received letters and emails from many of my neighbors expressing their concerns about this. Tonight you'll be hearing from several neighbors who have dealt with past flooding and have fears of more dangerous flooding to come should surface mining be allowed. A large abandoned strip mine on the left side of the watershed has caused a high level of sedimentation, which has been documented by biologists. To the residents it is obvious that the creek has filled in and narrowed over the last decade and that it now has less carrying capacity for floods. Jack Spadaro, a mining engineer – who, while working for the Mine Safety and Health Administration, investigated flooding from the Buffalo Creek disaster and the Martin County sludge spill – has corroborated their claims.

Because protection of human life is the chief value by which the Cabinet should make its determination, I would also like to make you aware of public health research now underway. Dr. Michael Hendryx of the Institute for Health Policy at West Virginia University has completed a series of epidemiologic studies looking at the health of people living near surface mines. These studies show higher death rates from heart disease, chronic lung disease, lung cancer and kidney disease in heavy coal mining areas, even when controlling for age, smoking, poverty and many other factors known to contribute to poor health.

A 2008 follow-up study of air quality suggests why. The average Total Suspended Particles (TSP) for areas within a half-mile of mountaintop removal sites was more than five times greater than non-mining areas tested. On the worse day tested, the TPS was 40 in non-mining sites, but near mountaintop removal sites it was 812. Dr. Hendryx concludes one of his studies with these words: "The set of socioeconomic and health inequalities characteristic of coal mining areas of Appalachia highlights the need to develop more diverse, alternative local economies."

In other words, alternative land uses which are a higher benefit to the public than surface mining are consistent with the intent of Congress in creating the Lands Unsuitable process and our petition to keep Wilson Creek a safe, healthy place to live.

The second allegation speaks to the historic value of Cedar Cliffs, a magnificent rock formation in the petitioned area which has been a cherished part of the landscape for generations as evidenced by the dozens of rock carvings on the site, some going back to the 19th Century. Steven Boyd, a landowner, is currently seeking state historic designation for the site.

Our third allegation is that the Wilson Creek watershed is a hazardous area owing to the extensive deep mining that has been done throughout the area and auger mining that was done in the early 1960s. Paul Smithson, a professor at Berea College has used GIS mapping and state mine records to show the extent of abandoned deep mines. Dr. Smithson describes the mountains of the watershed as looking like a complete honeycomb. From the elders of the community such as Loretta Meadows, we know that water ran from these mines and is likely still present, so the residents have good reason to worry that blasting over the old mine works could cause a dangerous mine blow out.

The auger mining – which covered the length of Wilson Creek – resulted in numerous landslides. Nathan Hall, a student a Berea College and former underground miner, researched Abandoned Mine Lands (AML) records and found there have been two AML jobs on Wilson Creek, one to stabilize a large landslide caused by the auger mining and another to close a deep-mine portal.

The threat of landslides is not past. The Woods family at the head of Wilson Creek is concerned about an unstable area behind their house that might give way with nearby blasting.

The final allegation is that surface mining on Wilson Creek will destroy the community's water wells. Several families depend on wells as their only water source and many still have functional wells that are used for gardens and as backup to the city water line.

The Lands Unsuitable provisions of SMCRA also speak to the protection of "natural systems." Several speakers will discuss the rich biodiversity of the petitioned area, including biologist Julian Campbell and resident Elizabeth May. Again, there is a "higher benefit" in preserving the economic and ecologic value of the forests, streams and fields of Wilson Creek than in allowing its permanent destruction by surface mining.

In addition, residents are concerned about the dangers of coal traffic on our narrow one-lane road, dust from mining and damage to our homes from blasting.

We are aware that just last week the Miller Brothers Coal Company petitioned the Cabinet for Energy and Environment to declare our petition "frivolous." In other words, Miller Brothers considers our fears that surface mining will damage our community frivolous and irrelevant.

What appalling arrogance.

Tell that to Erica Urias, whose community of Island Creek in Pike County has been almost completely driven out by mining.

`Tell that to members of Kentuckians for the Commonwealth

WE ALL LIVE DOWNSTREAM

(KFTC) from Hueysville, who are currently dealing with blasting damage, dust and a dangerous, leaking sediment pond that is the responsibility of the Miller Brothers Coal Company.

Finally, I would like to call attention to a letter that has been received by several of my neighbors. It contains your agency's response to their concerns and includes the words "we are strongly committed to strict enforcement of our surface mining laws and regulations...."

Unfortunately, we have far too much evidence that your agency routinely issues permits that disregard the protections of SMCRA. The Division of Permits routinely issues waivers to the chief regulation that is meant to protect streams. Rather than requiring a 100-foot buffer zone around streams, your agency allows streams and headwaters to be completely buried by valley fills.

In 2005, 76 of the 137 new strip mine permits you issued granted full waivers of the stream buffer zone rule.

In 2006, 77 out of 140 new mines were granted full waivers.

In these two years alone your agency authorized the burial of 284 headwater streams in Kentucky.

In 1999, your agency was reprimanded by the federal Office of Surface Mining for allowing post-mining land use plans for fish and wildlife habitats on mountaintop removal permits. This is illegal, yet you have continued to allow this.

In 2005, all permits for mountaintop removal in Kentucky had the cynical post-mining land use plan of fish and wildlife habitat.

For years, your agency routinely issued permits which included waivers allowing coal companies to set off blasts greater than 40,000 pounds and instead allowed blasts of 80,000 to 100,000 pounds. The largest recorded blast found by KFTC members was 600,000 pounds at the Starfire mine in Perry County. The practice of allowing overblasting has been so routine that this is no longer found in the permit applications available to the public.

But, in the interest of open mindedness – and because the Lands Unsuitable designation is based on the assumption that any surface mining would occur in compliance with the regulations – I accept that you are committed to enforcing the regulations. But what I wonder is this: if you routinely give coal operators waivers from the regulations which would most effectively protect the public and the water supply, then exactly which regulations are you committed to enforcing?

The time to strike a rational and humane balance between the nation's need for coal and the survival of mountain communities is not after every mountain is laid low and every mountaineer driven off to a city. The time to strike that balance is now, here on Wilson Creek. I ask that you listen carefully to our neighbors and supporters; their fears are very well founded. And I ask that the Energy and Environment Cabinet then designate the Wilson Creek watershed unsuitable for surface mining.

Finally, I would like to address the representatives of the Miller Brothers Coal Company, which is the intervener in the petition:

I will not ever lease my land to you or any coal company.

I will not ever sell my land to you or any coal company.

I will not ever leave my home on Wilson Creek.

My land is a priceless gift from past generations that I intend to use carefully, protect and, in time, pass on to the next generation. It is likely you assume every landowner has some price for which they will allow their homeplace to be destroyed but I, my family and quite a few of my neighbors know you are wrong.

BEVERLY MAY, Kentucky

Speech delivered at the Wilson Creek Lands Unsuitable For Mining Petition public hearing on 1 December 2008

Moving from Faith to Works

What does it profit my brethren if someone says he has faith
but does not have works? Can faith save him? . . .
For as the body without the spirit is dead, so faith without works is also dead.
—JAMES 2:14 AND 26 NKJ

It was a triple "H" day in the nation's capital – hazy, hot and humid. A dome of smog hung over the city and extended far beyond the Capital Beltway. The weatherman told those with illnesses to stay indoors, but eight-year-old Etta and her brother went to a neighborhood playground.

I began my afternoon shift in the ER wing of the children's hospital while Etta and her brother were running through a sprinkler to cool off. As Etta exerted herself, her airways began reacting to the smog. The muscles that line the bronchioles of her airways involuntarily contracted, while the mucous cells began a pathologic overproduction of thick fluid. Within a few seconds, this fluid buildup became what we call an asthma attack.

Etta's brother ran back home for her inhaler, and bystanders called 911. Within a few minutes, a rescue unit was on-site and began treating and transporting Etta. They radioed ahead that things were not going well.

A nurse flipped on the lights in a trauma room, and we assembled there. The doctor in charge of the team called out what he wanted everyone to do. I was given the job of intubating Etta, if needed. The ambulance crew arrived. She was being "bagged," meaning that the paramedic was trying to oxygenate her with a mask over her mouth and nose and an Ambu bag that forced air into her lungs. Her thin, limp body was quickly transferred to our trauma gurney.

Etta's pulse was ominously slow, and her oxygen saturation level was barely readable. The Ambu bag was hard to compress because of the resistance in her clogged airways.

"Matthew, go ahead and intubate. Tammy, get an art [arterial] line in; I want her paralyzed too," the leader called out. I lifted Etta's small hand and held a few endotracheal tubes next to her little finger. Then I selected the one closest in diameter to her finger, a trick I'd been taught for quickly getting the correct size. I paused a second to lean down and whisper in Etta's ear, which is the only way to communicate with a patient in a crowded, noisy room.

"Etta," I whispered, "I'm Dr. Matt. I'm going to put a tube in your mouth and get you breathing right." I looked into her frightened eyes. "I'm not gonna let anything bad happen to you, sweetheart," I promised. Her left hand still rested in mine, and I thought I felt a weak squeeze.

Two images from that scene still haunt me. The first was her little finger held next to those plastic endotracheal tubes. That hand was so small and vulnerable in my oversize palm. The second image came thirty seconds after I intubated Etta. The team leader yelled for quiet. He held his stethoscope on her chest. "Give her a breath," he ordered, and I squeezed down on the bag. Etta had on a bathing suit the color of a fluorescent green hula hoop. Pictured on its front was a happy, smiling whale blowing a spout of water into the air. Etta must have loved that bathing suit. One couldn't help but smile at the frolicking whale. Trying to lift that whale by forcing air into her lungs is my second haunting memory. Despite the rescue squad, and despite the best efforts of an entire pediatric emergency department, I broke my promise to Etta. She died of air pollution on that summer day.

A decade ago, I would have told you that our family was concerned about the environment. I would have said that we were true "conservatives," working to preserve nature. That was talk. We have progressed from talking a good talk to walking a better walk. How did we go from saying we were concerned to actually making a difference?

When God called me to this creation care ministry, I was a physician – chief of staff and head of the emergency department – at one of the nicest hospitals in America. I enjoyed my job, my colleagues, my expensive home, my fast car, and my big paycheck. I have since given up every one of these things.

We now live in a house the exact size of our old garage. We use less than one-third of the fossil fuels and one-quarter of the electricity we once used. We've gone from leaving two barrels of trash by the curb each week to leaving one bag every few weeks. We no longer own a clothes dryer, garbage disposal, dishwasher or lawn mower. Our "yard" is planted with native wildflowers and a large vegetable garden. Half of our possessions have found new homes. We are a poster family for the downwardly mobile.

What my family and I have gained in exchange is a life richer in meaning than I could have imagined. Because of these changes, we have more time for God. Spiritual concerns have filled the void left by material ones. Owning fewer things has resulted in things no longer owning us. We have put God to the test, and we have found his Word to be true. He has poured blessings and opportunities upon us. When we stopped living a life dedicated to consumerism, our cup began to run over.

Today I am one of a growing number of evangelical Christians whom the Lord is using to witness to people about his love for them and for the natural world. The earth was designed to sustain every generation's *needs*, not to be plundered in an attempt to meet one generation's *wants*.

As I go around preaching and teaching, people share their concerns. Many want a less hectic daily schedule; others long for meaning and purpose, and the security of a rich spiritual life. Still others know what is keeping them from a closer walk with God but cannot overcome inertia to make the necessary changes.

I spoke recently with a group of men. Each described himself as born again, and yet one told how he could not stop himself from buying cars – cars he cannot afford. Another complained of a persistent problem with credit card debt. A third described the pain – both economic and emotional – of going through a divorce. Being born anew in the Lord is crucial, but spiritual growth must follow. Spiritual growth is a journey we must actively seek.

One area we must change is our dependence on coal. Despite what many think, climate change may not be the most harmful outcome of our fossil fuel habit. When people's lives become dependent on a substance, we call that addiction. The addictive potential of a substance does not necessarily correlate to the "high" it delivers. A more accurate way to judge addictive potential is to see how willing someone is to go without the substance, or how painful life becomes when it is suddenly withdrawn.

When we are addicted to something, we tend to start denying or overlooking things. We fail to question its side effects. We are willing to lower our standards.

As a Christian and a physician, I'm interested in the moral

implications of our fossil fuel dependence as well as its health effects. What does devoting so much of our lives to obtaining and delivering coal do to us as a country and as individuals? All over Appalachia, mountains are being exploded to supply our addiction to coal and the electricity it supplies. Because we are unwilling to turn off lights and hang clothes on the line, we are destroying in a few short years the streams, forests, wildlife and access to clean water and air that God created for generations yet to come.

Ours is not the first generation to be morally blinded by building a lifestyle based upon energy from foreign shores. Slavery was the importation of cheap energy without regard to its moral cost. States that initially forbade slave energy, such as Georgia, eventually sanctioned it out of envy of the material wealth of their neighbors. Upon meeting Harriet Beecher Stowe, the author of *Uncle Tom's Cabin*, President Lincoln is purported to have greeted her as the woman who started the Civil War. Stowe's father was among the evangelical ministers who preached the cause of abolition. Other preachers penned eloquent pro-slavery sermons. The church, like the country, found itself split by the slavery controversy. How could church leaders come to such different conclusions while reading the same Bible? Can we draw lessons from this defining moment in our history, or are we doomed to repeat it?

The Golden Rule allows us to see the moral side of many issues, including environmental ones. Love thy neighbor as thyself—one cannot claim to be a Christian and ignore the Golden Rule. It isn't a suggestion or a guideline; it is a commandment from God. What is the connection between the Golden Rule and the environment? Isn't our choice of homes, cars and appliances just a matter of lifestyle, and therefore not a moral or spiritual matter? Does God care whether I leave the TV on all night, use a clothes dryer or keep my computer on 24/7? The Bible doesn't mention any of these things. They didn't exist in Jesus' time. Yet Jesus taught the spirit of the law, not the letter. From the spirit of the law, and from the example of his love, we can determine the morality of our actions.

When I speak in a church, I bring along a case of efficient lightbulbs to give to people. I refer to the Energy Star website (www.energystar.gov) which urges us to consume less. Formed by the Environmental Protection Agency under George Bush Sr.'s administration, the Energy Star site states that if every household changed its five most requently used bulbs to compact fluorescent lightbulbs, the country could take 21 coal-fired power plants off-line tomorrow. This would keep one trillion pounds of poisonous gases and soot out of the air we breathe and would have the same beneficial impact as taking eight million cars off the road. A decrease of soot and greenhouse gases in the air translates into people who will be spared disease and death. Some 64,000 American deaths occur annually as a result of soot in the air.

Throughout my childhood, I knew of only one schoolmate with asthma. Now on a hazy day, dozens of kids in every school reach for inhalers to aid their breathing. God did not design the air to make us short of breath. It was meant to sustain us. The Harvard School of Health looked at the impact of one power plant in Massachusetts and found that it caused 1,200 ER visits, 3,000 asthma attacks and 110 deaths annually. Nationally, the soot from power plants will precipitate more than 600,000 asthma attacks.

These are just numbers, albeit large ones. For me, those numbers boil down to Etta – one young girl who died because of our poor stewardship of God's creation. For every action that we take, every item that we purchase, we must ask ourselves, "Will this bring us closer to God?"

Because of our consumer lifestyle, we are all responsible for Etta's death. Little sacrifices – changing lightbulbs or hanging laundry on the line – are the small gestures that can help us save the next little girl's life.

MATTHEW SLEETH, Kentucky

Reprinted from Serve God, Save the Planet © 2006 by J. Matthew Sleeth; used with the permission of Chelsea Green Publishing (www.chelseagreen.com)*

Revolutionary

I want to look up, above the lights
And praise God, whoever she is
For all those stars above my head
And know, that that's what truth feels like

I want to hug a tree to save its life
Knowing that it saves mine every day
And I want to drive to the mountaintop
And I want it to be there.

I want you to know my name
Even if you disagree with who I am
And I want to feel, each day, like
I feel this very second

I want to motivate screaming voices
And fists of fury to sit down
And exercise their right to peacefully assemble

I want blacks and whites
And the full color-spectrum of nationality
To take a deep breath and
Allow the earth a chance to change

I want to be the possibility
And I want to be the change I wish to see
I want to live, love, and grow without fear
My name is Cody True
And I want to be a revolutionary.

CODY C. TRUE MCCLANAHAN, *South Carolina*
College Sophomore

Memento Vivere

After an hour of standing in front of Mt. Greenhollow, the police began to arrive in small groups attempting to stop our protest. Dad and his crew were already threatening us before their arrival, but the waves of nightsticks proved to be a much greater fear. I'll admit that I had some second thoughts at this point, but deep down I had known this outcome was a possibility. Standing there, channeling out the derisive comments from the miners, I began to relive the events in my head.

"I repeat," said the commander through his megaphone, "you have one minute to disperse from the area, or we WILL remove you!"

My minute was dwindling to a close. In spite of all the oncoming onslaught of the police, in spite of the inevitable lawsuit, in spite of the massive trouble I'd get in at home, one single thought ran through my head: "How did I ever end up here?"

I guess it all started in June, just a few months ago. Of all the professions in the world, my dad chose that of an executive in the coal industry. Despite the fact that I'd lived in Louisville all my life, he saw fit to move to Edmundville, located in Eastern Kentucky close to the Virginia state line.

It amazes me just how much control money has over people's lives. He already had a steady job in Louisville, and my sister, Jody, and I were doing very well with school and friends. I pondered this during the ride to Edmundville. Was separating me from my best friends worth an increase in salary?

"I swear to God, Julian!" I recalled Dad screaming, "Do you REALLY want to be late on your first day of school?"

Uttering insults under my breath, I slumped out of bed and wandered aimlessly until I found the dresser. It had become my natural summer habit to simply pull something randomly from the closet, but that was the first day of school. Didn't I want to make a great first appearance? I found a clean pair of jeans and a band t-shirt and ran out the door faster than you could say "Hot Topic."

As was natural, I arrived late for first period and crept into a desk near the door. Mrs. Hurston didn't even notice and acted perfectly normal when my name came up on the roster. I sat down next to a guy with jet black hair hanging partially in his face. He wore a shirt of the same band I was wearing, which provided some excellent small talk. His name was Adam Lockhart and he would become my best friend in Edmundville.

I ended up having most of my classes with him, as well as lunch. There, we sat down at a table with two girls chatting secretly. One of them had reddish-brown hair and brilliant green eyes; the other had blue hair and a black hoodie.

"Hey!" called the blue-haired girl to Adam.

"Hola!" he replied. "This is Julian. Julian, meet Allison and Jesse."

Allison, the green-eyed girl, gave me a shy smile, and Jesse responded with a rather loud hello.

I had the remaining classes of the day with Jesse and Allison. My new friends made me feel very hopeful about moving, after all. My snobby sister, Jody, on the other hand, had a completely different idea of the area.

"But daddy," she pleaded at dinner that night, "the people all talk so bad. It's like they never learned grammar."

I rolled my eyes. Jody, who had mastered the delicate art of complaining, apparently didn't notice that "bad" is an adjective; she should've used "badly." However, she was also a proficient liar and would have denied the entire thing – or ignored it – so I didn't correct her.

"I know, sugar-booger," Dad comforted her, "but daddy has to make a living."

If I ever live to be 90, I'm sure I'll agree even then that there is nothing more irritating than hearing my father call my 13-year-old sister "sugar-booger." I guess my sister really knew how to be "daddy's little girl."

"You know," I started, "the people are cool here. And I love the mountains."

"How can you be happy living here?" Jody spat back, "Don't YOU miss your friends too?"

"Well, duh," I replied indignantly. "But I don't consider myself above the people here like you do."

The reprimanding look from Dad made the two of us end the bickering, but I'm sure Jody had some unintelligent remark repeating through her head. Dad's power over her was almost sickening. I can never remember an instance when Jody would think for herself; she usually just gave it her all to please Dad.

The many succeeding days in Edmundville really made me enjoy the place. Louisville was nice, but Edmundville was captivating. I regularly used the lush, verdant mountains as a subject in my watercolors. There was something about the way each tree was formed in such a different way, but the uniform design made the mountain look so alive.

Ms. Rochester, my art teacher, slowly emerged as one of the most supportive people in Edmundville. She noticed that my ornate paintings were of the mountains and gave me many different photographs of them as inspiration. My favorite part of the week was Wednesday when Allison and I would go to her room after school. Mrs. Rochester – we all called her by her first name, Catherine – shared my love of the mountains. And although she was originally from Edmundville, she didn't discourage my newfound attraction to them; in fact she loved it.

Many words can be used to describe Catherine, but very few of them do her any justice. She had the type of disposition that made you feel guilty even before you disobeyed her. She had the ability to make me laugh, even if my day was going horribly. Above all, she pushed Allison and me to stand up for our beliefs, which gave me the audacity to join my imminent protest.

"Hey, Catherine!" I called towards the storage closet, "did you watch the news yesterday? Supposedly, Mt. Greenhollow is in the works to be strip mined."

"Oh good Lord," shouted her muffled voice as she hunted for an easel. "It's just one mountain after another! When I was younger, our mountains weren't flattened out just for a bit of coal."

One thing I loved about Catherine was how she always used her childhood as a way to embellish her ideas. Her best story was that of her copy of "The Last Supper." When she was younger, she had a copy of it from a yard sale, and for the longest time she believed it to be the actual painting. I have no clue how that taught me about Leonardo Da Vinci, but it made me love her.

"Man, at this rate, we'll have no mountains left," Allison piped in as she sketched her outline of an autumn maple tree.

"And my nephew just *loves* to run around the hollers," Catherine replied as she began organizing her palette of acrylics.

That's another thing about her I loved. No matter what the occasion, she could relate it to her nephew. I can remember one instance where she let us do some free-drawing because she had to plan her nephew's birthday party. While we drew whatever came to mind, she painted a poster of Yoda and designed Storm Trooper masks.

"Catherine, we should go to a mountain and paint *en plein air!*" I exclaimed, almost dropping my brush on the floor.

We set November 5th as the date of our trip. With every new day, I grew more excited about it. Adam, on the other hand, didn't understand my elation. A week before my trip, he spent the night at my house.

"I don't see why you think these mountains are so amazing," Adam mentioned as he devoured his fifth slice of pizza. "I've lived here all my life and I can't wait to get out."

"Don't ask me why," I replied, wrestling open our second bag of chips. "I couldn't tell you what's so special about them."

"I wish I could paint like you," Adam mumbled.

"I'm sure you can," I told him, even though I had doubts.

"Hey!" he began, "maybe I could go with you on your painting trip."

"Sure," I sputtered, wondering why I suddenly had a conscience. "I'll ask Allison."

The day of our outing was a cloudless Saturday morning. The sun radiated down upon us as we drove along the way to Mt. Greenhollow. Half asleep, I glimpsed the array of fall colors while the car sped down the road. Miles and miles of ambers, oranges, yellows and reds flooded my view. Immediately, I contemplated different paint media I could use to illustrate the scenery. Impasto just wouldn't work – the thickness of the paint would make the trees look far too dense. Acrylics dry too fast and oil paints dry too slowly. As my mind leaned toward watercolors, another image struck me.

A dull, brown, flattened land engulfed the horizon. Dust, rocks and heavy machinery all encompassed the barren landscape. I looked at the other passengers, but they were indulging in their diversions. I guess they were simply desensitized to the subject, but it was abhorrent to me. Upon our arrival, we exited the car and set up our canvases.

"Now remember, Adam," Catherine instructed. "Watercolor

is like a teenager. You have to know when to control it, and when to let it go."

For three hours, we each worked on our own separate paintings. Allison's executed an amazing drybrush, and Catherine's gouache shone stunningly. Adam's simple wash, amateur as it was, was certainly not a bad first attempt.

Despite all my beautiful photo-inspired paintings of Mt. Greenhollow, I simply couldn't paint it again. Every time I put my brush to the canvas, the image of that barren space filled my head.

"Julian," Catherine uttered, "wha...what is this?"

My image was that of the flattened mountain we passed. Needless to say, Catherine was taken aback at my landscape. I told her about how the bleak mountaintop removal site just cut off my creativity. After the silent car ride home, I spent hours Googling mountaintop removal, trying to research the topic as best as possible.

I was astonished.

All these things the coal companies were doing to the environment – it appalled me beyond all belief. The valley fills, the flattened mountains, the dead streams. I'd lived in Edmundville for almost five months, and these images disgusted me. Even though the creative block was bad itself, what really affected me was how the people were wounded by mountaintop removal. The articles and excerpts I read painted a far better picture than my feeble watercolor. I kept all the articles saved on my computer so I could use them later.

Days and weeks passed in which I described all these events to my friends. Adam and Allison were just as astounded as I was, but Jesse was quite the opposite.

"But it would hurt the economy to end it!" Jesse exclaimed during lunch.

"So money is more important than life?" I retorted.

"No, but it would hurt the people more to stop mountaintop removal," she replied. "They wouldn't be able to work."

"Sure they could," Allison interjected. "The coal companies could put them to work underground, or help them get educated in other jobs."

Then it hit me.

My own father was a culprit. Why did I even come to this town anyway? So he could work for his coal company. We didn't get along splendidly in the first place. If I was going to be bold and stand up for my beliefs, I couldn't let him get in the way.

But he would definitely be an obstacle.

"Julian, get in here this instant!" Dad yelled from the other side of the house.

I trudged in to the living room. I wanted to do the quintessential "What is it this time?" but by the tone of his voice, I knew I shouldn't test my luck.

"Why on God's green earth do you have these *treehugger* sites on our computer?!" he asked angrily.

The way he said "treehugger" made me want to vomit.

"I was just researching mountaintop removal," I replied.

"Why didn't you ask me?" he proclaimed, growing more annoyed.

"I just wanted to figure it out for myself."

"Then explain why you went to the 'Save the Mountains' site."

Now I was trapped. I'm not a mendacious person – I could barely lie about missing homework. If anything, I abhor lying, but that didn't matter. I was screwed.

"Well," I gulped, expecting the fight, "I wanted to learn what is so bad about it."

"And were you convinced?" he replied, the blue vein on his head expanding.

"S...sorta," I stuttered.

"Well, did you ever think that it's what's gonna pay for your college?" he shouted.

"Yeah, but it's not fair how it hurts the environment and the people."

"Do not talk back to me!" he yelled.

That's one thing I never understood about him. Every time I had a good point that went against his, I was talking back. It's like since he knew I was right, he had to shut me up somehow. Well, if "talking forward" means lying, then I'll settle for backtalk.

"Don't touch the computer for a week," he said and walked to his room.

I sat down on the couch and thought for a while. *I could do without the computer for a week, but how could I live off my dad's money, when it came directly from the pain of others?*

"Why was dad yelling?" Jody asked.

"Because he saw my 'treehugger' sites," I responded rather aloof.

"How can you believe them?" Jody inquired.

"Dad isn't always right," I told her, "and from what I've learned, we're profiting from greed. It's just not right."

"What is wrong with you?!" Jody shrieked. "Why do you care? You live in a big house! You should be thankful for what Dad gives you."

"And I should also be allowed to disagree with how he does it."

Jody stormed out of the room, no doubt infuriated with me. I can't say I'm sorry – she deserved to be flustered. Had she been able to control herself, maybe she wouldn't get so mad when people disagree with her.

The next day in art, Allison, Catherine and I talked about mountaintop removal.

"You know, they got the approval to mine Mt. Greenhollow," Catherine said.

"But it's such a pretty mountain!" Allison protested. "When's it gonna happen?"

"It'll be a few months," replied Catherine, "but it's still inevitable."

We all came to the realization that there was very little we could do to stop the mining. Also, considering my dad was still sour about my "treehugger" studies, I would have to act in secret.

"Maybe we could talk to some political office," I suggested.

We decided to visit the Natural Resource and Environmental Protection Cabinet, which was a disaster, culminating in an absolute refusal to cancel the mountaintop removal permit or even listen to our side of the argument. Technically, we didn't even have an argument prepared, but I would've been happy to think off the top of my head. Impromptu orations are always the most heartfelt kind. But it didn't matter – we were pushed out the door.

Life went on. I immersed myself in other things, but the issue still lingered in my mind. Weeks passed and every couple days I posted on some anti-mountaintop removal websites. Surprisingly, we weren't the only ones upset about the imminent destruction of Mt. Greenhollow. In fact, a lot people discussed many different ways we could fix it – each as useless as the last.

However, one particular idea stood out – a protest. Through the Internet, a large number of us planned out how we could execute a demonstration. After all, the Constitution gave us the right to protest.

"I told you, Julian, I'm not doing it," bellowed Jesse over the phone.

"You *know* it's the right thing," I shouted back.

"No!" she screamed. "It's a dumb idea and I am *not* going to wake up and go stand around when it won't help anything!"

She hung up. I already had Adam and Allison willing to protest, but Jesse would've been a great addition. Catherine couldn't do it – she didn't want to risk losing her job in the county school system. I can't say I blame her now, but then I was a bit disappointed.

I stayed at Adam's house the night before our demonstration. His mom was supportive of our protest and was willing to take us there. Of course, Dad didn't know a thing about it; I hid my schemes from him.

"Are you ready?" I asked Adam when we woke up.

"I'm as ready as I'll ever be," he replied.

We dressed quickly and his mom drove us to the site. We met up with our fellow protesters and, more importantly, Allison. It was freezing cold in the middle of January, but I didn't care. The civil disobedience began.

"All right, time's up," shouted the commander.

The policemen rushed at us with a flood of black nightsticks. All the boldness gone, and completely unarmed, we were sitting ducks. I can remember being utterly terrified, but the rest is really a blur of pain.

When I awoke in the cold jail cell, I could barely remember what I had just gone through. However, the moment I realized what had happened, I completely froze. *What was I going to do? What charges was I facing? Was I really dumb enough to trespass?*

Well, apparently I was – why else would I be sitting in a cell – but no one was near me, except for the guard at the end of the hallway. I'd never felt as alone as I did then. *Did Allison and Adam*

We All Live Downstream

run away? Was I a fool for staying?

"I hope you're proud of yourself," said a voice from behind.

I spun around to see Dad standing on the other side of bars.

"I don't know where to begin, Julian," he said with a blank expression. "Did you really think you could get away with trespassing?"

I wanted to say "It'd be dumb to say 'yes' now," but I had bigger problems to deal with; my sharp tongue would have to wait.

"I don't know if I'm sorry or not," I replied instead.

"Well, I have to hand it to you," he told me. "You certainly do stand up for your beliefs. It's commendable, but it's not gonna erase your charges."

"I know," I responded, "but I can't help feeling like I didn't change a thing."

"Well," dad said, "you didn't."

I don't know if that comment made me angry or sad. At that point, my dad's attitude was of the least importance. I started to think about everyone I pulled in to this mess. I wonder just what Catherine would say if she could see me now – sitting in a cell, about to hear my charges. My public defender came to get me, and we headed to the courthouse for my arraignment.

As I walked up the steps into the courthouse I couldn't help believing that I really had changed something. I wondered if my actions and legal issues could actually bring about a change for mountaintop removal. Maybe there were better ways to get my ideas across than getting arrested.

Was a mountain worth criminal charges?

I stood outside the doors of the courtroom. My attorney gave me random bits of advice, but I wasn't listening. As he coached me on how to behave in the courtroom, I kept wondering what would happen to me. For that matter, what would happen to my friends?

I guess I can't explain what emotion I had at that time. It wasn't cheerful, but it wasn't exactly hopeless. I knew deep down that my life as I knew it wouldn't end here, but I was still frightened of what would happen next. It was like driving in the dark: you know where you need to go, but your headlights only let you see what's directly in front of you.

"Julian Milton," said a man from the courtroom, "we're ready for you."

I walked towards the doors. Although all I could anticipate were the immediate events, something inside told me that I'd eventually make it to my destination.

That was all the reassurance I needed.

JACK CARTER, Kentucky
High School Sophomore

Black Mountain Breakdown
for Jeremy Davidson, 2001-04

There are no outward signs of mayhem here
at the foot of Black Mountain. Things rest
as we left them, a plastic baseball glows
in the grass where you dropped it when mama called
for supper, a tricycle hides under the high deck
of the porch, a wading pool droops, leaf-littered
and frozen. Inside, the couch where you tumbled
with your brother, your video games abandoned,
your room marked with yellow tape, your crib
where you breathed easy as mama put you down to rest,
driven into the floor by strip mine spoil,
your brother's room littered with bright Christmas
dragged from the closet as the boulder dozed through,
squatted by his bed, spared him but memory and nightmare.

JANE HICKS, Tennessee

Originally published in Appalachian Heritage

Jeremy was killed by a boulder that plunged over 600 feet from the top of Black Mountain and crashed through the side of his family's home in Inman, Virginia.

Power Past Coal

"Clean Coal" is a dirty lie and coal is killing us all. It is poisoning our children and us. It is the number one cause of climate change. Coal is public enemy number one to humankind.

We're all brothers and sisters on this earth and the environment is the one thing that connects us all. We are the environment – we eat it, drink it, bath in it, cook in it, excrete it and then drink it again. The environment should be our first priority.

We should be preaching it to our children – green is the color that connects us all. It is the color of change.

I don't mind being poor or being made fun of for being a hillbilly, but I do mind being poisoned and blasted.

Don't you dare poison my babies.

We owe our children a huge apology. We told our children to clean up their rooms when we are leaving them a toxic mess to clean up.

Shame on us.

We're allowing the coal industry to clear-cut the world's most diverse temperate hardwood forest, located in perhaps the oldest mountains in the world. They use 3.5 million pounds of explosives daily in West Virginia alone to blast our homes and mountains. The rock dust, silica, coal dust and the mix of explosives poison and foul our air.

They end up in our homes and lungs. They poison and pollute our water and streams, and if we dare speak out, then we are threatened by the coal industry and ignored by the media.

The mainstream media don't want to hear about corporations poisoning neighborhoods of people of color or poor white hillbillies.

But we won't shut up and we aren't going away. We are organizing together for environmental justice. From West Virginia to Detroit, from Kentucky to the South Bronx, from Harriman, Tennessee, to Little Village in Chicago – we are just starting to fight for our children. Tennessee's toxic coal ash disaster has opened the eyes of people living near coal plants.

It is time to stand together. The mercury from coal-fired power plants is dumbing down our babies, causing ADD, autism, low IQs, mental retardation and behavioral problems. People constantly ask,

"What's wrong with our kids?"

We are poisoning them. That's what wrong with them.

If you saw someone putting poison in a baby's bottle, wouldn't you push them away, screaming "Stop it!" and "Don't come back or I'll hurt you!" among a few other choice words?

Well, then, let's stop them now! Our children are beginning to understand what is happening to them. They will hold us responsible.

We need more actions, more protests, more letters to the editor and much more commenting and blogging on the Internet. We need to encourage President Obama to implement his plans to better the lives of our children. Our actions will give our President the mandate he needs to silence his critics; he'll then be able to look to them and say, "See, this is what the people want." Our President needs our help, and he can't do it alone.

Get out of your seats and into the streets. Let's power past coal.

JULIA "JUDY" BONDS, West Virginia

A Mountaineer's Hate

The flooding ain't over
And the killin' ain't done
Caskets are being carried
By father and by son
And a mountaineer hates
As long as he lives
And the sun will never shine
On the day he forgives

Chorus   There's machinery in his mountains
    There's foreigners diggin' his coal
    And it's leavin' his people hungry
    It's leavin' his poor land broke

His burden is heavy
His nights have grown cold
He's strong as an oak
But too soon he's grown old
Yet for food for his children
And the love of his wife
He'll stand like a giant
And he'll give his life

Repeat Chorus

Jack Wright, Ohio

Prophet, Come Down

My friend Albie has seen the ocean. Not just pictures of it in books or on TV, but for real. He says it's bigger than the river and a lot more noisy. Albie says you can't see land on the other side no matter how far you walk along the banks. He says it rolls up and turns itself over, then flattens out thin when it comes back to the land. He says the rolling never stops and it's the same every time you look at it. Once it hits the land it gets slow and quieter and kind of crawls back out into itself again.

He said the ground along the edge of the water is nothing but sand. Just clean sand everywhere and no wet mud like on the river. And the sand goes all the way out into the water, lays under it as far as the water goes, he thinks.

Albie's favorite thing to do is to let the bubbly water chase after his bare feet. He says at first he runs from it, trying to get back far enough so it doesn't get him wet. But after a while he likes to just stand still and let it run across his feet. He says he can feel the sand wiggle out from under his skin and it's hard to stand up when it moves. It feels like something alive. He says he figures some of the sand wants to go wherever it is the water goes when it goes away in big rolling waves.

Albie moved away as soon as school was out for the summer and went to live at the ocean. When he left we promised to write letters to each other at least once every week. I asked Albie to write in his letters everything he could about what the ocean is really like since I've never seen it. He asked me to write to him about our special place on the mountain so he wouldn't forget about it.

Miss Mazie Lundy told us in our English class at school if we really want people to see what we're telling them about we should pretend the people we're talking to are blind. She said pretend they've always been blind and then try to describe things so well they can see them in their minds. I told Albie it's kind of the same thing when he's telling me about the ocean since I've never seen it before. When school starts back, I'm going ask Miss Lundy if I can read some of Albie's letters to the class. He writes such good pictures and I think Miss Lundy would be proud.

Albie told me the wind blows all the time at the ocean. He

told me to go up to the top of the mountain and stand with my eyes closed and let the wind blow over me without looking for a while. He said then I should pretend the air's hot and filled with mist, sort of like warm fog that you can't see. He says imagine I taste salt on my lips. He said that would give me a pretty good idea of what the wind is like at the ocean.

I've been going up to the clearing at the top of the mountain more than usual since Albie left. Me and Albie used to love it up there. If we'd had a really good day or a really bad day, either one, it seemed to be the best place to go. We always thought there was no place like it on earth. We'd just sit there in the pine needles and look out over the humps and bumps in the mountain that run all the way out to where the sky comes down to the ground. It looks like the lumpy quilts on my bed in the winter time – only mostly green or brown, depending on the time of year.

I always thought if I walked far enough on the tops of the hills, I'd eventually come to a place where I could touch the sky. Me and Albie used to talk a lot about how the sky would feel if we could get close enough to touch it. I like being with Albie better than anybody. We could always talk about anything, especially when we were upon the mountain. Some days I miss him so bad I think I'm going to die.

Albie's daddy said they moved away from the mountain because he loves Albie so much. To this day, I still don't understand how that can be. I don't see how taking a person away from a place where they want to be is loving them. And I know Albie didn't want to leave. He told me that in person and he says it in every one of his letters. I don't think Albie understands why he had to leave the mountain either. I only know I heard Albie's daddy telling my daddy that it was time to get out.

"Things are going to change, James," he said. "You know they are. This place is not going to be here anymore and that's all there is to it. Not like it is now, anyhow. If you're smart, you'll take your folks get out of here, too."

I held my breath when I heard Albie's daddy say that. I was scared my daddy would decide to move to the ocean. But I let it all out when I heard what Daddy said.

"I know there's a chance of it, Lewis. A good chance of it. It's already started all around us. But these hills. This mountain. This is who we are. None of our people ever lived anywhere else. I don't want my kids to grow up not knowing who they are, Lewis."

"You think this is what I want to do, James? Tear up my family and just pick up and leave the only place we've ever known? Well, it ain't what I want. But what choice do I have? It's going to come and I just don't see no way to stop it. Go up on the ridge there and look west, James. It's going to be gone. All of it. And pushing the top off the mountain is just the start of it. Who knows how far it'll go before it's over? It's not going to be a fitting place to raise a family anymore."

I get scared sometimes when I think about what Albie's daddy said. I can't figure it all out. I go up to the mountain every day, just to be sure it's still the same. I try to picture in my mind how it would look if the mountain was to be gone someday, but I just can't imagine it, no matter how hard I try. I don't like to think about it too much. And Daddy never talks about it. Not in front of me anyway. I worry about my mountain and what's going to happen to it.

And I worry an awful lot about Albie. I worry about where he goes now when he's sad or when he needs a quiet place to think. I hope he's found himself a new special place by now. I guess he goes to the ocean somewhere. I suppose the ocean is a nice place and all, for people who are used to it. I wouldn't mind going to see it sometime. I wouldn't want to go stay there forever, though. It just seems to me the sky would be awfully far away there.

I pray every time I go up on the mountain that I won't ever have to leave here. I pray to God that maybe He'll make the people who want to take the mountain away change their minds and that Albie's daddy will bring him back home. I just don't think I could bear seeing my mountain gone. And I don't think God could bear it either.

SYLVIA LYNCH, Tennessee

Right or Wrong?

Before this job, his life was always fearful
He would walk into the cave of black
It appeared to go on and on:
Never ending

He was frightened that the coal above would rain down,
Scared of receiving that career-ending call,
Worried for his friends alongside him,
And wondering if he will see the sun shine the next day

But now that's all behind him
He's feels safer, more protected
Mountaintop removal feeds his family
Provides him with a house, keeps them warm

The sulfuric smell fills his nose and mouth
The booming sound of shattered rocks
Rings in his ears
Up there he can see it all

He stands there on the mountain
Sees the destruction caused by his hand
The majestic colors are gone
A plain of gray and black fills their place

He blasts away God's beauty –
Destruction caused by one small button
All for the wealth of man,
For the black gold

His mind spins in his head
As he stands above the world
Were his priorities in the right order?
Did he pick right from wrong?

SARAH FRANCIS, Kentucky
High School Sophomore

The Roy Critchfield Scandals

It was the summer of 2000, and the political season was heating up, especially in West Virginia, where we had a young woman running for governor to stop cutting the tops off mountains. This is a pretty quixotic position to take in West Virginia where the coal companies own mostly everything, including the politicians. It wasn't that we hadn't seen the ugly pictures of what they do to the hills down in the southern part of the state, but where we live, in the northern part of the state, they've been strip mining for 60 or 80 years and maybe we just got used to it. I don't know. It isn't that we're ignorant — we know about those poor people at Buffalo Creek who all drowned, and we prayed for them when it happened, but we have other things on our minds. We live pretty well in Cooper County, and we never saw much point to going against the coal companies.

Besides, that summer we had something much more immediate to think about.

My sister Vashie likes to say she raised me, and while it's true that she was almost 20 when my mother — her stepmother — died, she immediately ran off and married Roger Collier, who soon deserted her, leaving her pregnant with my niece Ruth. Vashie got her teaching certificate in time to be my third grade teacher, which she counts as part of raising me, but I don't. She was a terrible teacher, indolent and whiney. I'm retired from teaching and a widow myself now, but I remember everything. I talk to Vashie, but I don't drive her to the doctor, and I don't pick up her groceries. Ruth doesn't either, but Ruth is a classic agoraphobic. Vashie was even worse as a mother than as a third grade teacher.

So we're all widows now, Vashie, Ruth me, and my friend Ursula Rose, who was having the tag sale in front of her late husband's mansion the day Vashie waded through the sale tables leaning on her walker, lurching dramatically from time to time and pausing to rest when she thought we were watching her.

"Well ye gods and little fishies," said Ursula, glancing up from the cash box. "Look who's coming. Do you see who's coming, Ann?"

"I see her," I said. "She's planning to stage a fall, and we'll have to call the ambulance."

"You're always so mean to her," said Ursula. "I can't give her my chair because I'm taking the money. You'll have to give her your chair."

Ursula and I started college together, but she dropped out to marry Mr. Rose and become a full-time bridge and golf player, cocktail drinker and shopper. She has gone to Pittsburgh to shop at Kaufmann's at least once a month since she got back from her honeymoon. After Mr. Rose died, she started having tag sales every summer. She fills the yard with sale tables. The Rose mansion is the biggest house in town, overlooking everything, the Masonic lodge and county courthouse, the high school and the old fairgrounds. It's a wonderful view, and that day there was a fresh breeze.

As Vashie got closer, she called out in her tiniest voice, "I've been having palpitations. I know I look fine, but my heart has been doing somersaults all morning."

Ursula said, "Ann's going to give you her chair, Vashie. I have to sit here and take money."

I got up. I'd planned to give her my chair all along. I pulled over a five-gallon Christmas popcorn can from the sale. I'm 15 years younger than Vashie, but it's more than age: I walk and I garden. Vashie sits all day peering out her window.

As I tell this, it occurs to me that I must appear to be very mean-spirited. According to Vashie, she spent her youth staying up nights when I had fevers. But as I remember it, I was a stupendously healthy little orphan, and even before I started school, I was babysitting Ruth so Vashie could go to the beauty parlor. And even if my memory from childhood is distorted, I have long since paid off my debts by listening to Vashie's complaints about my un-Christian ungratefulness.

I asked her how she got up the hill.

"Caliph Dickinson drove me in his car."

"I thought you and Caliph weren't on speaking terms." Caliph owns a lot of property around town and has money in the mining supply company and a string of coal trucks. He's also chairman of the board of trustees of the First Baptist Church of Kingfield.

"I've been advising him on hiring the new minister, and of course he never listens to me, and he made sure I wasn't on the search committee. In fact," and here she leaned forward and cut her eyes right and left to indicate something important was coming, "in fact, he told me they've hired an Interim Pastor. And you will never believe who Caliph Dickinson picked. To be interim pastor of the First Baptist Church of Kingfield. It's a scandal."

"Somebody we know?" said Ursula.

I said, "How can Caliph hire a preacher by himself? What happened to the search committee?"

"It's an *interim*. Besides, the search committee does whatever Caliph says."

You need to know that the Baptist church doesn't provide leadership the way, say, the Catholics do, or even the Evangelical United Methodists. There is no Baptist Church hierarchy to send you a new minister. Baptists get their preachers by stealing them from other Baptists. Search committees go around listening to preaching, and then the church sends out a Call, and then the preacher prays to find out if he's supposed to accept.

Vashie waited for us to ask for the name, and when we didn't, said, "Frankly, I think Caliph is getting senile. He was so handsome and smart, too, when he was young, and he ended up a dry-as-dust old tightwad. I practically had to beg him to bring me up here today, and then he wouldn't wait for me, he just abandoned me to get back however I can."

I tried to catch Ursula's eye, but she was taking 10 cents from a little girl for a plastic princess mug.

Vashie paused until Ursula was finished with her commercial transaction. "Well, are you going to guess?"

I said, "Just tell us, Vashie."

"I'm not even sure this *interim* is an ordained minister. He's been doing something with juvenile delinquents, and before that he was some kind of political radical, which means a Communist if you ask me." She pressed her lips together one more time, looked at Ursula, then looked at me. Finally, she said, "He hired that hillbilly hippie Roy Critchfield. To be interim pastor at the First Baptist Church!" Then she settled her chin back in her neck and narrowed her eyes to get our reaction.

Ursula said, "Who's Roy Critchfield?"

Vashie snorted. "Ann knows. She taught him."

"He was in the very first class I taught at the high school," I said. He had been big and gangly, all his height in his legs so that his knees and feet always seemed to be sticking out in the aisles. I remembered wide shoulders and a terrible haircut, and how he cringed when you called on him. "He was from up on Salt Lick Run. He went to some kind of hard-shell fundamentalist church and wasn't allowed to do perfectly innocent things like sing in the chorus. I remember Roy."

Vashie gave me a tiny nod with her eyes glittering, the closest to praise that I ever get from her, when I verify something she says. "That was because of his father, Preston Critchfield. Preston died a couple of years back and left his little shack to the boy. It's right next to Caliph's back acres. I have to think Caliph has something in mind about the property, hiring the boy."

"Well," I said, "he's not much of a boy now is he? He must be 45 if he's a day."

Vashie said, "Roy's mother ran off and left them, and oh it was the biggest thing that ever happened. Preston used to come into town and stand outside where she was staying and shout that she was going to hell. There was always some kind of trouble around the Critchfields."

"You sure do remember the good parts, Vashie," said Ursula.

I said, "I think Roy wasn't allowed to play baseball either. *That* was the scandal, forbidding that poor boy to do what the other kids did."

"And then," said Vashie, "Roy went off and became a Communist and a drug dealer and wore his hair down to his waist!"

I didn't remember any of that part. I had had a vague sense that things had happened to Roy, but I might have been confusing him with a different boy from Salt Lick who died in Vietnam. I said, "Vashie, are you saying Caliph would hire a drug dealer for a preacher?"

Ursula said, "Caliph might if the drug dealer was cheap enough."

At this point a woman we didn't know came up to ask Ursula the price of a glass vase. The woman didn't sound like she was from here. We had already had two cars with Maryland plates and at least one from Pennsylvania. I don't know how people find out about Ursula's yard sales, but they come from all around.

"I don't know what to charge for it," said Ursula. "What do you think, Ann?"

"I don't know," I said. "Is it good glass?"

"Probably."

The stranger woman's eyes opened wide, which suggested to me that *she* knew something about glass even if we didn't. "I'd offer a dollar," she said.

Vashie was right on it. "A dollar? That thing's Waterford crystal! Don't sell it to her for a dollar! She's a dealer, I can tell. She's going to go off and get eighty or ninety dollars for it! I'll pay you two dollars myself for it!"

The stranger said, "I'd go five."

"Six!" cried Vashie.

"Five dollars will be fine," said Ursula.

Vashie brings out the worst even in kindly souls like Ursula. I think our last preacher left because he couldn't stand Vashie sitting behind her curtain watching his family come and go and calling him in the middle of the night because her heart was palpitating.

Vashie shook her head. "That woman was laughing up her sleeve at you, Ursula. Sometimes I don't think you have good sense."

"Oh," said Ursula, "I just sell stuff for fun. I don't need the money."

"I wish *I* didn't need the money," said Vashie. "I wish *I* was in a position to throw money away. Me with the roof falling in on that old house and half the window locks broken so any evil young man could come right in and do what they do to women."

Ursula took a deep drag on her cigarette. "You ought to get the windows fixed, Vashie."

I wish she'd stop smoking. She has that cough, and she's always getting bronchitis, plus there are the tiny burns in her expensive clothes. It's prematurely aged her skin, too. I don't want to think about her lungs.

I said to Vashie, "So did you see Roy Critchfield? He was such a skinny boy. Did he ever fill out?"

Vashie shrugged. Narrative, not description, is her strong suit. "His hair isn't long any more. But let me tell you Roy Critchfield was a rough customer for many years. He finally stopped being a troublemaker long enough to get that job with the juvenile delinquents, which is the blind leading the blind if you ask me."

Ursula said, "How did Caliph find him?"

"He was camping out in his Daddy's house on Salt Lick. No water, no electricity. Caliph thought it was a vagrant and went to chase him out. But they talked, and Caliph found out that Roy had gone to seminary for a while and become a youth pastor."

Ursula said, "That doesn't sound so bad. That sounds sort of admirable."

"For the First Baptist Church of Kingfield? A youth worker? Maybe not even ordained? When my daddy was the chairman of the board of deacons at the First Baptist we would never of had anything like that."

I have to admit, she gets to me when she acts like Daddy was only her Daddy and not mine. So I said, "When *my* daddy was chairman of the board we didn't have women deacons either. It wasn't so wonderful, Vashie. But what I want to know is, why would Roy Critchfield accept?"

"He probably lost his other job. I don't know. And he gets the parsonage – "

"With running water and electricity," said Ursula.

"– that beautiful yellow brick parsonage that has housed some of the finest Christian men who ever lived. And now this poor excuse is going to try to head up the First Baptist Church of Kingfield!"

"Vashie," I said, "aren't you and I related to the Critchfields?"

"You are. Not me. Through your mother. I think this *Reverend Critchfield*'s mother was a second cousin to your mother. We are certainly no relation on Daddy's side."

So the first scandal was Caliph hiring Roy Critchfield at all. The second scandal was how bad Roy's preaching was. We've been losing membership for years, especially to a couple of nondenominational churches out on Corbin Creek, but we had a nice turnout for Roy's first sermon. I always sit in the back, and Vashie does too, in her wheelchair on the opposite side from me. The big surprise was when my great-niece Becky walked in. She's Ruth's daughter, Vashie's granddaughter, a big girl who rarely speaks, almost as anti-social as Ruth is agoraphobic.

I waved to Becky to join me. "Did Ruth send you for a report?" I whispered.

Becky ducked her head and shrugged. She wears her hair short and doesn't make eye-contact. There are those who used to think she was a lesbian, but I always thought she was just born with the worst case of morbid shyness I've ever seen. I taught her in high school, and she sat in the back and never raised her hand for anything.

The choir sang the call to worship. Caliph Dickinson in his shiny old blue suit led the opening prayer and introduced Roy, who had been sitting in one of the big carved chairs out of my line of sight. He was remarkably recognizable after all these years. Wide shoulders, long legs, short torso, a little less concave in the chest than when he was a teenager, but still thin. His hair was thinner, too, and his clothes were as all-wrong as they had ever been: a brown suit jacket short at the wrists and wrinkled khaki pants.

When he began to talk, you couldn't hear a word he said. We have a good sound system, but we like preachers who don't need it. We take public speaking seriously in the mountains, recognizing different styles, of course, but at a bare minimum we expect volume. Roy was mumbling, reading from sheets of notebook paper that he held in front of his face. He glanced out at the congregation just once, and he looked like the proverbial deer in the headlights.

Vashie said out loud, the excellent acoustics carrying her voice to every corner, "What's he saying?" and then a little later, "I can't hear a thing!"

Finally, Caliph Dickinson walked across the platform in his deliberate grim-faced way and fiddled with the switch on the pulpit mike. There was a great rumble as of thunder, and suddenly we could hear Roy's mumbling, very loud. Not the words, but the rhythm of the mumble.

On the positive side, his first sermon was short.

We sang "Blest Be the Tie That Binds," and Roy gave an acceptably loud benediction, and marched up the aisle to stand at the door and shake hands. I half expected him to run out in humiliation, but, no, he seemed to be enjoying greeting people. In fact, the line moved slowly, as if people were having a chat with him. I would have asked Becky what she thought, but she did one of her disappearing dodges, which is remarkable for a woman as tall as she is.

It turned out that while Roy was a terrible public speaker, he was personable and pleasant and was trading jokes and greetings like the Chamber of Commerce. He and the whole congregation seemed to be having a downright good time getting to know each other. Vashie jumped the line, or rather rolled right over people's toes. She stared up from the wheelchair at me accusingly, "That was Becky. What

was Becky doing here? Why didn't she have the good grace to come
and say hi to her grandmother?" But then it was Vashie's turn to
speak to Roy, and she talked to him longest of all. "I couldn't hear a
thing," she shouted up at him. "You have to enunciate more clearly,
Reverend!"

Roy seemed to be sincerely sorry, "Several people told me
that," he said.

"I'll help you," said Vashie. "I'm a professional teacher, you
know. And when I was a girl we studied elocution, so I'll help you
improve your public speaking skills."

Roy, poor lamb, seemed to think that was a good idea and
thanked her in advance for any help she could give. Then he saw me
and his face lit up. "Mrs. Harding, how great to see you!"

"Well, Roy, it's good to see you, too." I say that to all my
former students and I almost always mean it. "You sound like you're
surprised I'm still alive."

He tossed back his head and laughed a big baritone laugh.
"No, it's just that this wasn't my church when I was a boy, and I
didn't know who to expect. Are you still teaching?"

I shook my head. "Retired three years ago, and I don't miss it
at all." That was mostly true. I had liked teaching, but I was tired.

"Your mother used to come to church here," Vashie said to
Roy. She had locked her wheels right beside Roy as if she were part
of the reception line. "After she left your father."

The people behind me leaned forward expectantly to see Roy's
reaction to that.

"That was a sad time for my family," he said.

"Well," I said, "It's good to see you grown up, Roy. You seem
to have turned out very well."

He laughed and shook my hand again, and again I had that
feeling of being genuinely liked, and I understood why the line had
been so slow leaving church. "I do apologize about the sermon," he
said. "I haven't had a lot of experience preaching."

"We'll take care of it," said Vashie. "I'll give you a little
practice, milk and cookies. I always take care of the pastor. I live
right across the street, you know. You can always call on me." I passed
on by, and she was still talking. "I'll just wait here while you finish
greeting everyone," she said, "and then I'll let you take me over to
my house."

Ruth phoned later that afternoon. We speak on the phone almost every day. I ought to go see her, but it's painful to go in that cluttered house. She said, "Well, I hear my mother already has the new preacher in her clutches." In spite of agoraphobia, Ruth always knows more of what's going on than I do. "I hear he's nice but no preacher. I'm going to make Becky come again next week to tell me if he does better." Ruth's other kids are out in the world as teachers and engineers, but Becky, who I sometimes think might be a touch autistic, rarely does anything more social than her job attending to the library stacks at the university.

The second week's sermon was a big improvement over the first. Roy was still reading, and I'm pretty sure it wasn't his own words, but you could hear him. Becky wore an aqua summer dress that showed off her shoulders. She left during the benediction again, and Vashie rolled over to me and said, "Becky was here again? And had a dress on? And what about her hair? Her hair is different. What did you think of the sermon? I worked on it with him. The parsonage has a whole library of sermons, so all he has to do is pick one out and practice."

A little later in the summer there was a scandal over the sermon that Roy wrote himself. Most people were pretty pleased with Roy's work, especially with the youth. He had them into the parsonage and organized some hikes and softball games. He had discussions connecting Jesus Christ to the environmental movement that not everyone approved of, and he let a couple of the boys play electric guitars during the service. That didn't go over too well, but it didn't rise to the level of a scandal.

Roy even collected money and hired a bus for a weekend to take the youth downstate to help rebuild someone's house. The most unusual thing about this bus trip was that Becky went along as one of the chaperones. Ruth and I talked about it a long time, how Becky had gone out and bought an overnight bag and some new shorts and slacks.

The scandalous sermon was a week after the bus trip, the morning after the church picnic. We have the church picnic in the grove next to the town swimming pool, and that year we filled three shelters, one with teenagers alone. Roy came over to me from the teenagers' area. He had a bright colored shirt, a print between

Hawaiian and Abstract Expressionism.

I said, "Well, you're looking sporty."

He grinned and sat down beside me. The shirt was wrinkled, as if it had been recently pulled out of a bag, and it had a very faint odor of mothballs.

I said, "I hear your weekend with the kids was a big success, Roy."

He smiled. "I want to connect church to what's going on in the world." The shirt looked familiar to me. Roy said, "I wish someone had done that for me when I was a boy. I wasted my teenage years turned inward and suffering."

Vashie was under the third shelter, and I could see she was craning her neck to see what we were doing. I said, "Well, you've got my sister taking up your cause – when you let the boys play electric guitars. Caliph didn't like it."

"I heard from Mr. Dickinson. It never occurred to me that anyone would care about the music. It was a funny lapse on my part, if you think about it, because my church when I was a boy split up over instrumental music. But today I couldn't believe anyone would care."

"I don't know that anyone does care except Caliph. I expect he and Vashie are just using you as a surrogate for their private fight. Caliph is pretty well pleased with you, overall."

He said, "He won't be after my sermon tomorrow. He isn't going to be happy. Or Mrs. Collier either."

Vashie had finally lost patience and was calling *Yoo-Hoo* and waving.

Roy got up. "I'm not much of a public speaker," he said, "but the thing is, I may not be much of a Christian either. That's what I'm going to preach about tomorrow."

Well, that piqued my interest all right, but he was moving away, and not towards Vashie. He gave wide berth to Vashie and her *Yoo-Hoos* and walked downhill to intercept Becky who was just arriving with a cake, and wearing that aqua sundress again. They stopped and smiled at each other.

Well, well, well, I thought. I had not been mistaken. And then I remembered the shirt. It had belonged to Becky's father. He had been built big and rangy like Roy. And I began to wonder if it was Ruth or Becky who had given it to him, and when they had given it to him.

Vashie was watching them make eyes at each other too, her head stuck out between her shoulders, looking like Daddy in his final years, after he'd had his stroke and used to lie all day propped on pillows in the dining room snarling at the world, jealous of anyone with health and youth.

That sermon was without a doubt the best one Roy preached all summer. It was about the possibility that Jesus experienced a loss of faith. I don't know how closely people were listening, but for those of us who did, it was an eye-opener. Who ever thought of things like that? And if they thought of it, who would ever say it?

"We all want to know that someone really understands us," said Roy. "We Christians are taught that Jesus is the only one who can do that, and we're taught that he can do it because he experienced what it is to be human. But if all Jesus experienced in the way of being human was physical suffering – well, what kind of suffering is that? The worst human suffering isn't about physical pain. Our bodies shut down when we hurt too much. We pass out. But our brains can suffer on without end. The worst kind of human suffering is to lose hope.

"So my question is, how could Jesus really understand us if he never experienced despair or at least had serious doubts about what he was doing up on that cross?" Roy waited a few seconds, and then said, "'My God, my God, why has Thou forsaken me?' Jesus said that on the cross, and I believe he really meant it. That he really knew what it meant to stop believing. Not just to have a test of physical endurance, but to lose hope of God. And if he didn't know what that feels like, well, he was never truly human."

It gave me a little shudder. I don't spend a lot of time thinking about these things, but I had wondered about that, about why Jesus getting crucified was supposed to be so much worse than someone else getting crucified or the torture you read about in the paper every day or for that matter the suffering people go through with cancer.

Vashie had cupped her hands over her ears, which didn't mean she was listening but that she wanted people to think she was. Caliph Dickinson had his eyes closed. I think most of them blocked it out, that someone paid by the First Baptist Church could be standing up there saying Jesus Christ doubted the existence of God.

The ending rambled a bit. Roy said that if there is a heaven (and I'm sure he used the word "if"), that Jesus will let us all in because he understands, that he'll forgive us our disbelief. So we should pay attention to one another and be kind and (I'm sure he said this) try to stop them from ruining the mountains because we're part of this world and we're all in this together. When it was over, I shook his hand and thanked him. Most of the rest of them seemed to ignore what he had said the way you ignore an old person passing gas in public.

The final scandals were about sex and politics. Vashie called me to complain that Roy hadn't come home the night before. I said he probably just came in really late, but she said, no, there hadn't been lights even at 3 a.m., and he didn't answer the phone either.

"Maybe he's staying out at Salt Lick."

"Something is going on," said Vashie. "Where is he? What if I have a heart attack? Who will I call? What if someone breaks into my house?"

I said, "How were you getting through the night before he came to the parsonage?"

"Not well," she said. "All I know is, I heard a noise last night and called, and he never answered. I could have been murdered in my bed." She paused, and I could hear her breathing. Then she said, "I'll tell you what *I* think. *I* think he was out tomcatting."

It took her a couple of days to figure it out She called me again, and as soon as I answered the phone, she started shouting. "You and Ruth! The two of you! My own daughter and my sister I raised like a daughter! How could you treat me like this?"

I said "What are you talking about, Vashie?" Knowing exactly what she was talking about.

"You've known about it for weeks and kept it from me! Ruth doesn't have the sense she was born with. Letting that fat Becky do whatever she pleases– "

"Becky is 35 years old, and she isn't really fat anymore."

"I don't care! She's living in Ruth's house, and Ruth should keep a leash on her. It's Roger Collier's bad blood, that's what it is. To *have an illicit affair* with the temporary preacher! To have a preacher who is an adulterer!"

"I think 'fornicator' is the word you want," I said. "I don't think either Roy or Becky is married."

"Sneaking around in the night! First Ruth told me Becky has a boyfriend, and then she says 'Becky is entertaining menfolk!' Like it was a joke! I said 'Ruth this can't be allowed!' And do you know what she said to me? She said, 'Becky deserves some pleasure in this life!'" She had to stop and pant for a while before going on. "And besides, he's a-way too old for her."

I bit my tongue so I wouldn't say, *And you're too old for* him, *sister.*

"And that's not all. He came over to my house today as big as life bringing me my groceries and offering to take me to the doctor!"

"And you told him you couldn't accept help from a fornicator?"

"I let him know how I felt. I didn't say it in so many words, but I hardly spoke to him the entire time I was in his car. He knew."

In spite of fornication, however, I don't think Caliph would have fired Roy until they had the next preacher lined up, if not for the Mountain Party people.

On Friday, I picked up the phone for Vashie's first call of the day. She hissed, "Becky is at the parsonage right now! In fact, there's a whole house full of people," she said. "People with banjos! They're sitting on the porch of our parsonage." She paused. "It's the Communists from the Mountaintop Removal Party."

Now I've mentioned that it was an extremely busy political year – this was the year West Virginia put George W. Bush over the top with our five electoral college votes at the same time we were electing the usual Coal Company Democrat for governor, but we also had that girl from downstate running for governor on the Mountain Party ticket.

"Roy Critchfield is not only tomcatting at night," Vashie said with great satisfaction, "he's showing his true colors and turning the parsonage into a den for radicals!"

Now I have to confess that once I figured out what she was talking about, I wasn't so pleased either with Roy mixing politics with church. I may not take literally every word that gets preached to me every Sunday, but I like a calm Sunday morning service. That week Roy turned the Sunday morning service over to these political people with anti-coal company ballads and a slide show of ugly pictures of mud and raw dirt where beautiful trees used to be.

Everyone showed up: Becky looking like the cat that ate the canary, or maybe more to the point, like a woman who's been enjoying herself for the first time in her life. The teenagers were there, and people from the university, and there was even a reporter with a camera.

The Mountain Party people sat in the big carved chairs up on the platform with Roy, and they did everything except read the scripture. Roy did that, Psalm 46: "God is our refuge and strength. Therefore we will not fear, though the earth be moved, and though the mountains be toppled into the depths of the sea."

They had a slideshow and stories and songs about the awful things the coal companies had done to our state. Buffalo Creek where all those people who drowned because of the faulty dam for wastewater from the mines. But except for Psalm 46, there was no mention of God and no praying. The congregation ranged from bored to bemused to vaguely uncomfortable, except for Caliph Dickinson. He was outraged. Caliph has that part interest in the mining supply company, and I expect he would gladly sell the tops off all his mountains if anyone made him a fair offer.

By midweek, Roy was through as interim pastor. There was an emergency meeting of the entire church membership – deacons, trustees and all the rest of us. One of our lawyer members, also a member of the Republican committee, said it was partisan politics and therefore endangering the church's tax status. Most of them just said it was not what they come to church for. Vashie stood up in her walker and said she had supported Roy from the beginning and helped him in every way she could. As a Christian, she still had to love him, but he had gone too far. Roy sat through it all, nodding like he was in a counseling session, trying to understand their feelings. I voted to keep him on, but I wasn't all that sorry the way it turned out.

Before Thanksgiving, the First Baptist had hired itself a regular pastor with a wife and two kids. The wife, however, was a big disappointment to Vashie because she refused to let her husband run across the street every time Vashie's house creaked.

Roy moved in with Becky and Ruth, and spent a lot of time in the southern part of the state working with the Mountain Party. A few of us – Becky and me and Ursula because I told her to and Ruth by absentee ballot – voted for the Mountain Party. They never had a real chance, of course, and the regular Democrat won. He wasn't a bad governor by West Virginia standards, but he didn't run for a second term because he had an extramarital affair that came out in public.

After the campaign was over, Roy and Becky got married, which Vashie claimed was her doing. She said every time he took her to the doctor, she worked on him about the importance of holy matrimony. Then Becky got pregnant, so Roy took a job at the grocery store and eventually he got his certification for teaching, and he teaches social studies at the new middle school now, where he gets in trouble from time to time for the projects his students do. He still works against mountaintop removal, and he also runs errands for Vashie, who says she has forgiven him although she'll never forget.

I donate to whoever Roy says to, as I believe he's a righteous man.

Roy and Becky have turned out be wonderful parents, probably better at babies than at stopping the coal companies, but they don't give up, so I won't either.

Meredith Sue Willis, New Jersey

Sunday Drive Survival

Ada and Hank, back from the north,
struggle out of the mangle of traffic
past Wal-Mart's, and Bargain Resale Homes,
on up the hill by the Black Gold
Golf Course. They slow to a crawl

behind two behemoth coal trucks
which grind and snort, and on
toward that sweet park they remember,
the one with the stone fireplace
by the river where they used to dream.

They spot the fireplace ablaze
with broken glass and beer cans.
Perhaps they can find the old path
to the river. At what seems to be the bank,

ghosts of trees, prisoners in their shrouds
of kudzu, are hung with the white stuff
of flood leavings. Tires in muck block the path.
A rusty refrigerator lists in the acrid slime
like a frozen guard pushed over.

They have happened on a grand festival
of decay. Broken glass sparkles
in the sunlight like fire. Before them
spreads the strip job, a yellow scab of earth
as far as they eye can see. Trees left
by the bulldozers dangle from their roots
at bone crushing angles. They turn

back to the car, shove the gearshift in low
and grind silently back through the muck.

Noel Smith, New York

Battling a Giant: A Christian Response to Mountaintop Removal

When Kathy Lindquist wrote a half-page essay on mountaintop removal coal mining in the summer of 2005, she had no way of knowing the remarkable chain of events she had set in motion. Her essay, intended for the newsletter at Knoxville's Church of the Savior, was a heartfelt appeal to her fellow congregants, asking them to speak out against the growing threat of mountaintop mining in Tennessee. She wrote: "Where God put a mountain, do we have the right to remove it?" Kathy's words were a tiny stone flung at an industrial giant, and she surely must have wondered if she was wasting her time. She wrote anyway.

Just a few weeks later, near summer's end, Kathy passed away at the age of 45, having lost a decades-long battle against cancer. This story might have ended there if not for another heartfelt action, this one by a second church member, Dale Liles, a quiet woman of 70-something, who stood up during Sunday service to remind the congregation of Kathy's final appeal. "My husband and I fought strip mining 30 years ago," Dale said, "but mountaintop removal is worse. Something needs to be done, and somebody younger needs to do it."

After church that day, I stopped Dale in the parking lot and told her I felt called to help; she told me another church member, Dawn Coppock, had also volunteered. Several brainstorming sessions later, LEAF, the Lindquist Environmental Appalachian Fellowship, was born with Dawn and myself as co-founders, and Dale designated as LEAF's "godmother."

From the beginning, Dawn and I sought to shape LEAF as a memorial to Kathy that reflected not only her passion for environmental stewardship, but also her deep faith, a faith forged through long years of ill-health and frequent hospital stays. During one serious setback just a year before her death, Kathy had to be placed on a ventilator. Unable to speak for many days, she communicated by writing on a small dry-erase board. When told her condition was finally improving, Kathy responded by writing: "*God is amazing.*"

LEAF was subsequently founded in this same spirit – an attitude of gratitude in the midst of battling long odds. Our mission became the education of Tennessee congregations regarding the Biblical call to care for God's creation, with a special emphasis on protecting the state's mountains from the looming threat of mountaintop mining. The Bible contains literally hundreds of verses that speak of God's love for His creation and his continuing ownership of what He's made.

The Earth is the Lord's, and everything in it. (Psalm 24:1)

The teachings of the early Christian church display a strong stewardship ethic, something most contemporary Christians seem to have forgotten.

In the 3rd Century, St. Augustine wrote: *Some people, in order to discover God, read books. But there is a great book; the very appearance of created things. Look above you! Look below you! Read it. God, whom you want to discover, never wrote that book with ink. Instead, He set before your eyes the things that He had made. Can you ask for a louder voice than that?*

More than a thousand years later, Martin Luther boldly declared: *God writes the Gospel not in the Bible alone, but also on trees, and in the flowers and clouds and stars.* It seems that only in modern times has it become acceptable for Christians to view God's gifts as nothing more than a "resource" we can ruthlessly exploit for financial gain. The more Dawn and I studied, the more we realized how "green" Christian doctrine truly is.

In retrospect, Dawn and I were an improbable team to establish an environmental initiative. For starters, neither of us had any environmental expertise. I'm a freelance writer who has spent the past 20 years traveling the southeast for a variety of magazines, including *Southern Living.* Reserved by nature, I'm the blue jeans and tennis shoes type. Dawn, on the other hand, is a high-powered adoption attorney whose name consistently appears on the short list of Tennessee's best lawyers. Power suits are her normal attire, she's comfortable in heels, and she's never met a stranger.

But as different as we are, the two of us share a heartfelt belief that living out one's faith can, and will, make a difference in the world. In addition, we possess a bone-deep love of the mountains. Both of us can trace our roots to ancestors who settled in Tennessee during the 18th Century, about the same time Daniel Boone first made his way through Cumberland Gap.

Thanks to the generosity of members of Church of the Savior

who made donations in Kathy's memory, LEAF's first action was to purchase "creation care" materials and offer them, free of charge, to interested congregations. Dawn and I held lengthy meetings around my dining room table, sorting through books and films, seeking works that would capture the attention of busy churchgoers who'd never heard of mountaintop removal mining. Early on, we were delighted to discover a documentary called *Kilowatt Ours*. The filmmaker, Jeff Barrie, happened to be a fellow Tennessean, and it wasn't long before he'd introduced us to a pair of evangelical Christians, Matthew and Nancy Sleeth, who spend much of their time criss-crossing the U.S., speaking to congregations about faith-based environmental stewardship. Their book, *Serve God, Save the Planet*, became another core component in LEAF's outreach to churches.

Within the first two years of LEAF's existence, more than 150 congregations scattered across Tennessee were exposed to the message of creation care through LEAF's study materials, a remarkable accomplishment for a small committee from a small church with fewer than 200 members.

Although we rejoiced at the growing number of churches who were heeding the call to care for God's Creation, it was agonizing for us to witness the growing list of Tennessee mountains that were slated for destruction. We were moving as fast as we could, but the mining companies were moving faster.

That was why, in the fall of 2007, Dawn came up with the idea of proposing legislation to end the practice of mountaintop removal in the state of Tennessee. As an attorney, she'd helped draft adoption legislation in the past, but she knew she'd need help with the technical aspects of an anti-mountaintop removal bill. She decided to consult the staff of the National Parks Conservation Association (NPCA), whose southeast regional office is located in Knoxville, knowing they were deeply concerned about mining in the headwaters of the Big South Fork National Recreation Area, just north of Knoxville.

The NPCA agreed not only to help draft the bill, but also to partner with LEAF in lobbying for its passage. Introduced into the Tennessee Legislature in January 2008, the Tennessee Scenic Vistas Protection Act garnered support from a broad coalition of legislators, Republicans and Democrats alike. Although the LEAF/NPCA partnership was unsuccessful in securing the bill's passage during our first legislative foray, we came amazingly close, and we were heartened by the outpouring of support from people of faith across the state. As I write this, there are plans underway to reintroduce the bill in the future.

People frequently point out the David and Goliath aspect of LEAF's story. From its small beginnings as a church committee speaking out against an industrial giant, LEAF has grown into a network of Christians from many different denominations that are raising their voices in unison against the devastation of God's creation.

When Kathy sat down to write her anti-mountaintop removal essay, she had no idea if anyone would listen, but she wrote anyway. When we step out in faith – speaking to a politician, writing a letter to an editor, teaching a creation care class – we can never be sure our efforts will make a difference, but we do it anyway.

Sometimes God uses tiny stones to bring down a giant.

PATRICIA HUDSON, *Tennessee*

My Home

for the people of McRoberts, Kentucky

We moved into that one-story coal camp house
On the day he married me
He put that gold ring on my tiny finger
We made our home in 343
That man he loved me so tender
He was sure crazy over me
But one good man's love just can't hold up
To the cruel hand of a whole company
Not long after we made our home
They started taking that mountain down
We lived below in the shrinking shadow
We trembled when they shook the ground

Chorus   I don't know my home
               Lord, how in the world can this go on?
               Nothing's the same and it won't go back
               Oh, something's wrong

I knew I would lose my mind
I lived that mess every day
I told him I couldn't take much more
Told him I had to go away
He took me over into Virginia
And when we came back the next week
Crossing that state line back into Kentucky
I went cold and I couldn't speak
Plateaus sharp against the sky
Flat brown mounds like graves
In memory of something they chose to squander
Something it's too late to save

Chorus   I don't know my home
               Lord, surely I wasn't away that long
               Nothing's the same and it won't go back
               Oh, something's wrong

Bridge   One blue-black night in mid-September
                The sky cried heavy to the ground
                That valley-fill came pouring down
                He found my letter, the words warped from shaking
                I wrote, "I can't take any more"

Chorus   He can't stand me gone
                Lord tell me he won't have to stay too long
                Nothing's the same and it won't go back
                Oh, this is wrong

TIFFANY WILLIAMS, *Kentucky*

A Vacation To Remember

"Hey!" I shouted at my brother Jeremy. "Scoot your junk over!"

Our vacation to Disney World was going smoothly until we stopped to eat breakfast. At that first stop my brother added about an hour to the trip after he insisted on removing his backpack from the trunk. Removing Jeremy's bag was not the problem. When we go somewhere that is twenty hours away, like Florida, my parents always pack two of everything.

Jeremy's backpack was filled with practically everything he owned; candy, bubblegum, CDs and Star Wars action figures. The instant my brother unzipped it, his junk started to overtake the car. My brother is not civilized like most human beings. Instead of getting out one of his CDs, he will pour every one of them onto the floor, then he will decide to have a battle with all of his Star Wars action figures. And don't even get me started with all of the gum and candy wrappers.

Simple fact: my brother is absolutely the most disgusting person on the planet, and he makes more messes than three or four people combined.

After I told Jeremy to scoot his junk over, he pretended like I did not even exist. What's more, his eyelids suddenly dropped shut, and I thought I could hear Toby Mac's voice start to grow louder behind his headphones. I glared at him. Jeremy was always terrible at faking sleep, but this time really took the cake.

"Please, Jeremy," I said, trying to control my temper. "Move your junk!"

Instantaneously, my mother spun around in the front seat and gave us *the look*.

"Amanda, stop picking on your brother."

I felt my face turn red with frustration, but I knew that talking back would not get me anything except a punishment. I sat silently and looked out the car window for something to capture my attention. I noticed that at the side of the road there were little signs with numbers on them. After a few minutes, I realized that there was a new sign about every mile.

I started counting them. Before I knew it I had counted 16

signs. At the last one, mile marker 148, I saw a sign for a town:

Daffodil Ridge
Population 218
8 miles

I wondered why people paid to have signs put up every mile in the middle of nowhere. I turned to look at my brother who was lip-synching and picking his nose at the same time. He didn't seem to notice that I was staring right at him. Quickly, I turned my head away. *How could one person be so disgusting?*

I directed my gaze to the floor, the only section of the car that wasn't yet covered with Jeremy's stuff. I thought I saw a bracelet that I had lost under the backseat, so I reached down to grab it. My palms felt like they were clasping something foreign. I opened my hand, and staring back at me was the ugly face of Darth Vader. First, I thought about hiding my find, but then I got a better idea – *what if I just got rid of it?*

"Can we open the window please?" I asked my parents.

"Sure," dad said.

Slowly, I lifted Darth Vader toward the window as a tornado of candy wrappers started to form inside the car.

"Noooooo!!!!!" Jeremy wailed as my hand inched closer to the car window. His whole tough guy attitude quickly diminished into little kid tears.

I knew deep down that what I was doing was wrong. I also realized that if Darth Vader really flew out the window, I would never see the light of day. So I rolled the window back up and threw Darth Vader into the floorboard of the car.

I looked at Jeremy. He started to tattle, "Amanda tried to…" but he was cut off as the car slowed and pulled off on the side of the road.

At first I thought that my parents were going to ground the two of us for life, but they did not say anything. Jeremy and I looked at each other. We sat there as cars rushed passed us, shaking our car back and forth. My dad turned they key, but nothing happened. He repeated this, but still, nothing.

"I think the car died," Dad said.

"No duh!" Jeremy said under his breath. My father looked at him in the rearview mirror, eyebrows raised. *Great,* I thought, *now we don't get to go to Disney World.*

The next few minutes were pretty hectic. My dad tried to start the car a few times, until finally he popped the hood. I have no idea why he did this; he knows nothing about cars. In fact, the only cars I have ever seen him try to fix were Hot Wheels, which is why I wasn't surprised when he shut the hood and told my mom that he was going to try to call a tow truck. Of course, this didn't work; we were in the middle of nowhere and the black interior of our car was rapidly heating.

Then my dad remembered he had seen a sign for a town a few miles back, but he didn't know how far we were from it. Everyone was disappointed. I remembered I had seen the sign, too. It was just past the 148 mile marker.

"I saw the sign!" I shouted.

"Do you remember what was on it?" mom asked doubtfully.

"Yes!" I replied excitedly. "'Daffodil Ridge, Population 218, eight miles ahead.'"

"Okay," my dad said. "But I still have absolutely no idea how many miles back the sign was."

"Do you know what was the last mile marker we passed?" I asked.

"Mile marker 140," he replied. My dad looked surprised that I had been counting mile markers. He got out of his car and started walking toward the town. We waited patiently, and in less than half an hour a tow truck pulled up beside us.

The door of the truck opened and a short, stocky man jumped out to greet us. He had gray curly hair and a long beard that was in desperate need of a trimming. My father led him over to the scalding car and said, "Burl here is going to tow our car and give us a ride."

"Burl?" my mother asked with a worried expression. She had never been too fond of strangers.

"At your service, ma'am," he said.

"Yeah," my dad added. "He owns Burl's Repair Shop. He picked me up at the turn-off."

"I can see that," my mother answered, a frown forming on her lips.

I looked at the tow truck beside us. "Burl's" was painted across the side of it with the ugliest shade of mustard yellow paint I had ever seen. Reluctantly, my mother beckoned us out of the car and into the tow truck. I was so relieved when we got out of the car. Between the growing heat, the invasion of Jeremy's junk and the constant rocking back and forth of the car, it was all I could do to keep myself from shouting for joy once my feet touched solid ground.

Burl hooked the car up to the tow truck and waited for all of us to climb inside. When I opened the door, a repulsive smell almost knocked me back. There were French fries all over the backseat and a patch of mold beginning to grow on the ceiling. I moved back so Jeremy could get in first. Of course, he decided to sit directly below the mold. I followed, turning away from Jeremy so I didn't have to look at him. My parents got in next, and once Burl made sure we all had our seatbelts on, we started moving.

I closed my eyes, trying to relax, but that didn't last very long. Burl was the worst driver I had ever ridden with. I looked at Jeremy who was holding onto his seat for dear life. My father cleared his throat nervously and said, "Burl?"

"Yes?" Burl answered.

"Why did you decide to be a mechanic?"

There was an awkward pause, then Burl replied. "Well sir, when I learned to drive, I wasn't the best driver. I always wrecked my car somehow or another, and cars ain't cheap these days. So I decided to go to work fixing them. Now, whenever I wreck one I can just fix it!"

Burl grinned. An uncomfortable silence fell over the car. Then he let out a laugh so suddenly I just about jumped out of my skin.

My dad continued to fuel the conversation with small talk, and before long my mother chimed in, too. Jeremy and I stayed silent, hanging onto our seats. Once I had just about gotten used to the smell in Burl's car, I saw a sign that said:

Welcome to Daffodil Ridge
Population 218

Burl drove us up a gigantic hill. Once we reached the top we could see the town. Daffodil Ridge looked like the front of a vacation brochure. Burl explained that it was built on the side of a mountain. I looked out the back window and saw the mountain's ridgeline behind us.

I probably would have still been looking at that same

breathtaking scene if Jeremy hadn't tapped me on the shoulder.

"What?"

"Look at that," he said. We were going past an old building. "Is that a school?" he asked.

"Yep, that there is our school." Burl pointed out several other buildings. Despite being so small, Daffodil Ridge had a church, a school, a diner and, of course, a mechanic. The next building we passed had an old sign with mustard yellow lettering.

"This is it," Burl said.

I hopped out of the car and inhaled a deep breath of air. Burl looked at the car and told us that he would probably need to order a few parts.

"How long do you think it will take to fix the car?" my father asked.

"Probably a day or so," Burl replied.

"Does this mean that we might still get to go to Disney World?" Jeremy asked. Dad grinned in response.

"Do you know where we could stay tonight?" my mother questioned Burl.

"We don't have a hotel," he said. "But there's a bed and breakfast over by the church."

"Thanks so much for your help, Burl," she replied. We walked to the car and got out some of our things. Thankfully, Jeremy's backpack wasn't included. Then we made our way to the bed and breakfast, which was just behind the church in a quaint two-story house.

"This looks like a nice place," my mother commented.

The owner showed us to our rooms, both of which had extremely soft beds, as well as a bathroom, TV and telephone. I had almost relaxed when I realized I would be sharing a bed with my brother.

UGH!

After we were settled, Jeremy and I turned the TV on. We fell asleep, eagerly anticipating what was in store for the next day.

The next morning I awoke to a dark room. I wasn't sure that morning had come yet, so I stayed in bed a few minutes until someone began to knock at the door. It was my parents carrying our breakfast.

"Good morning!" my mother said. I felt like groaning, but instead I smiled. For some reason I had a feeling that something was going to happen today. I wasn't sure what, but I couldn't wait to find out.

They sat with us while we ate our delicious breakfast of flaky hot biscuits, crisp bacon and fresh fruit. I couldn't remember the last time I had tasted something so good.

After we finished eating, we left to see how Burl was doing on the car.

"How soon until we leave for Disney World?" Jeremy asked.

Dad paused. "Assuming everything will go as planned, we could be out of here tomorrow morning."

Jeremy shouted for joy, and then started to do some really strange dance moves.

"What in the world do you call that dance, Jeremy?" I asked. "The limping cow dance?"

He slugged me in the arm as hard as he could.

"Ow!" I yelped with pain.

"That's payback for laughing at my dance moves."

If we hadn't seen Burl's sign with the mustard yellow letters, I had a feeling my brother and I would have started World War III. Suddenly, I realized something very strange – we hadn't seen any other people since we got to Daffodil Ridge. We had seen Burl, the lady at the bed and breakfast, but no one else. There were no kids playing outside, no cars going down the road, no dogs barking. I felt like something was terribly wrong.

"Dad, don't you think it's strange that there aren't any kids playing outside?" I asked.

"Yes," he replied, "but people are probably on vacation."

"The entire town? I didn't even hear a dog barking last night." I said.

Jeremy agreed. "Something strange is going on."

When we reached Burl's shop, he was nowhere in sight. The inside of his shop was dark. My father knocked on the door. "Burl?" he said, but there was no answer.

He knocked harder and spoke louder: "Burl!" No answer.

Dad kicked the ground. I had never seen him act like this.

"David, you need to calm down," my mother said. "He's probably busy somewhere."

"I guess you're right."

A few minutes later, my mother knocked firmly. "Burl," she said.

This time, the door opened just enough for Burl to stick his head out.

"I'm not going to fix your car," Burl said.

"What?" my father demanded.

"Please don't get mad, sir. It's not that I don't want to fix your car, I just don't have the time."

"What do you mean?" Dad yelled. "There's no one else here!"

Suddenly, Burl looked sad. "Come in."

We were surprised at what we saw. At one end of the room was a bench with tools on it and a few containers of what looked like oil. A stack of tires was nearby, but across from that was a table with six chairs around it. On the other side of the room were two beds, a dresser, a couch and a TV.

"Please make yourselves at home," Burl told us as he pulled a chair out from the table. We walked over and sat down.

"I didn't tell you folks when you came, but the people of this town have been miners for decades," he explained. "Most people don't think very much of miners, but they're hard workers."

Dad nodded.

"The mines are on the other side of the mountain. Mining's pretty much the only job you can get around these parts, and it pays okay."

Burl sighed. "We'd all lived pretty comfortable lives until some people showed up. They were all dressed real professional-like. They bought the mines, and after that most people just left."

"Why did they leave?" I asked.

"Every man in the town pretty much worked at the mines, except for me. Their wives ran the diner and the bed and breakfast, hoping to make a little money from tourists. The only problem was tourists wouldn't come. It gets pretty hard when folks ain't got a job. My wife even left."

I thought I saw tears start to form in Burl's eyes. I felt really bad for him.

"Several weeks ago, I learned that those men who bought the mine planned on blowing the whole mountain up," he shook his head.

"They said it'd be easier than sending miners in for coal. They said we only had two weeks before the mining would begin. That was a week ago."

"That isn't fair!" Jeremy shouted. "They're going to blow up the very mountain you live on?"

"Yep," said Burl.

"I can't believe this," I stuttered.

"Don't think it doesn't happen, Amanda," my dad said. "I did an investigative report on this just a few months ago. The process is called mountaintop removal and it could eventually take out the Appalachian Mountains."

I couldn't speak. This sounded like something that was completely illegal. I knew that we had to help the people here, especially Burl.

"What can we do to stop this?" mom asked.

"We can't really stop it," my father replied.

"Dad!" I shouted. "We can't let Daffodil Ridge get blown to smithereens. It's so pretty!"

"The coal companies don't care if it's pretty," he said. "All they want is the coal and they'll do anything to get their hands on it."

We sat there, shell-shocked. No one said a word; we were all too busy thinking of ways that we could save Daffodil Ridge.

Suddenly, Jeremy piped up. "Dad, what if we took a picture?"

"A picture?"

"Yeah, you can write an article for your newspaper that tells people to come here if they don't want such a pretty place to be destroyed. People who are big into the environment will want to help, and if people go to the mountains for vacation, well…"

My dad's eyes lit up. "We could try. Don't we have a camera in the car?"

Mom nodded in answer.

"Crank up the tow truck, Burl!" I shouted. "We need to drive to the top of the mountain."

Within a matter of days, people started visiting Daffodil Ridge. The coal company was forced to rethink their plan, and all of the miners got their jobs back.

We had originally planned to go to Disney World for vacation last summer, but after our car died, our plans changed. We actually wound up helping to save an entire town: Daffodil Ridge, Population 218. When people look back on vacations, they usually remember their little brother who's things took over the car, the extremely fast roller coaster they rode or the sights they saw on the way. I will remember that vacation for another reason.

I realize that if our car hadn't died, Burl would have gotten no help and the town would not be the popular tourist destination it is today. I also owe a little bit of credit to Jeremy, too. Even though he is still the most absolutely disgusting kid on the planet, he does have some pretty good ideas. I just wish he would scoot his junk over when I ask him to.

SARAH KATHERINE SAYLOR, *Kentucky*
Eighth Grade

Field Trip

People have recently begun to ask me why it is that I care about the environment. They wonder why I bothered to start an environmental club at my high school. Some friends have suggested that I do it merely for recognition or for college applications, but these have nothing to do with it.

I can see why they might be skeptical. Until recently, I hadn't exhibited any real interest in the subject, and even now my efforts by no means fulfill my desires. I still find myself taking part in the daily destructive rituals of our country – driving 20 or 30 miles a day, consuming an innumerable amount of unnecessary products, not taking the time to rinse out and recycle my apple juice bottles when I am finished with them.

Seeing this outward appearance, I do not blame friends who have mocked and questioned me. At the same time, knowing my intentions and motivation, I am steadfast in my newfound activism.

It all comes back to one moment – a cool day in November 2000, the last day of my fifth grade field trip.

The leaves crunched beneath our feet and the cool air filled our lungs. Our adolescent bodies ached from a hard day's work. It would be over soon, though; the summit was within sight. As we approached it, we were filled with a new drive. Determined to reach the top, we pushed through the pain that wracked our clumsy frames.

When we finally reaching the clearing on the ridge of Pine Mountain, we were blown away by the brilliant reds and yellows of the changing leaves and the crisp wind that extinguished the heat of our sweaty faces. The mountains extended beyond our vision. We soaked in the serenity.

In one instant, however, this picturesque moment came to an end. As I turned, a striking abnormality caught my eye – a barren plateau in the center of a lush mountain forest.

Mountaintop removal.

A lifeless place riddled with machines that were harvesting what seemed to be the life from the earth. The devastation was overwhelming, and it all took some time for it to sink in as the guide explained what was happening.

When I recall this single day at Pine Mountain, I begin to realize why I am so concerned about the environment. It was in that split second that I first developed a sense of environmental awareness. I think back to that moment each time I hear or see news of destruction. Each time, I have the same childlike reaction. I find that the true reason for my passion is the fear created that day, the fear that soon there could be nothing left.

At this point, I am a bit relieved, but certainly not satisfied, with my activism. I am involved in a group called EcoLouisville, a coalition of high school environmental clubs from across the city. We are still in our nascent stages, but have successfully put on our first major effort – a week of events that included an auction, a dinner, a capture-the-flag game, community outreach and a "Ride Your Bike To School Day." Through these activities, we have already raised over $2,000 to be donated to Kentuckians for the Commonwealth to fund their efforts against mountaintop removal. Although we only consist of five schools, we hope that we will be able to expand and host more events.

Brennan Clark, Kentucky
High School Junior

The Worst Bad Neighbor

Turn on your television today and chances are good you'll be treated to a barrage of slick commercials about striving for American energy independence. These ads are all about ingenuity and freedom and pride. They talk about resolve and resourcefulness and wrap all their imagery and verbiage in the American flag.

No doubt some companies are indeed working to make ours a better country and a better world. At least I hope that is the case. But I'm jaded where energy messaging is concerned. I've been in public and media relations for more than two decades and I understand how corporate communications manage public opinion. Commercial wordmeisters solicit and elicit, incite and delight with carefully honed slogans. Nowhere was this more evident than in coal company ads that ran throughout the 2008 presidential debates in an attempt to influence votes and reinforce their "clean coal" brand.

Clean Coal – how it rolls off the tongue. How cool and sanitary it sounds.

Like most such slogans, *Clean Coal* is designed for a friendly appeal that masks a darker reality. It is re-branding at its finest. Pay no attention to the man behind the curtain operating the giant earth gutting machine.

While making coal energy cleaner and more environmentally friendly is a lofty goal, my skepticism is fueled by first-hand viewing of a means of mountaintop removal mining. *Clean Coal* is a tagline that redirects public focus to the end product and ignores how the natural resource is obtained. Energy companies should be grateful that in America the whole truth is not something they have to provide in their messaging. You may notice I wrote *energy companies* and not *coal companies*. Bush administration language consultants found it much easier to sell the idea of "exploring for energy" than "drilling for oil." Big Coal was quick to pick up on this simple, economic way to clean up their sooty image, and coal suddenly became an "American energy source." This term, designed to make us feel self-reliant, efficient and strong has had considerable impact on public opinion.

But *Clean Coal* is just another clever linguistic device used by those who most likely have never seen Appalachia and her coalfields except perhaps from the oval window of a private jet. If they ever looked down on America's largest and most diverse mountain range they would see entire sections missing. Mountains mowed down to bedrock. A flat, lifeless plane tracked through with dusty roads and ailing land for miles – the result of mountaintop removal mining.

When I saw my first mountaintop removal site I was confused. Where once stood two beautiful, green mountains, there was only a barren parking area scattered with massive earth moving equipment. I've since learned that this wholesale destruction started decades ago, but picked up steam when the Bush administration lifted restrictions that protected the mountains, streams and local people. With fewer buffer zone regulations to manage their process, coal companies now blast a mountain to bits, push off her top, scrape out a vein of coal and continue the process until there is nothing left to blast. Mountaintop removal is worse than the scorched earth policy of war. At least with that military tactic there is land left to regenerate. With mountaintop removal mining there is nothing left, absolutely nothing.

Energy company commercials tell us that coal is our most abundant energy source. That it "powers our way of life." They speak of "outdated perceptions about coal" and their "advanced clean technologies." All of corporate America knows that any message, repeated frequently enough, becomes accepted truth by most. And why should people care about the Appalachian Mountains? We're a stressed-out society. We've two wars to deal with and a sagging economy. We are losing our homes and jobs. We fear what tomorrow will bring, so if some corporation sends us a feel good message of patriotism and hope, *well, okay, who doesn't want to be patriotic?*

But no single energy source will save us. None is so bountiful or without costs as to be a clear choice over all other options, although if you watched any of the coal industry's ads you would think they could deliver us single-handedly. Most people never think about their home's energy unless that light switch doesn't turn on or steaks start to thaw in the freezer. But there is a massive industry behind providing light and refrigeration. And energy production ain't pretty. It is a dirty, costly business.

Coal-fired utilities are what most people see, and they are the focus of the push for cleaner coal production.

And while it is necessary to clean up our act in all forms of carbon-based energy use, people must realize that coal can never be truly "clean" while devastating the American landscape. Allowing coal companies to devour our mountains is akin to consuming ourselves as a country. We are reducing our future to rubble and turning our most lush mountain range into unproductive land akin to the rocky remains of Afghanistan.

Not for the first time, those most affected are speaking out against the coal industry. There is now a grassroots group of people using technology to spread the word about this destructive method of energy harvesting. Any search engine will bring up dozens of hits on mountaintop removal mining, most with graphic photography of the devastation usually hidden from view of highways and other public areas.

The corporate communications departments of coal companies bristle against what they view as the heartstring-tugging rhetoric of those who have stepped forward to speak out about mountaintop removal mining. But these protestors are not only pesky environmentalists who care about trees and salamanders and such. Most are just regular folks who'd like to have clean drinking water. They're people who object to a massive, poisonous slurry pond poised to slide down a hillside into their local elementary school. They are people who see the destruction of our natural heritage as egregious waste and mountaintop removal mining companies as the worst bad neighbor imaginable.

Shining a light on the darkness of mountaintop removal is a group of writers from Kentucky and other Appalachian areas. This group has been inviting other writers and interested people to take a plane ride to get an aerial view of the incredible destruction of some of the 500 mountains felled so far. This has spurred action – letters to editors, email campaigns, petitions, websites and anthologies of personal stories by people directly affected by mountaintop removal. Their stories are not sexy or patriotic or hip. They are not inspirational messages people want to hear, so these writers battle for attention in today's cluttered communications atmosphere.

Due to the efforts of writers like Wendell Berry, Silas House, Erik Reece and Bobbie Ann Mason, the message is finally finding its way into mainstream media. Mountaintop removal mining has been covered by *The New York Times* and NPR on various occasions. The issue was also covered by *Harper's* (April 2005), *National Geographic* (March 2006) and even the consumer entertainment magazine *People* found the subject important enough to run a four-page article in

October 2008. The actor Woody Harrelson has gotten involved with iLoveMountains.org and other celebrities are becoming concerned. The Sierra Club has covered mountaintop removal on its website and they have a page called *Exposed: The Truth Behind the Coal Industry's Ads* that can be found at www.sierraclub.org/coal/adwatch. And although it has yet to address the topic of mountaintop removal, a new organization, The Reality Campaign, is dissecting clean coal advertising on their website www.thisisreality.com.

This public information initiative by writers, environmentalists and affected citizens has been personally costly to many of those who speak out. Not only have they been criticized in the media, but many have had their homes and families threatened by frightened neighbors who hold some of the few remaining jobs in the local coal industry. Like all businesses responsible to shareholders, coal has been systematically finding ways to maximize profits and one way to do this is to limit the number of employees. Deep mining is costly and dangerous, but it employed more than double the people to do the same work, and when they were finished mining, mountains still stood.

I'm now in the loop to receive communiqué from mountain-loving groups, and a recent email I felt compelled to forward resulted in an unexpected reply from a coal company employee. The message was so apparently formulated that I immediately recognized its corporate communications origins. The reply was:

"Most of the people who work for NAME OF COAL COMPANY HERE also live in the community and they would never put their friends and families in danger."

This person, who refused to identify himself, went on to write that he was proud to have "sculpted" the mountains into useful land.

The idea that mountaintop removal mining is an act somehow akin to an artform is ludicrous. Still, it shows that while big coal is late to the game of language politics, they are learning fast. Like the ugly words *strip mining* and *clear cutting*, I'm sure coal will try to wipe the term *mountaintop removal mining* from their lexicon next. In its place we'll be treated to the happier, more obfuscating term "land repurposing." We'll be told that this newly "sculpted" land is repurposed for strip malls, hospitals, schools and golf courses.

That's right. Let's get rid of those pesky mountains blocking our view and throw up a few parking lots. Never mind the water sources ruined, the roads destroyed, the animals and people displaced by blasting, coal dust and danger. Overlook December's 5.4 million cubic yard Kingston Sludge Spill outside of Knoxville or three-year-old Jeremy Davidson who was crushed to death in his own bed by a boulder dislodged by mining.

America recently opted for a new moral compass. Now is the time for us to reevaluate the freedom coal companies have enjoyed over the past eight years. Mountaintop removal mining is an ecological tragedy on the level of rainforest destruction, and common sense dictates that it must stop.

In a country where image generally matters more than policy in public perception, even a toothsome argument can fail against shiny corporate ad campaigns, particularly if fear is invoked. One particularly dreadful coal company commercial states that if we are not supportive of their goals we "may have to say goodbye to the American way of life we all know and love."

Holy crap.

The authentic voices of grassroots protesters may not enjoy the format, flash or frequency of Big Coal, but fortunately they have truth on their side.

JANNA MCMAHAN, South Carolina

My Father's House

sits far back where no evening
or morning breeze of memory stirs,
as far back as a dream of Logan County,

West Virginia where folks sit at tables
and stand beside chairs in bald gullies
and stripped terraces, as if my father's

house were sucked up into air by a tornado
that lifted the heavy and left the light.

All the places where he and I would've lived
are torn open. Nothing – neither parking
garage nor vacant lot remains where strange

cars or chewing cows could wait and wander,
places where we might have grown up
and old across from each other's morning
cereal bowls and coffee mugs.

In my father's house, I am the one who
walks between walls and falls through
floors looking for a stair to climb, a bed
to raise dreams in, a closet to hang
shirts and pants, a tree to stand under –

all things that would wait
to be filled with our meaning.

Here, where he forgot how to breathe,
where I have still to live, we look out
at the ghosts of mountains
that used to be our homes.

Ron Houchin, West Virginia

Slow Voltage: Toward A Community-Based Renewable Energy Policy

PART I: FULL DISCLOSURE

I like electricity. As a documentary filmmaker, my livelihood depends on my ability to harness electrons to capture the stories I see in the world. Electricity powers the cameras and computers required to create my work as well as the televisions and projectors that allow me to share my films with others.

My dependence on electricity is probably not much different from yours. Our information age economy increasingly relies on electronic workspaces. We are told that the economy of the developed world depends on cheap reliable electricity. This may be true, but definitions of "cheap" electricity differ considerably. You probably know that burning coal produces about half of U.S. electricity. In the eastern U.S., most of that coal comes from the central Appalachian coalfields, according to the United States Department of Energy. And, as you may have guessed, most Appalachian coal is mined by removing the mountain on top of the coal – mountaintop removal mining. The price utilities pay for the coal and the subsequent cost consumers pay for the electricity does not include the damage mountaintop removal mining inflicts on drinking water, roads, communities and ecosystems. These expenses are left for coalfield communities to pay.

This is what drives my documentary work – a desire to explain how our national addiction to fossil fuels places an unjust burden on rural energy producing communities, especially here in the Appalachian coalfields. Mountaintop removal coal mining is a clear example of how the costs of producing "cheap electricity" are shifted from the companies that mine the coal and generate electricity to coalfield communities.

As I work on my films, I am painfully aware that every watt that powers my camera and computer is part of a mountain that has been blown up. Am I actually blowing up mountains as I claim to be working to save mountains? What is a documentary filmmaker to do? For that matter, what is anyone who needs electricity and cares about mountains to do?

At first glance, our choice appears to be either to move off the electric grid or to risk hypocrisy. However, we have more options – we just need to look behind the household electrical outlet and connect to the source of our electricity.

Connecting to your source of electricity may sound a bit abstract. It's just wires, right? To explain further, I have chosen to create a manifesto of sorts, a document that provides a few basic principals we can use to gain more control over our energy choices. I approach this task with some hesitation, as manifestos have a long, sordid, and often pretentious history. It is my hope that you all can take this manifesto with a dose of salt; laugh a little, learn a little, and leave with something to ponder.

PART II: THE SLOW VOLTAGE MANIFESTO

Slow Voltage applies the Slow Foods philosophy to electricity. You may be familiar with the Slow Foods movement – an international effort to promote local foods grown with sustainable agricultural methods and fair labor practices. The Slow Foods philosophy asks consumers to explore their connection to the food they consume, and therefore to the bioregion in which they live. In the process, people learn about their community while enjoying fresh, healthy meals.

Slow Voltage employs a similar approach to electricity. Just as the Slow Foods movement connects people to the source of the food that nourishes our bodies, Slow Voltage seeks to connect electricity consumers to the source of the energy that drives much of our economy. The result will be a more just energy policy – and the end of mountaintop removal coal mining.

What would a fully-formed Slow Voltage movement look like? In a nutshell, Slow Voltage encourages local governments, communities, and businesses to invest in locally available renewable energy. This is a lofty goal, and plenty of small steps are required to make it happen.

Let's start by defining the basic principals of the Slow Voltage Movement.

Slow Voltage Principle #1: *Know your source of power*

If you produce renewable electricity in your home or business, then you've got this one covered. Skip ahead to principle #2. If you buy your power from an electric utility, a good way to disover where that electricity comes from is to look at your power company's annual report. For more specific information about how you may be connected to mountaintop removal, Appalachian Voices, a regional non-profit, has created a project called *What's My Connection* (www. ilovemountains.org/myconnection). Once you reach this site, just type in your zip code and find out if your electricity comes from mountaintop removal coal.

If you discover that you get your electricity from power plants burning mountaintop removal coal, here are a few simple steps you can take to reduce the damage caused by your electricity consumption:

Most electric utilities offer green power options. Purchasing green power helps increase demand for renewable energy. This is a good start. Next, get involved with nonprofits and other groups working on renewable energy solutions. Finally, take a close look at how you use electricity. Everyone who uses electricity has a connection. Find out yours, then use your connection to advocate for fair and just energy policy.

Slow Voltage Principle #2: *Less is more*

In his essay "Ban the Bulb," Lester Brown, author of *Plan B 3.0: Mobilizing to Save Civilization*, explains that a shift from incandescent to compact florescent lighting will reduce electric demand enough to facilitate shutting down 80 coal-fired plants in the United States. Brown believes that simple act of changing a light bulb can have an impact on mountaintop removal. Besides saving mountains, electricity conservation and investments in energy efficiency can also save a great deal of money. A 2002 study by the Southwest Energy Efficiency Project projected that energy efficiency policies will reduce demand for electricity by 30 to 40 percent nationwide. This energy savings will eliminate the need for new coal-fired electric generation and keep more money in the pockets of electricity consumers by removing the need to finance new power plants through ratepayer increases.

We cannot spend and consume endlessly. We have got to learn to save and conserve. We do need a "new economy," but one that is founded on thrift and care, on saving and conserving, not on excess and waste.

WENDELL BERRY

As we move from mountaintop removal coal mining and other destructive practices that exploit fossil fuel reserves, energy conservation becomes an increasingly important survival skill.

Slow Voltage Principle #3: *Choose the right tool for the job.*

> *Heating with electricity is like using a chainsaw to cut butter.*
> JOSHUA BILLS, Kentucky-based solar installer

The U.S. Department of Energy's Consumer's Guide to Energy Efficiency reports that electricity produced from oil, gas or coal converts only about 30percent of the fuel's energy into electricity. The report concludes that: "electric heat is often more expensive than heat combustion appliances, such as natural gas, propane, and oil furnaces."

A Slow Voltage mindset looks at the task to be done and then decides the best way to make it happen. For example, when building a home on an abandoned strip mine bench in Letcher County, Kentucky, I discovered that installing a solar hot water system large enough to heat my house cost just a few more dollars than installing an electric heat pump. After the house was built, my electric bills averaged $30 per month. My neighbor, who chose an electric heat pump, told me he spent about $100 per month for his electricity. This is a perfect example of how small investments in energy efficiency can provide immediate economic benefits.

Slow Voltage Principle #4: *Stop, Look & Listen (for Local Renewable Energy)*

This principle connects very closely with the Slow Foods movement and is perhaps the heart of the Slow Voltage philosophy. Use your senses, curiosity and imagination to engage your local environment. Look around you – where are the best sites for solar exposure and wind located? Listen to your neighbors and attend community meetings – where is natural energy going to waste?

In West Virginia, local people looked at the Summersville Dam on the Gauley River and saw untapped hydropower potential. The City of Summersville hired Gauley River Partners Inc. to work with the Army Corps of Engineers to create a hydropower station by simply connecting to the discharge tunnel on the dam.

The Gauley River is a National Recreation Area, so project managers involved the National Park Service and local outdoor outfitters to design the hydropower station to have minimal impact on the river. Today, the project is a model for low impact hydropower and is featured on the website of the Low Impact Hydropower Institute.

A glance around the Central Appalachian coalfields reveals a number of similar-sized lakes where low impact hydropower may work. The Flannagan Dam in Dickenson County, Virginia, The Carr Fork Reservoir near Hindman, Kentucky, and Buckhorn Lake near Hazard, Kentucky, are just a few examples of dozens of small flood control dams in the coalfields that have low impact hydropower potential. Find one near your home and ask your local government to develop unused hydropower potential. The Summersville Hydroelectric Project provides a great model for how local governments can invest in renewable energy.

A basic principle of ecology is that biological diversity helps create a healthy ecosystem. Slow Foods encourages ecological diversity by encouraging farmers to replace massive monoculture crops such as corn and soybeans with small farm plots that grow a diverse variety of produce. Applying this approach to electricity is not that big a jump. Instead of gigantic power plants, what if Appalachian communities created small-scale electric systems that powered a hometown, county or creek?

Slow Voltage Principle #5: *Articulate the Alternatives*

In Raleigh County, West Virginia, a citizen's group called the Coal River Mountain Watch looked up and saw enormous wind potential on the 3,300-foot-tall Coal River Mountain. The mountain has significant coal reserves and subsidiaries of Massey Energy had applied for permits to mine the coal by removing the top of the mountain. Members of Coal River Mountain Watch teamed up with Downstream Strategies, a group of environmental consultants from Morgantown, West Virginia. The team prepared a report that demonstrates how a wind farm on the ridges of Coal River Mountain will provide more jobs AND generate more electricity – in the long run – than mountaintop removal mining. The best wind sites on Coal River Mountain are above 2,400 feet, so removing the mountaintop will destroy the mountain's potential to generate electricity by wind. The report also points out important facts about employment:

Jobs in coal production last only as long as there is coal to mine. In the case of Coal River Mountain, this will only be for 17 years. A wind farm, on the other hand, will employ over 275 local residents during the construction phase, and create approximately 40 permanent maintenance jobs afterwards.

That Coal River Wind Project report (www.ColdRiverWind. org) also explains that development of a wind industry will diversify the local economy:

A wind farm will also allow the mountain to be used for other economic purposes, thus creating additional jobs numbering far more than the proposed mountaintop removal mining, and the opportunity for stable, supplemental income for local residents.

The catch is this: most of the land on Coal River Mountain is owned by absentee land-owning companies and leased by mining companies – and, although an investor for a wind farm has been identified, work on the proposed wind farm cannot move forward as long as the mining permits are in place. A local energy policy that designates funds to invest in renewable energy is part of the solution to this problem.

Slow Voltage Principle #6: *Make Your Own Local Energy Policy*

Not all of us can go to Washington, D.C., and lobby for a just national energy policy, but almost everyone can work to create local policy that connects people to renewable energy. For example, the city of Berkeley, California, responded to citizen's requests for a renewable energy policy by creating a financing system for residents who want to install their own renewable energy system.

Cisco Devries worked for Berkeley mayor Tom Bates. In an article for Grist.org, Devries writes:

Buying power from your utility is a simple, pay-as-you-go service. Solar and energy efficiency projects, on the other hand, require tens of thousands of dollars up front and a long-term commitment to see a return on investment. Put another way, how many of us would have cell phones if we had to buy 20-years of minutes upfront? People are simply uncomfortable with pre-purchasing 20-years of electricity, even if it is a good deal.

The Berkeley FIRST plan is designed to make paying for solar and energy efficiency projects much more like paying a utility bill. Devries explains:

Berkeley pays the upfront costs through the issuance of a new kind of municipal bond. The bonds are repaid from a new line item on participating property owners' property tax bills over 20 years. Participating property owners pay for only the costs of their energy project... and property tax expenses remain unchanged for those who choose not to participate.

The program began in late November 2008. If successful, Berkeley FIRST will serve as a model for more local governments to encourage home and business owners to invest in renewable energy. Perhaps we need to think about replacing our "trickle down" economic philosophy with a "trickle up" energy policy that begins at the local level.

Slow Voltage Principle #7: *Don't Mourn, Organize*

This phrase, attributed to labor organizer Joe Hill, has a long history in the Appalachian mountains. These words inspired miners during their struggle to be represented by a democratic union. Today, as we look at 500 of our Appalachian mountains destroyed for electricity, "don't mourn, organize" can call coalfield citizens together to create a future beyond coal. Community organizing is a crucial step to stopping destruction caused by mountaintop removal coal mining and creating a grassroots movement that includes renewable energy solutions.

The best part about organizing is that you don't have to start from scratch. There are dozens of citizens groups working to create policy that moves us from mountaintop removal coal mining to renewable energy sources. Find a group that is active in your community and get involved. Rural electric co-operatives are membership owned; if you get your electricity through a co-op, run for election to the board of directors and advocate for investment in locally-available renewable energy. Whenever possible, get involved with local government planning committees and work with them to create a renewable energy plan. This type of grassroots action makes democracy work – but it demands your participation.

PART III: KEEP YOUR EYES ON THE PRIZE (AND HOLD ON)

I realize all of this may sound a bit naïve and optimistic. I find myself walking the line between the hard reality of the political power that the coal industry wields in states like Kentucky and West Virginia and the optimism brought on by the election of a community organizer to be the 44th President of the United States. Yet even in these optimistic times, I am concerned that the development of renewable energy potential in Appalachia is likely to follow the same path blazed by the coal industry more than a century ago. The momentum of an economy fueled by capital from outside the region is an incredibly strong force. All too often, campaign contributions made by coal and gas interests to local officials guarantees that local policy is sympathetic to exploitation of the region's fossil fuel reserves. We should not forget that it is a long, long way from Harlan, Kentucky, to Berkeley, California.

Still, for the first time in my life, I believe that a national ban on mountaintop removal mining is politically possible. However, strong environmental regulations do not necessarily guarantee healthy communities.

A ban on mountaintop removal will certainly save our mountain streams and preserve the most diverse hardwood forest on the planet. But you can't save the land without also saving the people. Plenty of coalfield residents have been telling us this for a long time. In fact, one of the first groups to organize against strip mining was named "The Appalachian Group to Save the Land and People."

Much of the historic pattern of exploitation in the Appalachians is connected to the dominant definition of development in America. Unfortunately, the development of renewable energy in Appalachia may be no exception. In the introduction to his book *Uneven Ground*, Ron Eller, a coalfield historian writes:

> *Americans have an enduring faith in the power of development to improve the quality of our lives. …Many public policies are still based upon the naïve assumption that poverty can be seriously addressed without structural change, that growth is good for everyone, that urban lifestyles and institutions are to be emulated, and that local and regional markets are not important in a global economy. Such assumptions weaken the democratic conversation about the goal of government and the quality of our lives.*

Eller explains that the traditional views of development and growth have historically disenfranchised poor rural people and "displaced our collective responsibilities for the land and for each other onto the vagaries of the market."

The Slow Voltage movement, like the Slow Foods movement, questions the concepts of growth and development that continue to dominate our choices about how we obtain food, shelter and energy. By slowing down and paying attention to our connections to the world around us, we can work together to meet our needs through methods that increase democracy and promote justice.

Energy is so intertwined with economy, ecology and even the culture of the Appalachian region that imposing a "top down" solution from the federal government or allowing the free market to develop renewable energy is likely to perpetuate problems the region has experienced for more than a century. A sustainable solution for the central Appalachian coalfields must include grassroots organizing that empowers coalfield community members.

Furthermore, this organizing needs to move beyond single-issue organizing on mountaintop removal to include the sustained growth of democratic institutions free from the influence of big industry. We need more public spaces where citizens can work together to articulate their hopes and dreams and to begin to open a new path toward healthy communities.

Healthy, sustainable Appalachian communities will not come to life overnight. Any gains made too quickly will soon be lost. Lasting change of our institutions, of our energy policy, of our electricity consumption habits will need to happen over generations – and that's why the movement is called Slow Voltage.

TOM HANSELL, *North Carolina*

Climate Change; Change of Heart

I want to tell you a story.

On March 8, 2003, approximately two weeks before the United States invaded Iraq, thousands of individuals, largely women and children gathered in Washington, D.C., for a Code Pink rally in the name of peace. It was also International Day of Women. We walked from Martin Luther King Park through the streets of the nation's capital to Lafayette Park, located directly in front of the White House. When we arrived we were met by a wall of D.C. police outfitted with black combat gear, bulletproof vests and rifles. We were not allowed to proceed on to the public park.

Medea Benjamin, one of the organizers of Code Pink, began to negotiate with the police captain. While these negotiations were underway, Rachel Bagby, an African-American poet and musician, stood directly across from a policeman and focused her attention on one officer in particular, also African American. She began singing with all the power of her God-given voice, "All we are saying is give peace a chance." Over and over she kept singing those words.

Other women began to join her. She never took her eyes off that man, but just kept singing to him in her low, dignified voice. In that moment, it was clear neither one of them would be who they are or where they are, without the voices of dissent uttered by their parents, without the literal acts of civil disobedience practiced by their parents' parents and their parents' parents before them.

The African-American policeman quietly stepped aside, creating the opening. We walked through.

This is what the open space of democracy looks like.

"Disobedience to be civil has to be open and nonviolent... Disobedience to be civil implies discipline, thought, care, attention... Disobedience that is wholly civil should never provoke retaliation... but love." So speaks Gandhi.

Henry David Thoreau understood this when he chose to spend a night in jail for refusing to pay his taxes because of his opposition to the Mexican-Indian War.

"Cast your whole vote, not a strip of paper merely, but your whole influence," wrote Thoreau in his essay "Civil Disobedience."

Martin Luther King, Jr. understood this when he choose to

spend time in the Birmingham Jail and wrote:

> *I am in Birmingham because injustice is here. Just as the prophets of the 8th Century B.C. left their villages and carried their "thus saith the Lord" far beyond the boundaries of their home towns, and just as the Apostle Paul left his village of Tarsus and carried the gospel of Jesus Christ to the far corners of the Greco Roman world, so am I compelled to carry the gospel of freedom beyond my own home town. Like Paul, I must constantly respond to the Macedonian call for aid.*

> *Moreover, I am cognizant of the interrelatedness of all communities and states. I cannot sit idly by in Atlanta and not be concerned about what happens in Birmingham. Injustice anywhere is a threat to justice everywhere. We are caught in an inescapable network of mutuality, tied in a single garment of destiny. Whatever affects one directly, affects all indirectly. Never again can we afford to live with the narrow, provincial "outside agitator" idea. Anyone who lives inside the United States can never be considered an outsider anywhere within its bounds.*

> *In any nonviolent campaign there are four basic steps: collection of the facts to determine whether injustices exist; negotiation; self purification; and direct action...*

> *One of the basic points in your statement is that the action that I and my associates have taken in Birmingham is untimely. Some have asked: "Why didn't you give the new city administration time to act?" The only answer that I can give to this query is that the new Birmingham administration must be prodded about as much as the outgoing one, before it will act.*

> *For years now I have heard the word "Wait!" It rings in the ear of every Negro with piercing familiarity. This "Wait" has almost always meant "Never." We must come to see...that "justice too long delayed is justice denied."*

And in my own city of Salt Lake City, a University of Utah student, Tim DeChristopher, chose not to wait but to confront through direct action a flawed and flagrant system that profits the interests of oil and gas companies rather than the community at large – a community that includes all life, plants, animals, soils and rivers and human beings.

He raised his hand in the name of civil disobedience, his

hand which held a bidder's paddle and exposed the Bush-Cheney administration's midnight maneuver for what it was — a wholesale grab of our public lands.

He said, "our future is imperiled" and "we have a history of bravery in this nation and we must call it forward now. Our future is guaranteed only by the degree of our personal involvement and commitment to an inclusive justice."

To engage in responsive citizenship, we must become citizens who respond. Passionately. This is how we can make a difference.

Secretary of Interior Salazar reversed the decision and freed over 100,000 acres that were slated for oil and gas exploitation.

This is ultimately, about climate change. Climate change as the heating up of the planet. Climate change as a change of minds and hearts, inspiring direct action, both politically and personally.

Thomas Jefferson said, "I believe in perilous liberty over quiet servitude."

May we commit ourselves to perilous servitude. Call it a peaceful uprising. Call it the open space of democracy.

It is easy to believe we the people have no say, that the powers in Washington will roll over our local, on-the-ground concerns with their corporate energy ties and thumper trucks. It is easy to believe that the American will is only focused on how to get rich, how to be entertained and how to distract itself from the hard choices we have before us as a nation.

I refuse to believe this. The only space I see truly capable of being closed is not the land or our civil liberties but our own hearts. The human heart is the first home of democracy. It is where we embrace our questions.

Can we be equitable?

Can we be generous?

Can we listen with our whole beings, not just our minds, and offer our attention rather than our opinions?

And do we have enough resolve in our hearts to act courageously, relentlessly, without giving up — ever — trusting our fellow citizens to join with us in our determined pursuit of a living democracy?

The heart is the house of empathy whose door opens when we receive the pain of others. This is where bravery lives, where we find our mettle to give and receive, to love and be loved, to stand in the center of uncertainty with strength, not fear, understanding this is all there is. The heart is the path to wisdom because it dares to be vulnerable in the presence of power. Our power lies in our love of our homelands.

It is time to ask, when will our national culture of self-interest stop cutting the bonds of community to shore up individual gain and instead begin to nourish communal life through acts of giving, not taking? It is time to acknowledge the violence rendered to our souls each time a mountaintop is removed to expose a coal vein in Appalachia or when a wetland is drained, dredged and filled for a strip mall. And the time has come to demand an end to the wholesale dismissal of the sacredness of life in all its variety and forms, as we witness the repeated breaking of laws, the relaxing of laws in the sole name of growth and greed.

A wild salmon is not the same as a salmon raised in a hatchery. And a prairie dog colony is not a shooting gallery for rifle recreationists, but a culture that has evolved with the prairie since the Pleistocene. At what point do we finally lay our bodies down to say this blatant disregard for biology and wild lives is no longer acceptable?

Twelve thousand students at the Power Shift Conference this weekend have said, "Enough."

We have made the mistake of confusing democracy with capitalism and have mistaken political engagement with political machinery we all understand to be corrupt. It is time to resist the simplistic, utilitarian view that what is good for business is good for humanity in all its complex web of relationships. A spiritual democracy is inspired by our own sense of what we can accomplish together, honoring an integrated society where the social, intellectual, physical and economic well being of all is considered, not just the wealth and health of the corporate few.

Climate Change.

I do not believe we can look for leadership beyond ourselves. I do not believe we can wait for someone or something to save us from our global predicaments and obligations. I need to look in the mirror and ask this of myself: *If I am committed to seeing the direction of our country change – how must I change myself?*

We are in need of a reflective activism born out of humility, not arrogance. Reflection, with deep time spent in the consideration of others, opens the door to becoming a compassionate participant in the world.

"To care is neither conservative nor radical," writes John Ralston Saul. "It is a form of consciousness."

Climate Change.

Are we ready for the next evolutionary, revolutionary step?

The restoration of justice for all species, not just our own.

This is the open space of democracy.

TERRY TEMPEST WILLIAMS, *Utah and Wyoming*

From a speech delivered at The George Washington University, 1 March 2009. The event, called "Artists For the Climate," also featured Wendell Berry, Bill McKibben, Janisse Ray and Kathy Mattea, among others. It was held in conjunction with Power Shift 2009, a conference on climate change that attracted 12,000 young people from every state in the nation and over a dozen foreign countries. The next day, Williams and over 2,500 protesters engaged in the Capital Climate Action, a mass act of civil disobedience that succeeded in shutting down the Capitol Power Plant, which uses dirty energy to power Congress.

This Hand Is My Hand
based on "This Land Is Your Land"

Chorus   This hand is your hand
              This hand is my hand
              So let's come together
              And heal our land
              From Appalachia
              To the High Sierras
              These mountains were made
              For you and me

As I was walking
A winding trailway
I saw above me
An eroded mountain
I saw below me
A muddy stream
This is not the land
For you and me

Repeat Chorus

I was wondering
If we work together
For all these mountains
Could they be protected
So grab my hand
And don't let go
Together they will be
For you and me

Repeat Chorus

LINSEY CLARK, *Kentucky*
Fifth grade

The God of Birds' Nests

If you happen to come upon a bird's nest along the way, in any tree or on the ground,
with young ones or eggs, and the mother sitting on the young or on the eggs,
you shall not take the mother with the young.
— Deuteronomy 22:6

This verse kept going through my head when I, along with about a thousand others, marched on the Kentucky state Capitol recently. We were there to protest mountaintop removal, particularly the devastating effect it has on our waterways, which are being forever affected by the ravages of this irresponsible form of coal mining. So, in honor of that, we first gathered on the banks of the still-beautiful Kentucky River, united by a common goal: to lift up our voices and ask that our mountains and our water be protected.

I don't even remember ever being taught this particular verse. But there it was, floating before me as we marched up that avenue, and it was a comfort throughout the day. While out there protesting it was empowering to see all those people standing up for what they believed in. Walking up the capitol steps holding that sign of protest (NOT ONE MORE MILE) while chanting with everyone else ("Whose mountains? Our mountains! Whose streams? Our streams! Whose future? Our future!") was a incredibly moving moment. Together, we were a force to be reckoned with. Together, we were loud enough to be heard throughout the city. Together, we were making a difference.

Ashley Judd was there, and we all knew that's what the media would latch onto. But she was not there as the movie star Ashley Judd. She was there as a concerned citizen, a proud Appalachian, someone who always cares for the bird's nest. People like to criticize celebrities when they speak out. They say they don't want someone famous "telling them what to believe." But Judd was simply there voicing what *she* believes. And she believes in what she's saying. She gave her time to be there, paid her own way, asked for nothing in return. I introduced her as "a great light," as someone who "loves and loves and loves." She was there because she believes in protecting the environment and she believes in everyone being good to one another. This is a lesson the coal companies and the government and big business would be well-served to learn as well.

There were dozens of children (the youngest was so little she was strapped to her mother's chest), some of them chanting into the bullhorn, holding their signs high above their heads. One teacher, Blossom Brosi, brought over a hundred students from her high school. That's the kind of teacher who becomes a hero to kids. There were college students, emboldened by the possibility of change. The oldest marcher, Marie Cassidy, is 96 years old. And I saw so many people who have fought tirelessly and bravely for years and years now. They are not about to give up. Among them were people like Teri Blanton, Carl Shoupe, Jim Webb, Bev Futtrell, Sue Massek, George and Connie Brosi, and so many more.

But the person I want to pause to point out particularly is Patty Wallace, a woman from Louisa, Kentucky, who has been fighting the coal industry for years. She once recounted to me that she "ran down" a coal truck driver to thank him for driving safely when the companies so often force them to speed to keep up with production. "I was once told by my boss that I let other people's problems become too important to me...but I just could never stand by and see people taken advantage of because they were afraid or didn't know how to fight," Wallace told me that day. She also talked about the late Hazel King, who fought tirelessly against the coal industry to protect her land, recalling King saying: "When they haul the coal out of Black Mountain, it's just like tearing out my heart."

Ironically, Wallace had a heart stint put in just a few days before the march. But she was out there walking that line anyway. According to her friends, Wallace's heart rhythm was struggling. As we came up Capitol Avenue she grew tired, but she refused to stop. Police officers, stationed along the route, offered to drive her on up to the Capitol steps, but she refused. "I can rest while I walk," she said. She was determined to make her voice heard, to stand up for what she believed in, to give of herself to protect the water and the mountains.

Patty Wallace is a protector of birds' nests. And one of my heroes.

But it was a frustrating day, too. Frustrating to see little children holding jars of rusty well water, polluted by coal companies who claim to be making our land a better place. Frustrating to see people having to march to save their *water*, our most precious commodity. It's mind-boggling, like something out of a science fiction novel, that people would actually have to fight for *that*. Even more frustrating to know that our governor refused to come out and hear our pleas, even though he *did* come out to greet coal mining officials on the front steps of the capitol less than a year ago.

What's even more frustrating is that Governor Beshear is a good man who has stood up to the industry in the past. His refusal to come greet us worries me that the industry has gotten through to him, too.

I think what Deuteronomy 22:6 is saying is that we have to be kind to even the smallest creatures. I believe it means that we should be compassionate, and thoughtful, and responsible. And I believe that it means we should not be short-sighted or mean-hearted or greedy. To be good people, the verse says, we must all be protectors of bird's nests.

However, I believe that the Bible is a living thing and that its wisdom is only as good and thick as its readers allow it to be. People have been misconstruing the Bible for ages for their own benefit, and have done a great job of it, using it to hold up slavery, anti-suffrage and intolerance. That's not what I'm trying to do here.

I choose to seek the positive in the Bible. The light. The God I believe in is one of love and compassion, not wrath and jealousy. I believe in a God of Birds' Nests.

And I am turning to the Bible to seek knowledge and wisdom, to help me understand the ways of people and the world. And this is what I have taken from it. To me, finding something of light, something positive, is just as amazing as coming upon a perfect little bird's nest in a low branch. Like my friend and great poet Lisa Parker says of such nests: "It's all in how you carry 'em, brother."

Now that's the truth.

Years and years ago, the coal companies stumbled upon a rich, beautiful bird's nest called Appalachia. But instead of acting with responsibility and taking only what they needed, they took *everything*: the babies and the mother. They mishandled the nest. They plundered and robbed. They were short-sighted, not looking ahead to the future. Because if you take the mother and the babies, what do you do with the future, when you need more songbirds? You have nothing but an empty nest, tumbling away in the wind.

SILAS HOUSE, **Kentucky**

Kids at I Love Mountains Day.

BETH BISSMEYER, Kentucky

Iconic footbridge over Troublesome Creek on the campus of Hindman Settlement School in Kentucky.

CHEYENNE HOUSE, Kentucky
Eighth grade

WATER

I gave my heart to the mountains the minute I stood
beside this river with its spray in my face and
watched it thunder into foam, smooth to green glass over
sunken rocks, shatter to foam again.
I was fascinated by how it sped by and yet was always
there; its roar shook both the earth and me.

WALLACE STEGNER, *The Sound of Mountain Water*

East Kentucky Water

Well the coal companies came down to Eastern Kentucky
Blew the tops off all the hills
Then they poisoned the wells and the rivers
With their dumping and their spills

Everybody prayed for city water
'Cause there's sulfur in the well
Little girls' curls lost their luster
And the moonshine went to hell

Chorus   Don't tell me 'bout Mexico and its water so bad
         'Cause the East Kentucky water is the worst I've ever had

Well we couldn't wear white when we were kids
Like the other kids could do
Had to change them old school colors
To gray and navy blue

And the bleach couldn't help the washing
And the filters couldn't help the taste
Thank God for the old spring on the hill
On long, hot summer days

Repeat Chorus

Well the EPA just sat on their hands
For far too many years
And there ain't no fish in the river
And there's sulfur in the tears

But I'd love for these mine owners
To have to swill from their own brine
And have their own shirts turn to yellow
From their white-collar crime

Repeat Chorus

STEPHEN COUCH, *Kentucky*

Black Water

Black and oozy,
down the creek it comes.
The company didn't tell anyone
the spill happened.
Sludge, cleaned-off coal,
filthy,
seeming unstoppable —
even a dozer can't stop it.
Secrets, cover-ups,
Wolfcreek sludged!

SEAN ANGERMEIER, Kentucky
Fifth grade

Upstream

In the early afternoon, the clouds begin to make. After a sun-hazy Saturday morning, unusual hot for the middle of May, and humid to where the air is a seen thing, gauzed all over the hills. The clouds clot and rise, white at first, darkening gradually to pearl, and they roll a little as they thicken, throwing enormous shadows over the ground. The shadows mottle the heaped hills, ripple over the heave and fold of the land. They dim the green ridgetops, shade the leafy hollows and creeks, and to the east, the clouds reach almost to where the mountains turn veinblue with distance. But before that, among the mountains closer, the shadows sweep, too, over vast tracts of ground the same color as storm color, as though the ground here reflects the cloud-dulled sky. The land stretching level for hundreds of acres in a dozen shades of gray. Immense flatnesses where flat doesn't belong.

Hundreds of feet below one of these flats, a man and a boy fish, even though they don't anymore eat what they catch. They come out of habit and for the peace of the place. The man watches wary the shift in the weather while his son turns over creek rocks, looking for crawdads. A year ago, they would have sat this cloudburst out, sheltered in the car, or even squatted under a hemlock, welcomed the relief from the heat. Now the man calls twice to the boy, who after the second time stands and spreads his arms, his palms up, begging for more time. The man shakes his head, repeats what he said, and then hustles his boy to the car and on home.

The thunderheads mass and swell. They stand up on their knees, blooming, then they rise all the way to their feet. Charcoal now, they jostle each other. They throb in their billows. The people can watch the clouds, predict, but they can't watch the flat places under them. Those places are hidden from the people hemmed in the hollows, in the narrow river bottom, the tight creekbeds, even from the few people on the hillsides, hidden by those mountains not yet taken and by the leftover trees. Some of the people know what is there. Others have just heard about it. Many of the flattened mountains are only half as tall as they were five years, two years, six months ago. In a few places, a whole range has vanished. A person could walk a day or more and not come to the end of skun-open flat ground.

The clouds have mounted into pillars. They bulge and they strain.

In a tiny town, a woman finishes cutting her grass. She kills the motor, and in the sudden silence, hears what could be thunder, a low distant rowl, but might also be coal pouring into a train car. She look above her, past the belts and tipples of the processing plant that dwarfs the town, and she reckons how short it will be before the clouds break. The fresh mess it will make. All around her, barely visible until it meets a sill, a car, a barbecue grill, a roof, the constant coal dust, a fine black snowing. But the muck is the just the most likely of her worries, and the one that scares her least.

Way up a dirt road in a broad pretty clearing at the foot of a mountain, two dogs pace outside their houses along the creek. Each is on a chain just long enough to let it drink. No one is home in the clapboard house with the sag in its porch. The mother and father have gone to their part-time jobs, Wal-Mart and a tire dealership, and the kids are at her mom's. When the thunder starts, the younger dog stops pacing, lowers his head, and begins to sound, something between a bark and a howl. Moan in it. The thunder gives one last muffled rumble, then draws away, but the dog does not. He sits back on his haunches, stretches his neck, and settles into the monotonous hooing. Unrelenting, inexhaustible, at an object secret to everyone but himself.

An elderly man and woman hurry to get their beans in ahead of the storm. It's already late in the season, but he's been sick a lot this spring. When the sky darkens, each stretches up for a moment, studies the clouds, then bends back over and works even faster. They have to get the seed covered good so the cloudburst won't wash it out, and besides, they're due at their youngest grandchild's T-ball game late this afternoon and they don't work on Sundays.

Finally the clouds can't any longer hold. Where the rain spills over trees, hills, it is cupped by leaf, held by shrub and brush, seeps into the soft ground around roots and logs. On the vast dead flats, the first drops pock the hard-packed dirt, spit up a little dust, and bounce right back. Even where the men have sown the sharp yellow grass, only a few drops find a little soak, while everything else is driven away. Now it's a downpour, lashing, drops rushing into drops into drops, those fast-riveling into even more, all of it rushing now to wherever the naked ground lies a little lower, but still, the earth doesn't take them. They torrent towards the hacked edges of the plateau, to where the creek used to start, but when they get there, they find the creek gone. And the water keeps coming.

A few miles outside of Prater, a teenage girl walking home after visiting her uncle sees by the color the wind makes the leaves that the rain is almost to her. She hurries down the path, breaks off to climb to a rock overhang she knows, and reaches it just before the first spatters. She crawls back as far as it goes, then turns to sit crosslegged where rain never touches. She picks up in one hand the dirt under her. Sifts it through her fingers, savors its silky grain.

A miner passes the guard shack at the foot of a mountain and switches on his windshield wipers as he pulls the long steep haul road to where he'll start his shift. Ten minutes into his climb, clawed raw earth spreads out his windows in all directions, continuing into the middle distance. Unlike many on this job, he is local. He has had to learn to look away. He thinks instead of his wife, his two little daughters. The sturdy addition he's having put on the house for the baby coming.

The elderly man and woman are still bent in their garden, rain darkening their shirts, them covering seed with their hoes as quick as they can. Until they hear the roar. Not a sound they've heard in the forty years they've lived up this hollow, and both of them swivel rustily – to see the creek coming at them, four times the size the creek should be. The old man drops his hoe and grabs his wife above her elbow, pushes her towards the house, his body going forward while his head looks behind, his eyes rolling like a horse's. She thinks better, wheels, struggles with him a second, then pulls him to the hill, and there they scrabble up the bank on all fours, the wet dead leaves slick, them slipping and catching hold of saplings, of roots, they stumble higher . . .

In the broad pretty clearing, the younger dog has hushed his moaning and curled up out of the wet in his house. The older dog has climbed above hers, as far away from the creek as her chain lets her go. She sits with her head lowered, rain leaking off her muzzle, it turned a little so she can see upstream. The old dog waits, shivering.

ANN PANCAKE, *Washington*

An excerpt from an early draft of the novel Strange As This Weather Has Been

Letter To The EPA

Honorable Stephen L. Johnson
Administrator, Environmental Protection Agency
Ariel Rios Building, 1200 Pennsylvania Avenue NW
Mail Code: 1101A
Washington, DC 20460

Dear Administrator Johnson:

I am writing to express my opposition to the Office of Surface Mining Reclamation and Enforcement's (OSM) proposed clarifications of the Stream Buffer Zone rule.

Kentucky is the third largest producer of coal in the nation, and as America's energy demands continue to grow, coal is a critical component in our national energy portfolio. Coal is a driver of the Appalachian economy and keeps electricity rates low, especially in my home state of Kentucky.

At the same time, Kentucky's water resources are essential to economic development, not to mention Kentuckians' health and quality of life. As such, we cannot allow our ecologically sensitive and interconnected creeks, streams and rivers to be fouled any more than is absolutely necessary.

The Stream Buffer Zone – established in 1983 to prevent mine spoil and waste from being dumped within 100 feet of any perennial or intermittent stream – is under attack by this proposed rule. The rule would remove existing protections which would, quite simply, make it easier to put spoil and waste in our creeks, streams and rivers. Numerous studies have confirmed that the harm caused to aquatic resources does not end with buried stream segments under the valley fills, sludge impoundments and other waste disposal sites in the mining regions of Appalachia, but continues far downstream.

The Programmatic Environmental Impact Statement (PEIS) on mountaintop removal and valley fills completed by the current administration in 2005 determined that more than 1,200 miles of streams have already been degraded or destroyed by mountaintop removal since 2001. This is by far the most significant destructive force on the region's waters. The cumulative impact study that accompanied the PEIS concluded that without additional environmental protections, the amount of damage to the region could double by the end of the decade. Therefore, weakening the Stream Buffer Zone rule is a move in the wrong direction.

Kentucky Governor Steve Beshear and I are united in our belief that this rule change is unnecessary and, in fact, damaging to Kentucky's economy and its people. Coal has a long history in our state and will play an important part in our future, but OSM's proposed overhaul of the Stream Buffer Zone rule does nothing but harm the Appalachian communities it purports to help.

I appreciate your consideration of this matter and urge the EPA to decline to give its written concurrence to this rule. Please contact me if I can be of any further assistance.

Sincerely,

BEN CHANDLER, Kentucky
Member of Congress

Please, Leave Them Be

They tear down our mountains
They pollute our streams
I ain't gonna tolerate this
Please, leave them be!

Please help me fight this
O how can you leave yourself be?
O please help me fight this
And leave them be!

Short Instrumental (banjo and fiddle recommended)

Bridge   O I'd fight for all my life
                  To get these mountains freed
                  But everyone just sets 'ere
                  While they ruin our streams
                  Leave our mountains be!

Please help me fight this
O how can you not see?
O please help us all fight this
And leave the mountains be!

OLIVIA JEAN-LOUISE HOUSE, Kentucky
Fifth grade

Losing Normalcy

The creek was once filled with crawdads. I spent three long summers with my best friend fishing them out, always aware of the water moccasins my dad had warned me about. Allison and I were terrified of them. We actually saw one once, swimming toward the boulder on which we sunbathed. We sat there, frozen, unsure whether to scream or run away, or to watch its body twisting in the water.

The backyard of my family's vacation home in Normalville, Pennsylvania, was the most beautiful haven I have ever known. At night, I would fall asleep listening to the trickling stream and an owl's hooting, a friendly competition.

Immediately outside of our backdoor stretched a labyrinth of hedges. Every spring the walls turned white because so many poplar blooms lay tangled in the paddle leaves. We used to play hide-and-go-seek every weekend, getting lost in the oblivion of sweet aromas.

In 2000, just before we moved away, my family and neighbors were impacted by a coal company's decision to strip mine an area behind our house. Across from the stream, each family owned about an acre of mountain land, supposedly full of coal. When we originally moved there, the creek had just started recovering from the last mining expedition – all the fish beginning to replenish their populations, the water starting to regain its nutrients.

Land in the area had been strip mined for years because it was easily accessible.

A few neighborhoods over in Ligonier, home of the wealthy Rolling Rock Country Club, no mining had occurred. The trout there were huge and sweet; my dad and I used to go there to fish, as there was nowhere near our house where the fish were in plentiful supply.

My dad and other neighbors decided they needed a petition to stop the proposed mining. Their efforts were unsuccessful. The stream was destroyed, and the run-off toxins from the mining have again killed the fish and poisoned the earth.

One of the families had a child about a year after the mining began. He was born with cystic fibrosis and almost didn't make it through his first weeks. Now, he struggles to breathe because of the filthy air that was left behind by the mining. Their wooden, four-bedroom house required repairs, as the ground had shifted from the effects of soil erosion.

This community is not a wealthy one. They are people who live in the mountains, either because they love the land or cannot afford the city. Unlike us, this wasn't a vacation home – this was their everyday life. When we sold our house, they remained to suffer the air contamination, soil damage and stream pollution.

This place was a paradise, and now it is left barren.

ALEX MASTERSON, *Kentucky*
High School Junior

Black Waters

Oh black waters,
will you cease to exist?
Oh black waters,
you look like a road.
Black as asphalt.
Oh black waters,
black from sludge,
black waters,
show mercy on
the culture we love.

WILL NELMS, Kentucky
Fifth grade

Pay Attention

If John Updike spoke to a rally of 1,200 people on the icy steps of the Massachusetts state Capitol, declaring himself ready, "all other recourse having failed," to get in the way of the legislature's refusal to save its own land and people from ruinous industrial practices, do you think the *Boston Globe* would report it? If citizens from across that state had made a "Save Our Mountains" banner that stretched halfway down the tunnel between the annex and the Capitol, do you think there'd be a photo or do you think they'd mention that school kids, wearing tee shirts and buttons they'd made, came not just to see the floral clock, but to try out democracy and see if it works?

Well, this and a lot more happened in Kentucky on Valentine's Day [2008] when Wendell Berry and Kentuckians for the Commonwealth rallied citizens from the west coast to the east coast of our endangered state to demand that HB164, the Stream Saver Bill, get out of the House Natural Resources committee and on the floor for a vote. But the local coverage consisted of a photo of a handful of people, and no mention of the lobbying, the bill, the speakers or the number of Kentuckians who turned out on a frozen day in February to plead for "our mountains, our streams, our future."

This proposed legislation, held in committee for three years, would end the practice of filling valleys and destroying streams with the trees, rock and dirt that are left over when you blow off the top of the mountain to get at the coal.

Why has this bill been held back so long? Because the coal industry has a chokehold on this state. Because Jim Gooch, chair of the House Natural Resources committee, is in the business of producing the gigantic equipment used in mountaintop removal mining, and because most Kentuckians, if they think about it at all, believe the Kentucky Coal Association's lie of cheap coal and are going about their business while mountains (470 so far) are being blown to Kingdom Come leaving behind a hell of buried headwaters, polluted air and ground water, unstable toxic waste lakes, fierce floods, plummeting property values and broken lives.

Here are Wendell Berry's closing words, spoken into a bitter wind after 40 years of protest & argument against the devastation caused by mining methods that put profit above all else: "If this

General Assembly and this administration give notice as usual that they are blind by policy to the ongoing destruction of the land and the people they are sworn to protect — and if you, my friends, all other recourse having failed, are ready to stand in the way of this destruction until it is stopped — then I too am ready."

Shame on the *Herald-Leader* for neither heralding nor leading to inform its readers of the content and magnitude of the lobbying and rally which took place on this third annual I Love Mountains Day. The Louisville *Courier-Journal* and Ashland's *Daily Independent* gave it significant coverage, as did the Corbin *Times Tribune*, *The State Journal*, *The Winchester Sun* and *The Kentucky Kernel*. My hometown paper, *The Harlan Daily Enterprise*, did likewise because Harlan Countians Carl Shoupe, an underground miner, and Ronnie Banks, a 13-year-old student, both spoke at the rally. I know Governor Beshear's plea for casinos was the big news that day, but there was room for a story about 1,200 Kentuckians come to the capitol to bet on the promise that their voice still counts.

GEORGE ELLA LYON, Kentucky

Originally published as a letter to the editor in The Lexington Herald-Leader

Horrified

It was so bad that it didn't seem real.
The color was a greenish-black
like liquid rubber.
I was horrified to see it.
"Where are they going
to put the sludge?"

DAVIS DEJARNETTE, Kentucky
Fifth grade

We All Live Downstream

Did you really think God got it wrong
When He put that mountain right there?
Or do you believe Mother Nature had no clue
When She populated it so fair?
And what was the crime of Father Time
Who set it all in slow, slow motion?
Still, you know best, don't you, Little Man?
Now, where'd you get that notion?

Chorus Well, you brought your D-9 dozer and you bought the law
You'll even use the Good Book to scrape the earth's face raw
So, blow it up, tear it down, claim you're a righteous taker
Rip it out, push it off – just be prepared to face its Maker.

Do you really think nobody cares
Just because your own heart's a stone?
Can you comprehend the life that thrived up here
Before you came along?
Until you poisoned them for power and for greed,
These headwaters were clean
But you don't care, do you, Little Man,
That we all live downstream?

So, you brought your dragline, oh and you bought the law
You'll even use the Good Book to scrape the earth's face raw
So, blow it up, tear it down, claim you're a righteous taker
Rip it out, push it off – just be prepared to face its Maker.

KATE LARKEN, Kentucky

My Wake–Up Call

The four cars from Louisville wound around the narrow mountain roads of Eastern Kentucky. I was awed by the majestic mountains covered in lush, untouched trees and bushes. But I was in disbelief at the sight of their brown and misshapen treeless siblings. As the cars drove deeper and deeper into the mountains toward Pike County, the roads narrowed as the elevation increased. Once our car reached the end of the paved roads, we moved onto gravel and dirt. The dust, overwhelming and suffocating, made everyone sneeze and cough. A speaker asked us to imagine 50 or more big trucks kicking up dust like our four cars had. By law, the roads were to be watered regularly, but the residents said that water trucks came by as rarely as once a day.

When the air finally cleared, I could see a few run-down houses deep in the woods. The blast of the explosives had wrecked their foundations and made them uninhabitable. I was baffled and confused as to why I hadn't heard more about Pikeville and its neighbors when I live in the very same state.

For the people living nearby, the coal company delivers gallons of clean drinking water, but they are still forced to bathe in water the Environmental Protection Agency (EPA) calls unsafe and unsuitable for use. A local woman, Erica Urias, plays a game with her three-year-old daughter at bath time called "Squeeze your eyes shut as tight as you can." The water is toxic, and if it seeps into her eyes, it is extremely painful and probably damaging.

When the presence of a domineering company starts to affect the supply of water, a simple necessity, then it is too obvious that those with money can get away with anything.

Mountaintop removal previously existed in my mind as a theory, an abstract process. But nothing could compare to the total shock I felt when I saw the devastation with my own eyes – the destruction of a diverse ecosystem.

It hit me, standing atop a cliff in tenth grade, gazing beyond a valley to the vast mountainous horizon. My heart plummeted into my shoes. I was watching the big yellow machines eat away at our country's oldest mountains.

The coal companies use explosives to shatter the mountaintops and expose the coal seams beneath. Machines return later to dispose of tons and tons of rock and soil waste by dumping it into the valley below. While the streams are buried on the surface, the underground aquifers are contaminated by the blasting, leaving little water for drinking.

Any land that was available for development had been carved out of the mountains; entire towns were visible from the highway. Overloaded trucks thundered through the town at unsafe speeds on their way to processing stations.

These were the first signs of a community dominated by coal mining.

Coal mining is an awkward situation in Eastern Kentucky. It has provided job opportunities for a few in the mountain communities, and our economy is heavily dependent on fossil fuels. However, for the health and safety of the land and people, coal companies have to be restricted and regulated. In the past, the companies have made themselves exempt or found loopholes to escape the laws, so keeping them in check is an uphill political battle. Citizens of Kentucky need to be assured that these companies will not be given special treatment just because some politicians have dollar signs in their eyes.

Kentuckians for the Commonwealth (KFTC) is an organization that offers some hope for the people and the environment of Eastern Kentucky. KFTC works inside the system to gain power in the Kentucky legislature and to spread awareness and gain support throughout the state. By lobbying state legislators, KFTC promotes bills that would restrict coal companies.

After absorbing the horrific sights in Pikeville on the Mountain Witness Tour sponsored by KFTC, I needed to do something. I took the opportunity to visit the state Capitol and follow a seasoned lobbyist to meet legislators to discuss the Stream Saver Bill.

Sponsored by Rep. Don Pasley, this bill would prohibit coal companies from depositing their overburden into the valleys below. If passed, it would greatly reduce the use of mountaintop removal mining. The rock and soil debris would have to be put back on the mine site, which would be a tedious and expensive process. This bill is absolutely necessary for the survival of the ecosystem in Eastern Kentucky.

I went to Frankfort because I believe that if this region is neglected any longer, we will lose the oldest mountains in the world. This experience was both incredibly exciting and disappointing.

I met with three representatives who all seemed oblivious of what was happening in their own state. The most depressing meeting was with Rep. Hubert Collins. His constituents live in four of the Eastern Kentucky counties most affected by mountaintop removal, but he seemed the least interested in listening to us. He tried to explain that many bills have become laws in the past and they just haven't had time to work yet.

In reality, Collins knows if he were to support a bill against the coal companies, he would lose their campaign contributions and, more than likely, his political office. Probably, this legislator knows better than anyone the problems in Eastern Kentucky, yet he refused to think morally.

Over 400 miles of streams have already been buried by valley fills, contaminating drinking water for more than a million people. Living in the United States has provided me with privileges and luxuries that I adore. But with prosperity comes responsibilities. Our culture has allowed us to ignore the truth behind the façade of wealth. The reason we allow such destruction of the environment in Eastern Kentucky is the lack of visibility.

There are areas all over the earth that are hidden from the eyes of the average person. Our nation, which has the most wealth in the world, is in desperate need of a wake-up call.

ABBY MILLER, *Kentucky*
High School Senior

Black Waters No More

It's official: The first shot has been fired in the legislative battle to end the devastating practice of mountaintop removal mining in central Appalachia.

With the quickly growing and extraordinary nationwide support of over 115 co-sponsors, including 17 members of the Transportation and Infrastructure Committee in the United States House of Representatives, Rep. John Yarmuth from Kentucky's embattled state of coal joined Rep. Frank Pallone (D-NJ) and Rep. Dave Reichert (R-WA) in reintroducing the Clean Water Protection Act today.

The Clean Water Protection Act was introduced originally to challenge the outrageous executive rule change by the Bush administration to redefine "fill material" in the Clean Water Act, which has since allowed coal companies to blast hundreds of mountains to bits, dump millions of tons of "excess spoil" into nearby valleys, and bury hundreds of miles of streams. An estimated 1,200 miles of waterways have been destroyed by this extreme mining process.

The end result: toxic black waters and poisoned aquifers that have denied American citizens in the coalfields the basic right of a glass of clean water.

Today's timing couldn't be more urgent: On the heels of a 4th U.S. Circuit Court decision that overturned greater environmental review of mountaintop removal actions by coal companies, scores of mining permits are flooding through the gates of the U.S. Army Corps of Engineers this month.

"Congress meant for the Clean Water Act to protect our nation's water resources; the Administrative rule change endangers those resources," said Rep. Pallone, the heroic author of the legislation. "The dangerous precedent set by the Bush Administration's rule change undermines the Clean Water Act."

The breakthrough role of Yarmuth, a Democrat from Louisville, has Kentuckians on their feet with applause.

"I am so thankful that one of Kentucky's politicians is stepping forward and showing true moral courage," said bestselling author Silas House, from the coalfields of Eastern Kentucky. "It's just a shame that the Act isn't receiving support from Eastern

Kentucky's politicians, where the water is most endangered. They should be ashamed that Yarmuth is having to do their job and his, too."

George Brosi, a long-time Appalachian activist from Berea, Kentucky, also praised the co-sponsorship of Rep. Ben Chandler from central Kentucky: "They are dramatically demonstrating that those who live downstream from the scourge of mountaintop removal mining must protect their water supply even if it means standing up to the most rich and powerful private interest in their state – the coal industry."

"Unlike some other members of this state, John Yarmuth isn't being cowed by the coal industry," noted Stephanie Pistello, an Eastern Kentucky native and legislative associate for Appalachian Voices in Washington, D.C. "He understands the devastation being wrought upon his state by this horrific method of mining. He is showing the courage to do what's right for the people of our great state and nation."

Pistello added that Lexington's consumption of high-burning coal fuel was singled out recently by a Brookings Institution study that ranked it as one of the cities with the worst carbon footprints in the nation.

As blasting continues to shatter peace and prosperity in the coalfields of West Virginia, Kentucky, Virginia and Tennessee today, anti-mountaintop removal advocates also continue to make their appeal to President Barack Obama, who told a campaign rally in Lexington, Kentucky, on August 27, 2007, "We're tearing up the Appalachian Mountains because of our dependence on fossil fuels."

JEFF BIGGERS, Illinois

Originally published by The Huffington Post, *4 March 2009*

The Black Panther's Stare

There was a panther as black as the night sky, his eyes as bright and piercing as the stars. As the panther's paws fell upon the forest floor, not a sound was heard. It was said this panther could jump a mountain with ease. All that its prey saw before it pounced was a pair of piercing yellow eyes.

One night, he was prowling the forest when he noticed that the water of a usually clear stream was brown and muddy.

"I've got to get to the bottom of this," he thought.

So he followed the creek bank upstream until he came to a clearing next to the water. In the clearing, there were some chainsaws and heavy machinery. As he looked to the side, he saw that the stream ran by a mountain. When he looked closer, he saw the entire top half of the mountain was gone.

He knew he had to put a stop to it. He decided that he would have to scare them out. So he put some long gashes in the upholstery of the machinery, and then went home to his den.

The next day when the men were packing up and heading back to camp, he waited until nightfall and then appeared about fifty feet away. He made sure at least one person saw him. All they could see were two bright yellow eyes. Then, after he was sure somebody had seen him, he disappeared into the trees.

He did this night after night.

After awhile, the men began to get spooked. Everybody had seen the piercing stare.

One night, the manager came up to check on the men's progress. That night, the panther reappeared. This time he made sure his eyes were visible for a good long time, then growled and backed into the shadows.

The manager thought the land was haunted, as did the other men. So they stopped working and backed out.

Eventually, the trees reappeared on the top of the mountain and the stream's water cleared up, and everything was back to the way it should be.

WALTER KING, *West Virginia*
Fourth grade

Shattered Mountain

The natural law says a flood like this comes
Once a century
But why it's happened twice in the past five years
Ain't no mystery to me.
They set the charge and blew that ancient
Mountaintop away.
They can pack it down, they can pile it up,
But shattered ground, it will not stay.

Chorus   When the rain came on I heard those
                Mighty waters rage.
                Washed away the shattered mountain
                That has stood from age to age.

I've walked my mountain land, I've felt its
Strength beneath my feet.
I tried to catch my shattered mountain as it
Washed down the swollen creek.
What some might call an act of God or a
Sad coincidence.
Has changed the way I understand
Forever, ever since.

Repeat Chorus

The river rose and the earth it fell,
The foundation, Lord, it shook.
No solid ground to set my feet, loss was
Everywhere I looked.
I couldn't catch my mountain
In my hands. I'll fight to
Keep another whole.
These hills hold me to Creation, they're where I rest my soul.

Repeat Chorus

BROOKE CALTON, *North Carolina*

Is It Mine To Mine?

"Almost quittin' time," remarked Joe, looking at his watch. "Let's see how much more we can get done."

The barn-sized scoop reached down into the ground and grabbed up more coal, again and again, until Joe's radio crackled. It was the Boss.

"Send Hand down to the shack, will ya? I'd like to talk to him before he leaves."

Hank stood. "I guess I'd better go. Might see you down there."

He climbed out the door and Joe could see him scrambling down the ladder to the muddy ground.

At the worker's shack, Hank greeted the Boss; his name was Willard, but everyone referred to him as "the Boss."

"I've got a new employee and I want you to train him. You know, teach him our kind of mining."

Hank was silent for a moment, as this would be the first person he would train. He nodded.

"Tomorrow at noon Sam will be here and you can get started," the Boss said.

"Welcome aboard! I'm Hank. Been working this Virginia site for about seven months. I'll show you around and teach you the tricks of the trade," Hank told Sam.

All day they walked around talking about the aspects of mountaintop removal mining. The site was loud with moving machinery – the draglines and coal processing facility.

Hank liked his job and was good at it. He enjoyed passing on the knowledge of his work. Later that afternoon, Hank and Sam watched as workers dumped ammonium nitrate into holes to blast away more of the mountain and expose the next seam of coal. They also helped start building a dam to hold the slurry away from the town below. Hank had an apartment down there for the duration of this job.

As he talked with Sam the next day, Hank actually started thinking about his job for the first time. *Was it really okay to tear the tops off mountains?* He thought about it hard that night and decided to talk to Joe about it the next day.

He sprang the question as they were getting out of the truck.

"What? Are you questioning the perfect job?" Joe jumped. "I get good pay, have reasonable hours, have friends and get to operate this big excavator. What more could you ask for?"

"I know, I know," Hank replied. "But I've just been thinking about the mountains and the people who live here."

"Since when are you so mindful about that?" Joe asked. "It doesn't matter, and the people, well, they never look at the good side of things. Are you all right? You're acting odd. You should see the Boss."

Hank sighed. "Yeah, I'm fine."

Hank did talk to the Boss, who told him that Joe was right – he really didn't need to wonder or worry. But during the next few days, Hank could see both sides of the story as he talked with Sam. He didn't enjoy the work nearly as much. Everything he did bothered him.

Three days later, Hank was watching TV before bed. The drone of the commentator was broken by a news flash – a slurry dam had broken in Kentucky and dumped black mud throughout a whole town.

Hank jolted awake. *They were building a slurry dam right now.* He'd never worried about it, as it looked sturdy enough, but now he'd have to make sure it was strong and stable.

The electric hum of the TV died as Hank turned it off. He couldn't listen anymore. That night, he didn't sleep. He now knew that nature was worth worrying over. This little nook in Appalachia would never be the same; all the mountains and valleys were gone for just another vein of coal.

Hank remembered when he began to dig. It was in his backyard as a kid. He remembered what it was like to have his creation torn apart. *That was how these people must feel about their mountains.*

Getting up the next morning, Hank drove to the site. He looked at the mountains through the windows of his truck. No longer was it an annoyance – all those trees left to dig up, all that dirt and rock burying the prize of the coal – but it was nature and Hank liked it. He worked as usual, but his heart wasn't in it. He was upset about the whole idea of mountaintop removal.

Everyone could tell. Joe asked what was wrong and Hank replied that he just couldn't do this anymore. That afternoon, Hank talked with the Boss.

"What's wrong? Are you still bothered by this?" the Boss asked.

"Yeah," Hank responded. "It all just seems wrong."

"Well, there are some bad things about it," the Boss admitted. "But it helps the community. It provides jobs for people like you. It makes flat land for houses and industry."

"I suppose so," Hank pondered. But not matter how hard the thought about it, he could not see mountaintop removal in a good light anymore.

The following day, Hank went to town to talk to people. Most of the residents thought the whole business was terrible. It was ruining the mountains, wildlife and creeks, they said. One lady was talking to her friend about how she had to buy bottled water now because her well was poisoned with heavy metals from washing the coal. Someone else was saying how his whole house was covered in coal dust.

There was no end to the dreadful aspects of the mining. Hank looked up at what was left of the mountains. He could see why the people in town hated mountaintop removal – the beauty was gone, the quiet was gone, the calm was gone.

He got back to his apartment and knew he could no longer be a miner. He couldn't go on tearing up the land. Tomorrow he would tell the Boss.

That wasn't going to be easy.

When Hank told Joe he was leaving, Joe looked astonished and started to respond. But he just shrugged and shook his head.

Leaving a note on the Boss's desk, Hank went out for a last day of work. While they were digging coal, Joe refused to talk to him. Sam knew he'd soon get a new working partner.

I have to get through this day, Hank told himself. *What have I done?*

It was through training Sam that Hank had come to see

mining in a new light. The dam break in Kentucky was part of it, too. He wondered if he'd made the right decision and worried about being unemployed. It was something he decided to think about later.

At the end of the day, Hank got a polite note from the Boss saying he wished for Hank's success at whatever he tried next. It didn't sound like the Boss, so he figured it was probably from the secretary.

Hank left Virginia and went to North Carolina. He started working as an excavator for a small construction company. That was much better. He still got to dig, but he wasn't destroying the environment and people's lives. Two weeks after starting his new job, he heard on the radio that there had been a protest against mountaintop removal in his old town. The mining company had been blasting and had started a rockslide, which buried several buildings. They had almost been shut down, and Hank knew there would be lawsuits.

Maybe because of this they'd realize the destruction they caused. He doubted it.

Ellen Robertson, Virginia
High School Sophomore

Lies and Secrets

I sit and look
up at my old mountaintop
wondering
why it had to be this way.

When you come
down the road you'll
see the streams,
poisoned,
choked.

Don't get out
to look at them
for what you will see is
what the coal companies have done
to these poor little streams.

Loud noises from miles away,
but that's just the trucks leaving
with my tears,
my mountain dirt,
my used-to-be memories,
just all drifting away.

Everyone asks why –
"Why does it have to be this way?"
I ask, "Why does this have to be us
and our land?"
Some will say it can be fixed.
As we both know
it's gone.

Forever.

Now my neighbors have
gone and moved to the city.

Is there any way
to fix the broken?
And the destroyed?

Will they ever get that God
made mountains
for people to see,
not to destroy?

Kaitlyn Klaber, Kentucky
Fifth grade

Crank's Creek

Early one morning without any warning
Seventeen miles of West Virginia lives were washed away
Pittson took the coal, left a dam that wouldn't hold
For the raping of that mountain for even one more day.

Chorus   But you know that something's rising up on Crank's Creek
              People rising to turn the tide
              Something's rising up on Crank's Creek
              People say it won't be the water this time

Nellie Woolum fought for years, through the courts she voiced her fears
That the sludge pile above her home would bury her alive.
Everyone in Ages Holler knows that almighty dollar
Talks louder than a single voice and she did not survive

Repeat Chorus

There have been so many floods they just seem to run together
No one talks lightly about the weather anymore.
Will we all wind up the victims or can we send our own storm warning
Floods of protest coming – let our voices swell and roar!

Repeat Chorus

Bridge   Shall we gather at the river
              And stop the floods of Babylon's greed
              Shall we gather at the river
              Before these mountains are washed to the sea

Repeat Chorus

BEV FUTRELL, Kentucky

View of what once was Kayford Mountain.

FRANCES BUERKENS, Kentucky

HERITAGE

Look how they've cut all to pieces
Our ancient redwood and oak
And the hillsides are stained with the greases
That burned up the heavens with smoke

BILLY EDD WHEELER, "The Coming of the Roads"

I Mark This Gone Place With Foxfire

Buchanan County, Virginia

At the edge of coal country
I pull the car onto a switchback,
stop where road and hollyhock run together
where used to you could go this road
to the top of Drill Mountain.
I abandon the car to this unkept place,
walk between overgrowth of briar and honeysuckle vine,
walk until I find the crevice – large enough
to walk into – where Granddaddy hid blackberry brandy.
But I am too long in the city, too afraid
of fast-moving critters who covet these dark niches,
I reach in with only my leg, toes pointed,
sweeping the floor for that bottle.

I come away with nothing, gone
as the road we used to drive together,
gone as these mountains, peaks missing, lopped off
by draglines that decapitate it all, leave
this strange, foreign landscape, absent
the rush of the Dismal River, even the creeks dried up,
or gone underground.

I find a poplar stump, sit against its damp wood,
breathe deep and imagine apple blossoms,
patches of pennyroyal, hillsides unvanished.
This place gave you love and children, mandolin
and shaped-note singing, a taste for squirrel gravy
and fried bluegill, and those black lungs
that finally slowed you to a stop.

I stand and dig up the forest floor with the toes of my boots,
break this rotting poplar up with my heels and push it in chunks
beneath the ground, cover it over again. You taught
me this trick. You said,

I know this to be true: sometimes
when you bring up things, rot and all,
you get a queer thing of light,
glowing even as it dies.

LISA PARKER, *Virginia and New York*

Kingdom Come
for my father

Ben waits for the green arrow to let him turn at the Pineville bridge, while his dad reads the signs at the Exxon station out loud. Richard always refers to this as the new gas station because it is not the one that sat on the corner for the first half of his life. The new station has an Arby's and a Little Caesar's Pizza inside it.

"Five dollar pizzas, all day, every day," Richard reads from a sign that lights up at night. "Son, when I used to drive through here, I didn't have five dollars to give 'em for a pizza." He says this every time they make the trip back to Kentucky.

Since Ben was a child, he loved being in the mountains. Each trip was another chance to memorize the twisting lines of rocks and trees against the sky. In those days, Richard drove on what seemed to Ben like such a long trip from their home in Knoxville to this place where Richard had grown up in Kentucky. It felt like a great voyage made more monumental by the fact that they crossed into a new state.

Now, it is Ben behind the wheel, and Richard complains he is driving too fast even when below the speed limit. "My nerves are bad," his dad reminds him. "Don't scare me today out on this old road. If I had known you were going to drive like a damn NASCAR driver, we would have stayed home." Music of any kind also makes him jittery, so there is only their conversation to pass the time – and Richard reading every road sign along the way.

"Kingdom Come Parkway," he reads after they cross the bridge. That is the official name of this road, although everyone just refers to it by its number – 119. This highway takes them deep into what Richard likes to call the Dark Hills of Kentucky.

"City of Pineville Water Treatment," he reads from the driver's side door of a utility truck parked on the side of the road. "Wonder what they do to it?" he says in the form of a question even though he never expects an answer. "When I was young, you could find the cleanest drinking water at any little stream you crossed. It was the best tasting water ever was."

Farther up 119, Richard tells again how he remembers when the first eight miles of this new road were built. That was 1958 – half a century ago – but to Richard it is still the new road, and after all these years and all the trips they've made back, Ben thinks of it as the new road too.

"I hadn't ever seen a road so good as this was then," Richard says. "I was going to Corbin to look for a job when they opened this road up. I wasn't out of high school yet, and they had closed the mines. There weren't any jobs. You couldn't buy work back then."

"Would you have gone in the mines?" Ben asks.

"I would have worked at anything if I could have stayed here. But there wasn't anything. No jobs at all. I guess it was better for me anyway. Forced me out of these black mountains."

They pass some pretty bottom land that lines the banks of the Cumberland River. These are the only flat pieces of ground for a long time. When Ben was a little boy, his dad would talk about how the first settlers had planted their corn here over two hundred years ago. He would talk with fascination about how the river flooded every spring like the Nile and made the dirt rich. Richard thought it must have been wonderful to turn that earth for the first time and plant that precious seed in hopes of a summer crop, and Ben did too.

Richard doesn't mention this anymore though, now that he is older. It is always about this time in the trip that he is tired of sitting in the car for so long, and he wonders why they have made the journey anyway.

"Maybe we shouldn't have run off up here today. I'm tired. I wish we had just stayed home. It's an awful gray day."

It really is an awful gray day, dry but with the promise of rain to come. It is late in October. The leaves have already passed their prime and now resemble a uniform blanket of rust. It's not an ideal day, and Richard only sees the land through winter windows. His eyes focus only on the houses that are run down, the businesses that have closed, the scrawny puppy on the roadside.

"Look at this ground," he says. "It's so poor it won't even grow a good weed."

This is the road to Harlan County; Patty Loveless singing "You'll Never Leave Harlan Alive" always comes to Ben when he's on it. But Ben can also see new homes on hillsides, gas stations and stores with plenty of activity, smiling kids everywhere. Ben knows the land is steep and rough and worn out, but he thinks there is still a lot of life in these hills, and certainly a rugged beauty he loves.

Ben was born in Knoxville. He has lived there all of his life. He is a Tennessean. Richard also thinks of himself as a Tennessean, but he is not. He was born a Kentuckian and has always remained one. Granted, he's been a Kentuckian-in-exile for most of his life, but it is this basic fact of geography that has colored his perception of the world. The pinnacle of Black Mountain is always in the landscape of Richard's mind like the 1982 World's Fair Sun Sphere is always in Ben's.

"For someone from Kentucky, you always have a lot of bad to say about it," Ben says.

"I'm not a native. I can say it." Richard says this fast, maybe so Ben won't argue. Richard is an intelligent man. He knows what the word native means, but he'll use any trick to get one over on his son.

"You are too a native. You were born in a potato patch in a coal camp in Harlan County." It's a story Ben has heard too many times to ever forget.

"I wasn't born in a potato patch!" Richard is in a huff at the thought he was born out in the dirt, as if his family were too poor or stupid to have children in a proper way. Ben knows all of this, but he likes to make a point sometimes too. "They were digging potatoes the day I was born," Richard says, "but I wasn't born out there. Besides, my people just came here to mine coal."

"Your people followed Boone through the Cumberland Gap. They became coal miners a lot later."

"Well, my mother was born in Virginia," Richard says, as if he judges the argument won.

He changes the subject by pointing out an eastern hemlock tree along the road. He knows all trees, some by their bark, some by their leaf. This is a gift Ben wishes he had, but he seem to have not inherited that gene. Ben thinks he might have also had to grow up on Cumberland Mountain to keep the names of trees so close to his heart.

"Community of Black Star," Richard reads from a wooden sign painted in bold letters of black against red. They follow the sign's direction and follow the smaller road until eventually trading pavement for gravel. Ben is not exactly sure where the line is, but he knows they have crossed into Harlan County. They come to the cemetery where Richard's parents are buried. Not only are his parents here, but so are most of the people he knew in childhood.

Richard does not have one bad memory from growing up on this mountain. Even the stories that sound wild and terrible are retold in a reverence for the past or with the excitement of a thriller. He loved this place as it was in his youth. He worshipped the people he knew. They are never far from his thoughts no matter how far away Knoxville is from Harlan, or how far he might wish it to be. It is this place he retreats to in his dreams.

As they move over the cemetery's car path, both men are quiet. Ben parks the car above his grandparents' graves. Richard stopped getting out of the car a long time ago, but Ben asks him if he wants to get out anyway. Ben always asks him. Now though, it is all Richard can manage to ride here, to realize he has already lived decades longer than either his mother or father, to pause for a moment and accept the fact that the past can not be relived. Ben will walk to the graves and read the familiar dates carved into their stones. He will walk there and stand there for both of them.

Today though, the air reeks of wood fire. The smoke is so diluted Ben squints his eyes to distinguish it in the wind. His nose recognizes the smoke though. Ashes land on his clothes like snow, and he looks around to see where the fire is. A massive heap of timber burns on a nearby mountainside. A bulldozer pushes more logs and brush into the flaming pile. A great section of trees have been torn off that piece of the mountain, and heavy equipment is working overtime to demolish more. Ben has stopped still before making it halfway to his grandparents' graves. He stares at this new view until he suddenly sees the trees are not all that is gone. Across the narrow valley, the entire top of a mountain has been removed, chopped off like the head of a convicted criminal.

"Lord, Lord!" Richard says behind him. He stands outside of the car, holds onto the door for support. His look of panicked amazement echoes how Ben feels. Both men feel the same endless drop in their chests.

"If you'd have told me 50 years ago they'd just tear the tops off those mountains, I'd have never believed it," Richard says. "I thought if anything at all stood on the Day of Judgment it would be the face of that mountain. It might have been the one thing able to look God in the eye without shame. Not even it now."

A huge flock of starlings blacken the sky like a scourge. They fly overhead and land on a row of sycamore trees that line a ditch below the cemetery. The trees' white wood, smooth and parched like bones forgotten in the sun, stands sharp against the birds' black feathers.

Richard thinks every trip he makes back to Harlan will be the last. He says this every time he visits the ground where his parents lie, but he always comes again. Ben realizes today, though, it may truthfully be too painful for Richard to come back to this place, with the curving line of the mountain's highest summit now made straight.

The men are always more quiet on the way home, but words are a complete failure to them now. The weight of the missing mountain sits too heavily upon them.

DENTON LOVING, Tennessee

mr. coal

he don't care I was born in a house
used to stand back there, orchard was here,
over there now entirely gone was a stream
along which beech trees dropped their nuts and our hogs
fed on them.
beech stealer.
watch out for mr. coal.
he steals your home,
he steals your trees don't care
who planted them.
he steals the pretty pink color
in your lungs, he steals the picture
in your heart that shows you what home
looks like, shows you how always to go back
there, home.
dirty thief.
steals your neighbors, some sell out
to him, some go down to him, some like the money
like green leaves waving in their hands,
some go to work for him and think, think, think
they doing the world a favor –
you like to burn your lights
don't you? and they quit
waving.
friend of mr. coal's no friend of mine.
i done heard too much about the man.
too many disappearances.
my daddy, my brother, my
good neighbor.
we are a remnant people
up in these hollers,
buried: 500 miles of streams
we played in, rocky
mountain creeks, springs and
clear sand bottoms.
tell me why my wellwater has turned

orange, why it smells, why
it has black specks floating in it?
mr. coal sent papers, says
mining is to begin
a half-mile from our house,
do we want a pre-blasting
survey? in case the old house
tears apart, pillar from post.
he sends machines with tires taller
than our tallest, he sends bull
dozers and a fleet of open
mouthed hauling trucks, tells the machines
to go to eating.
they ate the mountain
above the house, and the next mountain
and the next. I have lived with
these mountains all my life, have seen them
covered with ice & snow, fog
& mist, the greenest green, with bright yellows & reds.
like now.
my god, every morning I have woken
& looked out, glad to be alive
in these old old hills.
there's a map drawn on my heart
and it looks exactly like
breathitt county, kentucky
and right where the blood comes in
is where mr. massey's torn down
the entire mountain.
mr. coal, he lives down there
under the ground. wants to pull us all
under there with him:
your people are all sick, what you
got to live for, he asks.
down here, we can make us a bright
light, come on down, he says this
with his face black, his teeth black,
the little halfmoons under his fingernails
pitch black. his tongue is black.

his heart is blackest of all, it ain't nothing
but a rock. mr. coal carrying around
a rock like the rest of us carry memories
until the overburden hits us
and that's gone too.

JANISSE RAY, Georgia

God's Country

"God's country" is a phrase often used to describe the rich tapestry of life woven in Appalachia. But the destruction of Creation and injustice toward people caused by mountaintop removal mining has raised the concern of people of faith across America. Five major religious denominations have already passed resolutions opposing mountaintop removal.

The coal companies are destroying God's country. They raze a mountainside, using dozers to plow up the earth, ripping trees from the ground with huge tractors. Brush is cleared and then the debris is set ablaze. Dynamite is used to blow up the landscape. Holes are dug for explosives, charges are set and mountaintops are literally blown apart. As much as 800 to 1,000 feet of the mountaintops are blasted off in order to reach the coal seams that lie underneath. Huge draglines push the resulting millions of tons of wasted rock, dirt and vegetation into surrounding valleys, burying miles and miles of streams under piles of rubble hundreds of feet deep.

I'm against mountaintop removal. So is my family. And despite what others say, so are most people in West Virginia, Eastern Kentucky, Southwest Virginia and East Tennessee.

My family's heritage comes out of the mountains of Kentucky. Like my mother, I plan on taking my children and showing them where our heritage began.

Tell me: who would even do this to our land? Who would be able to sit back and watch our mountains fade away? I wouldn't.

Do you think our troops serving all over the world want to come home and see our mountains gone?

So when it comes down to it, are you for it or against it?

Stop mountaintop removal for the sake of our land.

SCOTTY COX, Kentucky
High School Sophomore

Erratics and Wanderers

My uncles lived in the mountains of West Virginia. Renick, Marlinton, Cass, Durbin, Ronceverte, Exchange were their towns. In the 1920s and 1930s they came up to Akron by train to work in the rubber plants. After they were hired on at Firestone or Goodrich and rented rooms on South Main Street, they looked for pretty and competent girls to marry. Some of them found the Haberkost girls who lived at 624 Grant Street. This is the way the mountains got in the blood of my aunts, and one of the ways the Appalachians got in my blood too.

My father and his father also brought the mountains here. The *northern* Appalachians. In 1923 my grandfather drove his young family from the anthracite mines of Scranton, Pennsylvania – where he had worked and where his young son, my father, had already begun to separate coal as a breaker boy.

I live in the same county in Ohio where I've always lived. There are officially no mountains here. The Appalachian foothills begin in *southern* Ohio – and I'm from a northern county in the Western Reserve. I have to drive almost an hour before I feel their deep contours under the wheels of my car, and hear its motor surge. The mountains came to me through the stories my uncles and my father told. Later, they came through trips my family took to West Virginia. My uncles and my aunts, my father and mother – all are gone now, so the mountains come to me only in the summertime, when I go to find them, alone.

But before any of this – before I was old enough to hear the stories, before the early visits to hollers and hills in my parents' Hudson hornet, and long before all the trips I've made alone – I lived in a place of stone. I lived my first five years amidst the remains of ravines and ledges and glacial rock. It wasn't a place of mountains, but, nevertheless, it was a place of stone. My uncles always felt comfortable here, in this hard place, and I think I know why now. It was in Wolf Ledge that I learned the lesson small stones, as well as great ones, teach children who encounter them.

Western Ohio experienced far more erosion than eastern. Sandstone and limestone were worn down to a flatness not to be found in the eastern half of the state. You can feel the difference between the two halves very suddenly as you drive from Akron, or from the town a little north of it where I live now, and head west toward Toledo, Ohio. Eastern Ohio – the place I've always called home – kept its sandstone, and all the old rock that rested under it. The grand river known as the Teays, that flowed from the Appalachians west to the Mississippi, cut deep valleys into Akron's sandstone, but left hilltops and ridges and ledges intact. Because our small Akron hills stand above these deep valleys – valleys later carved even deeper and wider by glaciers – they seem taller than they really are.

The glaciers, according to Frances McGovern and others who have studied and written about Akron geology, also brought huge boulders to Akron – enormous pieces of granite from the Canadian Shield called "erratics" or "wanderers." They're everywhere, and towns in my county have no trouble knowing where to mount their historical plaques. You see strangely shaped boulders on random corners and in parks, in the middle of cemeteries and small farms.

Ledges, ravines, boulders – they all were in Wolf Ledge when my grandparents were young. There was a thirty-foot cliff in their backyard that began near a street now known as Spicer and continued toward the Ohio & Erie Canal by Main and Cedar. Streetcar construction expanded in the 1890s, bringing the Loop Line down Grant Street – the main street in the neighborhood. Strangers discovered a natural wonder. More people suddenly wanted to live in this dramatic place, so over the next two decades some of it was leveled and landfill brought in. A boom began. Houses grew instead of trees and corn. Before the streetcar line expanded to the neighborhood, there were only a few houses south of Wheeler to the steep ledge that boxed things in. Slowly, the ledge was destroyed, fields surveyed and . . . more houses.

By the time my mother was born on Grant Street, Sumner Street had been graded, a bridge had been torn down, a gorge filled in. But there still were a few log bridges over steep grades, Wolf Run hadn't yet been routed through a stone culvert, the ravine remained, and a cave known at various times as Indian Cave, Under the Rocks, and Old Maid's Kitchen – with its enormous Steps at the entranceway – still was a favorite picnic spot, a place to go to fall in love. You could dam Wolf Run at various points and swim, climb rocks, pick berries and wildflowers, gather witch hazel to make home remedies that took the itch of poison ivy away.

By the time I was born, and lived on Eagle Street, just off Grant, there were still odd elevations in Wolf Ledge that the landfill could not disguise and a precipitous dip at the corner of Grant and Cross that Wolf Run had etched on its way to the canal, though its water was now hidden underground and I never saw the stream. I sometimes thought about wolves, though, because their name was as common to me as my own. I don't think anyone in my family had seen a wolf in Ohio. Ohio paid the last bounty for a wolf skin in 1842. There were many stories, though, about early settlers in the region hunting them. Everything was still named after them. The community was Wolf Ledge. Even the old Burkhardt Brewery on Grant Street was originally called Wolf Ledge Brewery. Old Washington Street underwent reconstruction during urban renewal and is now named Wolf Ledges Parkway – the plural an error very few even sense anymore. The wolves had long ago been ravaged, but you could still feel them here, the way you could the ledge. Along with Indian arrowheads, their bones were in the ground – hips, femurs, spines, snouts – and their stories were in fairy tales about little girls who wandered in the woods looking for Grandma's house.

The surface of the land had little of its original drama when I lived in Wolf Ledge, but there were signs that remained of that rocky place. What was still visible were massive boulders – the "erratics" and the "wanderers."

Across from Grandma's house, at the northeast entrance to Thornton Park, was one of them. We loved that rock. I lived in Wolf Ledge only until I was five years old, and when you're that small, a boulder takes up a lot of space. To us, it presented every bit as much adventure as the old ledge in Grandpa's day, or the ravine in my parents' time. From our progenitors we had inherited a fondness for glacial rocks and glimmering sandstone. It was in our blood. We couldn't stay away from that rock. There were steps carved into the hill that led up to it – probably meant to discourage people from climbing the grassy slope and ripping the lawn. We'd run up them to see who could reach the top step first, then mount the stone and ride it through space. My cousins and I were always racing, testing our legs and speed. We were constantly in motion, our brains and hearts still unformed. We didn't think or love yet. We just moved.

When we were young, rock seemed so permanent. Even when

the three of us tried to push that rock in Thornton Park and make it move – our little palms pressed hard against it and our feet pumping – its resistance was absolute. We'd laugh, then groan, when we failed, but I think if it had budged a single millimeter our world would have come undone.

Perhaps children have always loved boulders for this reason. Certainly Wolf Ledge children did. Earlier generations of our families had seen rock everywhere, not just on hills, for decoration, the way that we did. There were sandstone cliffs thirty feet high, completely perpendicular. Sandstone quarries in Wolf Ledge were as common and frequent as mini-marts today. There was one on nearly every corner – Adam Rohner's quarry on Sherman Street, Anthony Hunt's at Allyn, the Henry Zinkand quarry, the Peter Brown quarry, the Wohlwend quarry at Washington Street. Even though the cliffs were gone when I lived in Wolf Ledge, I still saw some of the stones. Downtown buildings were made from Wolf Ledge sandstone, including the Everett Building at Main and Market. Concordia Lutheran Church, the church the Haberkosts attended, was built by stonemasons from Wolf Ledge – and some of them were family. My grandma's brothers, owners of Golz Concrete Block Company, were the general contractors for the church. They hauled sandstone from local quarries and laid the brick.

My relationship to the mountains has some distance to it. I'm a wanderer, an erratic, I suppose. I know more about landfill than valley fill. But when I remember that stone in Thornton Park – and the solid ledges and ravines that were there when my grandparents grew up and that I could still feel beneath the land my own feet rested on – I sometimes wonder what it might be like to be a little child who watches a thousand vertical feet of rock blown away by dynamite. Maybe see it from her bedroom window. It was there when she went to sleep, and then it wasn't anymore, when first light poked through the morning glass. *Now you see it, now you don't.*

Children need softness, but they also need rock. They depend on it. How can you explain a thing like that to a child? My world, and all the steadiness I had built day by day, would have vanished if that single rock in Thornton Park – a glacial bit – had suddenly disappeared. How can I *not* wonder what dark thing enters children's heads when they see a mountain severed from its tip? I think, if it were me, if I were a small child again, I would scream and never stop. I would become all dark, hollow mouth, all empty – all sound, no shape. How can a child know the form she will take without measuring herself against a rock? Against something that's always been there – and that she expects always *will* be.

JOYCE DYER, Ohio

A Poet's Work

The aim of the poet and the poetry is finally to be of service, to ply the effort of
the individual work in to the larger work of the community as a whole.
—SEAMUS HEANEY

For Jeremy Davidson – 2001-2004

Spare me the post-modern pout
about dog piss in the gray snow
near the subway entrance,

Or the academic angst over a shaft
of light like the one in a scriptorium
of an obscure Tuscan monastery.

Witness meth labs that spring up in our rural
gardens, a quick pay out or fuel for three
piddly jobs, two to live, one to pay daycare.

Recount farm foreclosure, our food modified,
altered atrocities, the domain of agribusiness
conglomerates, the family farm a curiosity.

Clutch the child who sobs silently,
her mama a nurse in the Guard, called up,
goodnights from a webcam image from Basra.

Behold mountaintops removed, laid low by greed,
hollows filled, wells poisoned, God's majesty
flattened, fit only for Wal-Mart, the new Ground Zero.

Support the woman who tosses in fitful sleep as a dozer
strips her mountains under cover of dark, who wakes
to thunder, boulders tumbled upon her baby in his bed.

Revile the judgment of life's worth in coal country,
a fine levied at fifteen thousand, less than the price
of a good pickup truck, how the law measures a baby's life.

Spare me the post-modern pout, the academic angst.
Travel ruined roads, moonscape mountains, failed farms
and ponder judicial disregard, mindful
of a poet's work, the naming of what matters.

Jane Hicks, Tennessee

Originally published in Southern Ledger

Nature Doesn't Vote

As a young radio reporter in the 1970s, I loved doing stories about Appalachia. The people of Eastern Kentucky are natural storytellers, whether they're spinning a well-rehearsed yarn or simply describing last Saturday's trip to Kroger. The music in their voices makes them born radio stars. The other attraction was having the field almost to myself. The national press wasn't interested in Appalachia unless there was a horrible disaster, a rancorous labor battle or some excuse to revive hillbilly stereotypes of feuds and moonshine for a feature story during a slow news period.

In recent years I've gone back to hear Eastern Kentuckians tell me that the very mountains that shape their culture and define their heritage are being destroyed, and once again this is barely a blip on the national news radar.

Estimated to have formed nearly 300 million years ago, the Appalachian Mountains are America's oldest. During the last Ice Age, the central and southern Appalachians were spared. When the ice melted, the dense, lush, green forests of Appalachia re-forested the rest of the continent. Is it possible that people would visit such a historic natural wonder and blow it up? An outraged public wouldn't allow that to happen, would they?

We would. We want electricity and we want it cheap. More than half our electricity is produced by coal-fueled power plants. Eastern Kentucky's mountains contain a fortune in coal – the original black gold. For a century, we've burrowed tunnels into those mountains and laboriously extracted the coal in carts and on conveyor belts. It's an expensive process and very dangerous work. Mining companies have concluded it's easier to remove the mountain from the coal than to remove the coal from the mountain.

Using a mixture of ammonium nitrate and fuel oil, coal companies blow off the tops and sides of the mountains to expose the seams of coal. The valuable trees, topsoil and the rock are pushed over the side into the hollows between the mountains, often burying streams running through the hollows. So far, hundreds of thousands of acres of forest and thousands of miles of streams have been lost as a result.

Retired mine inspector Jack Spadaro maintains that the

process is illegal, that there are laws requiring mining companies
to observe buffer zones near streams, save the topsoil and return
mountains to their approximate original contour. Spadaro is right,
but state and federal government agencies routinely grant variances
allowing the coal companies to get around the laws. Legal challenges
to mountaintop removal have failed in court.

Do Americans know this is happening? Why isn't it getting
more attention? If the Adirondacks or the Catskills were being blown
up, wouldn't New York camera crews be in helicopters shooting video
of the devastation? Why is there so much outrage over plans to drill
for oil in the Arctic National Wildlife Refuge and so little notice paid
to the destruction of our oldest mountains? Why was there so much
news coverage of the Exxon Valdez oil spill when a coal waste spill
30 times bigger in Martin County got hardly any national press? Do
Kentuckians care about the loss of mountains, forests and streams?
Is there concern about silt and mining chemicals spoiling the drinking
water? How can a state with so many hunters and fishermen tolerate
the loss of habitat for fish and wildlife?

Those are some of the questions that sent me to Hazard,
Hindman, Whitesburg, Pikeville, Inez and parts in between and
beyond. The people directly affected by mountaintop removal coal
mining recited a litany of horror stories: cracked foundations from
blasting, wells poisoned by mining chemicals, streams and yards
ruined by spilled coal waste, relatives killed by overloaded coal trucks
driven recklessly on narrow mountain roads, and houses flooded by
rainwater finding new runoff patterns down reshaped mountains.
Eastern Kentuckians with whom I spoke are battered but not
defeated. They are fighting back. Organized by Kentuckians For The
Commonwealth, they are demonstrating, testifying, protesting and
talking with writers in the hope that their stories will reach a broader
audience. They are a hearty bunch, but they are outnumbered and
overmatched.

Opponents of mountaintop removal coal mining are battling
companies currently enjoying unprecedented freedom from regulation
by the Bush administration, whose leaders once were energy industry
executives and may be again someday. The very agencies charged
with protecting our environment and keeping wise stewardship of
our water and land are making it possible for mountains to be leveled
and streams to be buried. The Department of the Interior, the

Environmental Protection Agency, the U.S. Army Corps of Engineers and a host of others are all onboard. So are Congress, the courts and the Commonwealth of Kentucky. Even the major environmental advocacy groups are much more concerned about the burning of coal than the mining of it. Except for their neighbors similarly afflicted in Virginia, Tennessee and West Virginia, the people of Eastern Kentucky stand alone.

Finding villains in Washington and Frankfort is the easiest thing for a reporter to do. I might also look in the mirror. I'm writing this on a computer kept running by electricity supplied by a power plant that may be burning coal. I like my electric lights and my air conditioning. Would I pay a higher utility bill if it meant preserving a few more mountains in my native state? I would, but perhaps others can't afford to do that. We'll never know because our leaders aren't asking us to sacrifice our lifestyle or to invest our tax dollars in developing other sources of energy. In the name of "freeing our country from dependence on foreign sources of energy," we are blowing up our natural heritage. We are not asked to sacrifice, so nature must sacrifice. Nature doesn't vote.

BOB EDWARDS, Virginia

Originally published in The Courier-Journal

In My Town: West Virginia

There's a cluster of similar houses, two streetlights, a one-room post office, and a stop sign that circle like wagons against the outside world, each familiar as the items of a bedside table in the *kumbayah* of self-protection.

Each house has local-color shutters that stutter a chorus in wind, the same small porches that support two pots of geraniums as if an ordinance were passed some years ago against mums, and a curious cabbage garden that infects each backyard.

Two streetlights that work always, except in very high winds; until 2001 we had only one. The R&R track splits the town like a slash through a theta. Each of us as teens spent hours out there with a friend, maybe two, listening to the dying rail hum of distant places.

Our post office, rumored to have been a Norman Rockwell model, has the wood from the pilothouse of a riverboat lodged there so long in the water the tiny town accrued around it. If our village's growth were a cancer, the patient would never die.

The mail slots in the post office wear everybody's first name, except Ricky Morris's and Ricki Lewis's. Their boxes have the ♂ and ♀ signs for last names, the postmaster's acknowledgement that gender similarities exist.

The stop sign at the town limits stands its red watch. And the last thing everyone sees before leaving is this warning to look both ways and watch as the road opens up to the mountain that's no longer there outside our town and has just begun the eternity of being gone.

RON HOUCHIN, West Virginia

Farewell To The Mountains

In seventeen hundred and seventy-three
My grands first saw your face
They loved your rocks and hollers
Said, "We'll settle in this place."

They built their cabins by your branches,
Strapped on their powder horns
And you provided them with game
And new ground for their corn.

Chorus　　　　　How I love you, lovely mountains,
　　　　　　　　In summer or in snow,
　　　　　　　　For the sweetest song I know is here
　　　　　　　　Where your little branch-waters flow.

One day a stranger came around,
By coal men he was sent;
He bought Great-Grandad's mineral rights,
Each acre, fifty cents.

Repeat Chorus

Their railroads found your valleys,
They tunneled you with mines.
But still my branch ran sweet and clear
And greener grew my pines.

And then the coal so hard to get,
They came one awful day,
Drove their machinery up your sides
And they tore your crown away.

Repeat Chorus

Sometimes I think God's turned away,
He's forgot us in His plan.
How can he let the greed of men
Despoil this fairest land?

Put money in a few men's hands
While a million starve away?
And let your sides run down in mud,
Your branches choke with clay?

> Farewell you lovely mountains,
> The only home I know.
> Goodbye, you little branch-waters,
> For I guess you'll have to go.

My uncle he lives in Detroit
And he says that's the place for me;
Well, a cardboard box in a concrete yard
Just won't be home to me.

But still, my family's got to eat,
Have clothing to put on –
I pray the Lord to look after you,
Sweet mountains, when I'm gone.

> Farewell you lovely mountains,
> The only home I know.
> Goodbye, you little branch-waters,
> For I guess I'll have to go.

JEAN RITCHIE, New York

My Home

The mountains are
my home.
That's where I lived
all my life. I have
two kids growing up and
I hope they'll be
all right.

My home is being
destroyed
by the mountaintops
getting knocked off.

Please, Lord,
make this stop
right now.
Is it too much to ask?
Is it too hard to do?

My family and
my life
are depending on you.

My life is over.
I'm lost forever.
My home has
been destroyed,
my kids are
losing everything.
They're trying to
get their lives back
on track.

Lord, please
give them that —
they need it back.

BRIANNE GOLDBERG, *Kentucky*
Fifth grade

Roots and Foundations:
What Are We Doing To Appalachian Culture?

Early on Saturdays when I was a child, I watched my grandfather and brother Jarod putting on their overalls, preparing to head out into the mountains behind our house in search of ginseng. After spending most of the morning traipsing through the thick forests of Cutshin Creek, they would come home, each with a brown paper sack in hand. My grandfather's held ginseng roots and the occasional bloodroot. My brother's held any kind of root or weed that he thought looked remotely like ginseng.

Poppy sorted through his findings, dusting dried dirt from the roots, examining each one for size and to make sure he hadn't damaged it while digging it out of the ground. My brother watched closely, learning from each move Poppy made. Poppy then emptied my brother's bag, making a big deal about all the different kinds of roots he collected, although there was rarely one of value.

Still, my brother learned. Years later, after my grandfather passed away, my brother continued to go into the hills behind our house in search of roots, taking along friends who loved the mountains. It was a tradition.

Mountaintop removal affects more than just the environment. It affects the people, culturally and spiritually, who live near the mountain that is decapitated. Erik Reece, with his book *Lost Mountain*, brought the topic to a national audience, focusing on herb and root gathering as one sign of cultural change. He writes of Daymon Morgan taking him to a hillside on Bad Creek in Leslie County, Kentucky. Morgan tells him of the different herbs that will cover the hillsides later in the season – black cohosh, trillium, goldenseal and ginseng – and how one root of ginseng can bring $400 in Asia. Mountaintop removal ruins these harvestable herbs, and with them goes a second paycheck for many Appalachians.

Important as those paychecks are, losing them is not as traumatic as losing a part of Appalachia's folk heritage. Ginseng and goldenseal are not the only roots that get lost when a mountain disappears; a culture's roots go missing, too. In Appalachia, families live in certain areas for generations, never straying far from home.

But blasting, flooding and land battles lead to displacement.

Families are forced out so coal companies can move in. Insurance companies that can't afford the risks simply refuse to insure homes located near blasting zones and mining areas. Foundations are cracked and destroyed. The citizens of communities surrounding mountaintop removal sites often suffer with walls and ceilings cracking, windows rattling, doors popping off hinges, pictures falling off walls and rocks crashing through their ceilings or landing in their yards almost daily. These cataclysmic side effects of mountaintop removal often drive the populace out, fearing for their lives, and leaving behind their heritage, the foundation of Appalachian life.

When I visit my home deep in the mountains, I have to be wary of barreling coal trucks. They have always traveled Highway 699, but I never paid much attention to them until I was older. I always notice the growing trails that have been cut by the logging companies, ripping all of the trees away. But the thing that always slows my car is the sight of a mountain disintegrating.

My brother Jarod is older now, too, and has a son of his own. I can only hope and pray that when my nephew is old enough to venture into the woods with his father that there will be a mountain there in which to search for buried roots and treasure.

JOCELYN WHITE, Kentucky
College Senior

Like the Mountains Richly Veined

I was brought up in the music of the church. As a church musician for over 30 years, I have especially enjoyed the witness of music. I've heard sacred and secular music, jazz, folk, pop, gospel and contemporary Christian music offered up to the Glory of God.

In thinking about the disgraceful mining practice of mountaintop removal, I kept returning to music, which led me to the place where I have always found my faith and where I continue to gain spiritual strength: the hymnbook.

I grew up in a Southern Baptist Church in Knoxville where I absorbed the rich music and poetry of traditional hymns. As a child I learned by heart many of the hymns that have nature themes: "For the Beauty of the Earth," "This Is My Father's World," "All Things Bright and Beautiful." And I sang them without paying too much attention, but I realize now that those songs, that I had learned in the church, helped me to see the wonders of nature, helped me to formulate a moral imperative of good stewardship of the earth.

The father of English hymnody, Isaac Watts wrote this hymn nearly 300 years ago:

We sing your mighty power, O God, that made the mountains rise,
Oh how your wonders are displayed, wherever we turn our eyes
If we survey the ground we tread, or gaze upon the skies.

Today, we have not so many opportunities to witness nature's wonders from the mountains' rise in southeastern Kentucky, where I now live, or in the mountains of Virginia, West Virginia and Tennessee. The scale of ecological destruction caused by mountaintop removal mining is unfathomable, frightening, heartbreaking. For instance, nearly a half million acres of Appalachian hardwood forests have been clear cut to make way for mountaintop removal, and the mining companies don't even attempt to salvage the timber. It goes down the side of a mountain with the rest of what the mining companies call the "overburden," usually into streams or valleys below.

In 1923, a Methodist minister from Kentucky, Thomas Obediah Chisholm, wrote this hymn:

Summer and winter and springtime and harvest
Sun, moon and stars in their courses above
join with all nature in manifold witness
to God's great faithfulness, mercy and love.
Great is Thy faithfulness,
. . . morning by morning new mercies I see.

I wonder what Thomas Chisholm would think about his Kentucky now, where morning by morning many residents experience not new mercies, but omnipresent noise, air pollution from mining dust and debris, buried waterways, mountain vistas irreparably altered, and the ruination of plant and wildlife habitats. A Kentucky where coal companies engaged in mountaintop removal have hundreds of coal sludge ponds where they store the byproduct of processing coal for energy use. This slurry – a toxic tar-like substance – contains arsenic, mercury, lead and copper. When one of these ponds failed in Inez, Kentucky, in 2000, the slurry killed aquatic life for 70 miles, contaminated ground water, and wrecked homes, businesses, schools and churches. The mining company argued in court that the slurry spill was "an act of God."

Could the Swedish pastor and politician Carl Gustaf Boberg have foreseen the irony in what has become the great ecumenical and international hymn he penned in 1885?

When I look down from lofty mountain grandeur
and hear the brook, and feel the gentle breeze;
Then sings my soul, my Savior God to thee; how great thou art.

The lofty mountain grandeur is fast disappearing in our part of Appalachia. The flattened mountaintops have variously been described as looking like highways on a lunar landscape, a once beautiful animal with a debilitating case of mange, or shelves of rock that are jagged, scarred, pocked. What were once pristine mountain ranges now resemble the harsh tablelands of the desert southwest.

In contemporary hymn books, we still have these traditional hymns in praise of nature, but what we also have are many hymns that implore God to forgive us for our devastating and destructive practices toward nature. Consider the hymn of United Church of Christ pastor and hymn writer Ruth Duck:

Forgive us for each flower and bird now vanished by our hand.
Teach us to treat with loving care the creatures of the land.
Forgive us that we threaten sea and air.
Teach us to tend life's fragile web with wise and tender care.

Or David Mehrtens' hymn titled "The World Abounds":

Give thanks for plains and valleys
spaced by mountains thrusting high
Give thanks by fighting greed and waste
that drain their treasure dry

Or the hymn of the ecumenical and well-known hymnist, Brian
Wren:

We thank you, God, for minerals and ores,
the basis of all building, wealth and speed.
Forgive our reckless plundering and waste.
Help us renew the face of the earth.

The focus in Christian hymnody has shifted from admiring
and extolling nature to taking responsibility for the natural world
our creator bestowed on us and entrusted to our care. All these hymns
continue to reinforce my responsibility as a steward of the earth.

I turn to the hymnbook because when I turn to mining
officials, I find no solace, and certainly no answers. The Office of
Surface Mining, part of our government's Department of the Interior,
is charged with protecting the environment during coal mining and
making sure the land is reclaimed afterward. But when I looked at
the Frequently Asked Questions on their website, I was alarmed that
they take no responsibility for mountaintop removal mining:

Question: What are the benefits of mountaintop removal
comparedto deep mining?

Answer: TheOfficeof SurfaceMiningdoesn'thaveinformation
comparing benefits of different mining techniques.

Question: Underground coal mining seems to have less
environmental impact than mountaintop removal
mining, so why is it being used instead?

Answer: The Office of Surface Mining doesn't govern the decisions to mine a particular coal deposit and the technique by which it is mined. This question is best answered by the mining industry or mining associations.

So I went to the mining associations. The West Virginia Coal Association calls mountaintop removal mining a "temporary disruption." And the Kentucky Coal Association claims this type of coal mining does not eliminate or block streams, that erosion of a mountainside does not contribute to flooding, that mountaintop removal improves habitats for wildlife in Kentucky, and that once a site is reclaimed, it still looks like a mountain. "What's left is flatter, more useful land on the top of the mountain."

Who will take responsibility for the people killed in Appalachia due to flooding, mudslides, rockslides, flying debris, overloaded and speeding coal trucks – all consequences of mountaintop removal mining?

Who will take responsibility for speaking with elected officials our shock and fear of losing another ecosystem and, for many of us, our mountain culture and heritage?

Who will take responsibility for finding and demanding alternative energy sources?

Of course, it must be us as a body of believers, as keepers of each other, as stewards of the earth.

In 1985, the Presbyterian theologian and poet Thomas Troeger penned the hymn "God Folds the Mountains Out of Rock." His poignant warning is a benediction:

God folds the mountains out of rock and fuses elemental powers
in ores and atoms we unlock to claim as if their wealth were ours.
From veins of stone we lift up fire, and too impressed by our own skill
we use the flame that we acquire, not thinking of the Maker's will.

Our instruments can probe and sound the folded mountain's potent core
but wisdom's ways are never found among the lodes of buried ore.
Yet wisdom is the greater need, and wisdom is the greatest source,
for lacking wisdom we proceed to waste God's other gifts.

Lord, grant us what we cannot mine, what science cannot plumb or chart

your wisdom and your truth divine enfolded in a faithful heart.
Then we like mountains richly veined will be a source of light and flame
whose energies have been ordained to glorify the Maker's name.

Amen.

Marianne Worthington, Kentucky

When They Came for the Coal

Sung to the melody of "Rank Stranger"

I wandered again to my home in the mountains
Where in youth's early dawn I was happy and free
I'd walk once again the paths of my childhood
Back to the old homeplace and the sweet used-to-be

Chorus   But I found there no home, no trees, no mountain
I could see not one trace of the places I'd known
They scraped off the past with the blade of a dozer
And hauled it all off when they came for the coal

After Mother and Dad died, I took a job in a factory
Bought me a house on a long city street
But I knew some day I'd go back to the mountains
Fix up the old homeplace and live there in peace

But I found there no home, no trees, no mountain
I could see not one trace of the places I'd known
They cut down my hopes like they cut down the timber
And hauled them all off when they came for the coal

I wish one more time I could climb up that mountain
Past the poplars and pines to a place I once knew
Where the wind whispered secrets to the trees on the mountain
Where once my wild soul like the wildflowers grew

But I found there no home, no trees, no mountain
I could see not one trace of the places I'd known
Nothing left anymore for a soul to come home to
They hauled it all off when they came for the coal

ANNE SHELBY, Kentucky

Strip Mining Black History Month

I am ready to act, if I can find brave men to help me.
— CARTER WOODSON

As schools, communities and politicians across the country celebrate Black History Month each February, they will be remiss if their lessons don't include the coalfields of Fayette County, West Virginia. There, in the 1890s, an African-American teenager followed his brothers into the coal mines, serving what Carter Woodson called his "six-year apprenticeship." In the evenings, the young Woodson would gather with other black coal miners, read the newspaper, and listen to their extraordinary stories of life underground, and their struggles during the Civil War and Reconstruction Era.

The daily history lessons among African Americans in Appalachia were not lost on Woodson. He later wrote that his "interest in penetrating the past of my people was deepened and intensified" during these sessions among coal miners in Fayette County. Woodson managed to return to high school in Huntington, West Virginia — the access to education for African Americans being one of the reasons his family had chosen to come to Appalachia — and earned his diploma in two years. He moved on to earn a degree at Berea College, which had been founded in the hills of eastern Kentucky by abolitionists in 1855, studied at the University of Chicago, and then earned a Ph.D. in history at Harvard University.

Woodson went on, of course, to become the "Father of Black History," and one of our country's most celebrated historians. Few people realized, however, that West Virginia once again played prominently in Woodson's career in 1920, when the young black professor lost his job at Howard University and became a dean at the West Virginia Collegiate Institute. There in West Virginia, Woodson finally received a substantial grant from the Carnegie Foundation that allowed him to return to Washington, D.C. and set his Association for the Study of Negro Life and History on a course for world acclaim.

Woodson's and Black History Month's largely overlooked origins in West Virginia are not the only casualty in our selective memory regarding American history.

A century after Woodson's tenure in the coal mines in West Virginia, another "first" took place in Fayette County. In 1970, the first mountaintop removal operation was launched on Cannelton Hollow in area once called Bullpush Mountain. Thirty-eight years later, mountaintop removal practices – the process of literally blowing up mountains, and dumping the waste into waterways and valleys, in order to cheaply remove coal – have destroyed over 450 mountains and neighboring communities, displaced miners and stripmined the cultural landscape in the Appalachian region.

This catastrophic form of coal mining has robbed Appalachia of too much of its history in the process. If anything, it should remind the nation that the neglect and degradation of a region and its history have always mirrored the neglect and abuse of the land.

In a speech at Hampton Institute in Virginia, Woodson once reminded the audience: "We have a wonderful history behind us... If you are unable to demonstrate to the world that you have this record, the world will say to you, "You are not worthy to enjoy the blessings of democracy or anything else.' They will say to you, 'Who are you anyway?'"

Appalachians understand this bitter historical reality more than any other citizens in the United States. Black Appalachians, especially.

In 2007 for example, I was supposed to speak at a school in Chicago in February. But the organizer called me at the last moment and asked to reschedule until April, since a book I had written about "those people down there" didn't relate to Black History Month. But Black History Month was launched by an Appalachian coal miner, I told my host. Booker T. Washington, the most celebrated black spokesman from last century, also emerged out of the coal mining communities in Appalachia; Martin Delany, the first black nationalist in the 19th century, who helped to launch Frederick Douglass' first newspaper, came out of West Virginia. So did Henry Louis Gates, the prominent African American literary critic at Harvard University.

I went on. Do you know that Bessie Smith, the "Empress of the Blues," took her songs from the streets of Blue Goose Hollow in Chattanooga, just as W.C. Handy, the "Father of the Blues," composed his masterpieces from the sounds of his native hills of northern Alabama? That Nina Simone, the "High Priestess of Soul," always performed folk ballads from her native western North Carolina mountains? That, in fact, black guitar and banjo players were the stylists for much of the early country music, gospel and folk songs?

Did you know that four months before Rosa Parks refused to give up her seat on a Montgomery bus in 1955, she took a seat at the Highlander Folk School in the backwoods of Tennessee, where she attended strategy session on social action led by so-called "radical hillbillies"? That the first desegregated school to graduate a black student in the South was in the mountains of Tennessee?

And did you know that the United Mine Workers have always been an integrated union? Coal miners and coal mining communities in Appalachia and around the country should be celebrated during Black History Month, not dismissed or forgotten.

The struggle of man against power is the struggle of memory against forgetting, author Milan Kundera wrote about his native Czech Republic. He added in an interview with American novelist Philip Roth, "Forgetting is a form of death ever-present within life."

There is a lot of "forgetting" and death taking place in our nation's memory about Appalachia's destruction today.

Carter Woodson, who was mocked when he first arrived in Washington, D.C. for his "hayseed clothes," never forgot the importance of his origins.

Hopefully, some brave men and women will act to preserve Woodson's and Appalachia's great heritage before it is stripmined into oblivion.

JEFF BIGGERS, Illinois

Originally published by The Huffington Post, *29 January 2008*

A Place Undermined

Like most young females, I live with the constant fear that I am becoming my mother. I sit in the library of an institution that gives me credit to write things, lots of things, and she's paying for it (or at least the part that remains after all the dollars awarded by rich families of dead important people). My mom works full-time at the front desk of the local YMCA. It is the most recent in a string of secretarial jobs she has used to supplement my father's income, to pay the bills of my sister's and my comfortable lives – the lives neither of them enjoyed growing up.

My mother has always written little poems every now and again, and she's finished at least one children's story, I think. And every once in a while she reminds us all, "I'm gonna be a writer when I grow up." Playfully, she avoids the real issue, which is that she has never been able to pursue the life she wanted when she was younger, when she was my age.

I once confessed my fear to her, that I am just a little 21st Century version of twenty-something-year-old Donna Lou. Her words of assurance were one of those instances when she actually surprised me by not saying what I expected. She told me that while we're laughably similar – and that's something she's excessively happy about – my self-initiated West Virginia life doesn't have a thing to do with her:

"Honey, I left West Virginia – you're trying to go there all the time. That sure don't look like the same thing to me."

I lacked appreciation for certain knowledge until very recently, when my friend asked me to explain what a holler is. I laughed a little, to think that a term so common to me could puzzle her. As I set out to explain this geography, I thought of the real reason that the geography and topography of my mother's homeland are worthy of definition in a unique way.

Holler refers to an area between two hills that is smaller than a valley. But it is more than a term of topography. In the Appalachian region, the curves of the land are as unique as the curves of a human body. They are natural. Knowledge of hollers and hills and valleys and bottoms is just a part of life. Information you inherit. It is more

than location, it is definition. Appalachians are a people defined
by their land, and the terms that define the land define the lives of
Appalachians.

Our House

There is a river in Southern West Virginia named for coal,
and this river names the valley that holds it. It names Coal River
Road that runs the length of it, one end of the Coal River Valley
to the other. Having many tributaries, each with their own identity,
the Coal River really names almost everything, and it is one of the
many geographical features that define this region. Every place
in the mountains has their own, as unique as the people who live
there. Or maybe it is more accurate to say that, since they came after
the mountains did, the people are as unique as the geography. My
friend from the mountains even went so far as to say he felt insecure
whenever he ventured out from their shelter for too long.

Our house, in a small town called Rock Creek, sits on a short
residential road parallel to the Marsh Fork of the Coal River, accessible
by a little bridge. Every morning and every evening, and at least once
in between, a green Suzuki crosses that bridge to come to our house.
It's stopped here since long before I ever came. The driver is Charles,
a gravelly-voiced old man still waiting on his compensation check for
black lung.

The house is not actually mine at all. Constantly filled with
volunteers from various places, the house is now leased to Rory and
Matt, who work for a small environmental organization up the road.
But when I first met this house, that organization leased it, and it
was called the Campaign House. It is still known to many by this
name, but I call it "ours."

"I'd go through hell and high water for you two," Charles once
said to Rory and housemate Matt. And he meant every word, the
bad and the good of it. Chain-smoking whatever is cheapest, Charles
drives up and down the road, visiting his friends and helping them
with random tasks. Mostly he loves to stop at our house, to make us
quit staring at a computer screen for a few minutes and sit with him
on the porch for a cigarette.

A kid named Dustin comes over to our house once in a while.
My first summer in the Valley, he rode around with the old man in his
Suzuki. He had a crush on me, and that resulted in such daring feats

as washing a sink full of dishes. Dustin eventually grew out of his teenage crush and found a kid his own age to bum around with.

"That boy's gonna be trouble," Charles said when Dustin left the porch for the gas station. Being around Dustin in those last fleeting weeks of childhood innocence and summer crushes on older girls from out of state, it hadn't occurred to me that his potential to become the worst of what the valley produces was becoming real, no longer potential. It also never occurred to me how hard Charles had been trying to save Dustin from himself, and from the Valley. The river has a reputation for drugs that is a common story in small coal communities in Appalachia, where jobs are few and dollars are fewer.

Last time I was in the valley, I was awake before the two other volunteers at the house, and Matt and Rory were still at the office from the night before (they often sleep there, taking turns on the couch while the other works). I put on my flannel in the morning chill and forced myself into the kitchen and made biscuits, shortly before Charles came by. By the time the sleepers got up, just as the workers pulled into the driveway, the sausage was done frying, with gravy, fried eggs, biscuits and coffee to go with it. It was the first time I'd pulled all that off on my own for a houseful – just like my aunt up in the holler did every day – and it happened there in our little river house with the old man there to help.

In the afternoon, when the two sleepers had gone out and the boys had gone back to the office, Charles and I sat on the porch.

"See that tree right there?" He pointed to a tall sycamore.

Yeah.

"If you gave me a rope, I'd hang Massey up there myself, right now, just watch him hang."

Yeah.

"I'd love to see that son of a gun up a tree."

The truth is, there no one actually named Massey, at least not someone who owns Massey Energy, the major conglomerate that Charles is talking about. But around here, Massey is the name of that big spirit monster of the mountains. He's been up there for more than a century, working men like my grandfather and my uncle and Charles to a literal and slow death, keeping all the profit off their blood and labor for himself. And he's still up there.

WE ALL LIVE DOWNSTREAM

We Sailed Away on a Winter's Day

A few weeks before Thanksgiving 2006, I drove from my college in Ohio down I-77 to West Virginia with my almost-partner Joe and two other friends. We were going to a student gathering in the Coal River Valley, just an hour from mother's home, in the southern part of the state. We were going to learn about something called "MTR." California harpist/singer Joanna Newsome was playing her first show in Cleveland the same weekend, and all my friends were going. But Joe's subtle persuasion about my wavering decision – "They're blowing up the mountains!" – sealed my loyalties long enough to at least get me in the car and on the highway.

The air was cold and wet, and Joe's old Volvo ran slow and loud through the winding mountain highways. I was missing a kickass show, but I was determined to make the best of things. Our friend said something about the hollers we were driving through, and it was clear – to me, anyway – that the double-wides and hillsides filled with old refrigerators that we passed on Coal River Road were something for him to wonder at. Having visited family not too far from here my whole life, I remember the surreal nature of being in coal country with college friends, of worlds colliding, of seeing this world through a lens of something other than family. Although it wasn't quite far enough south in the state, driving those mountain curves still felt like the ground my roots were planted in.

Arriving later than most of the other students, we walked into a small white house on the river, a hippie house really, with prayer flags on the front porch and rolling paper packages here and there. It was packed wall-to-wall with young people like us, mostly college students and dropouts, all gathered around an old wood stove. A guy who apparently lived there, named Matt, with very red long hair, was warming piles of homemade pita bread and hummus. Already I was dealing with reconciling such a scene with the West Virginia I knew. Where were the chili dogs and beans? My travel companions and I pitched our too-big borrowed tent on top of rocks in the dark back yard, grabbed a few beers by the campfire, and met some new faces before retiring to sleep in a freezing, shaking pile of four.

The next day, exhausted from the sleepless cold night, we went to the office of Coal River Mountain Watch, the organization up the road that has been working against this MTR thing – mountaintop removal coal mining – for over ten years. An engineer there told us about the mountaintop removal (MTR) process, how the coal companies use explosives to access seams of coal too narrow for a deep mine to get.

We went up a horrible mountain road after that to meet a man who has since appeared in *Vanity Fair* magazine because his home is being demolished, one blast for one tiny little vein of coal after another. Famous for his stubbornness in the face of the millions offered by the coal companies in exchange for his land, Larry Gibson has been showing his homeland view of one of the largest surface mines in the state for years to people from all over the globe, against death threats and gunfire.

Driving back to Ohio, I was still a little bewildered at the collision of what to me had always been two such different worlds. But it was a happy collision, as far as I could tell, happy enough for me to not regret missing the Joanna Newsome concert.

Survival Is Suicide

About five or six miles from our house on Coal River is a slurry pool that contains over 2.8 billion gallons of toxic sludge. It sits on the river, next to a processing plant. Across the river, just a few hundred yards away, is the Marsh Fork Elementary School playground.

It seems logical to most people, including people who have pleaded for years for the governor to build a new school in a safe location, that a pool of toxic anything could be detrimental to the educational experience of young students. But it also seems logical – at least to people who want to generate coal-fired electricity at the lowest financial cost possible – that a playground full of children could be an obstacle to the processing of coal and "safely" storing toxic waste.

What seems far less logical is that, generally speaking, these are the same people. Many of the kids at Marsh Fork Elementary are getting headaches, asthma attacks, and are just generally not feeling well. Many of their parents work for the coal companies. When people come to the Valley for the first time, they ask why in the world people would work in a job that's killing them – and their kids. It's a really good question. One good answer: they need to put food on the table. Death by coal dust or sludge seems less imminent than starvation, especially when that's the way it's always been.

Fifty years ago, things were different. All mines were deep

mines. "He gave his life for his babies," people said at the funeral of my uncle, a coal miner who died of black lung. Coal mining of yesterday was a *personal* sacrifice. An underground "deep" mine operates by digging small tunnels into the belly of a mountain. People enter to dig the coal and bring it out through the tunnel. The coal is removed, but the mountain remains intact. This mining practice is not healthful, but it doesn't have the startling impact on the land, water and people immediately around it that surface mines do.

Even though mountaintop removal disrupts everything and everybody in the region, most people in coal county would agree that coal mining is an "honorable profession." To die of black lung is to die a noble death, not because the work is highly skillful, but because it is a sacrifice for something more than a paycheck. "YES, COAL" still reads on many billboards throughout the West Virginia, sustaining the belief that *West Virginia is coal*. It isn't just a history, but a Mountaineer heritage. To question coal is to question our fathers and grandfathers and what they lived and died for.

The coal barons of the 19th Century found a wide-open market in the central Appalachian Mountains. Today the industry drags the economy more than drives it. As coal runs out in much of West Virginia, mining operations close up and move on, and people are left with little else to turn to for work. Many people who are employed are employed by coal, but many more people are unemployed. There aren't enough coal jobs to go around. The welfare-dependent hillbilly stereotype is unfortunately accurate, all too often. Worse is its implications of a West Virginia work ethic, when the need for assistance is created by a mono-economy driven by extractive industry.

What Else Is There?

I recently met an old friend in a coffee shop to cram the past few years into an hour. At the end of our visit, he asked about a pin I have on my bag that reads "STOP MOUNTAINTOP REMOVAL" with Larry Gibson's phone number listed underneath. He listened more than intently as I told him about the work I'm doing in West Virginia and central Appalachia generally. At the end of my spiel, he asked in all sincerity a question I hope everyone considers after first learning of MTR: *If coal goes, is there anything else for Appalachian people to do?*

What *would* the coalfields do without the coal industry? If the coal companies left, what would leave with them? Starting with the most obvious: mining equipment, mines, coal trucks, processing plants, valley fill construction, sludge pool construction, mining equipment manufacturing, reclamation. While the mines themselves do not employ as many people now that mountaintop removal is used, most of the jobs in the area are somehow related to coal.

What would be left behind? Logging, hospitals, police force, firefighters, libraries, city and government offices, and other daily life needs. There is no trade, no centers of tourism no art. Even farmers' markets are few.

There are some places to look to see what is left when coal jobs are gone. But it isn't quite accurate, not what we would see if coal left entirely. The places I'm thinking of are towns where decades ago coal was booming, but the coal isn't producing like it used to, and the mining that remains provides just a few jobs.

McDowell County has produced more coal in its lifetime than any other county in West Virginia. However, it is not currently the highest producer. If you drive on Route 52, the main road through the county, you can see what it means for a place to have loved and lost with King Coal. Mention towns in the county – Northfork, Keystone, Welch – to someone in the next county over, and they'll wonder why you've been hanging around there. Prostitution, drugs and petty crime are now the economy of the county. Boards shut up the windows in 95 percent of the businesses, and all the communities' schools have been closed, students now being bused to consolidated schools.

But there were jobs, at one point. And when there were, there was life in McDowell County. Some say that Welch, the county seat, was called Little New York. All of this was wrapped up in one expendable fossil fuel, but at least it was something.

There is a terror that strikes, a darkness felt in the hearts of those who know that change must come. It is the general opinion of friends of coal and friends of the mountains (who are often the same people) that coal is killing us. The difference is that some have accepted this as a fact of life, and hopefully someday somebody will find an alternative. Others have decided to be the somebodies today, by opposing the industry or by working for an alternative, and it's scary.

I don't know how to make an entirely new economic framework. I don't know anybody who does. Everyone who has decided to find a way beyond coal is afraid of failing, of bringing more harm than good to a situation that seems as if it can't get any worse. But can it? What would that mean for my family and friends who don't live there by choice, but because it is all they can do?

I'm scared because I don't know what would happen to my family. What if the plans I think are good, fail? How could I possibly know better than those who came before me, whom I respect. They are, after all, the ones who created the life and the world here that I've known since I was little, before I knew there was anything that needed changing. This is, after all, a place I want to be because I love it, not because I want to change it.

People say that there are some places you can only go up from. But I'm not confident that we've seen the worst in the coalfields.

Returns

I recently took a drive again down Route 52 through McDowell County. After Keystone, I veered right onto Eckman Road. The road takes me under 52, across the railroad tracks, past Eckman Bottom where everyone now lives after they had to leave the holler, past the tipple, and then there is nothing. I can almost pick out where my Aunt Sally's house was, and the church, and where Uncle Buddy's trailer used to sit, where he and his wife Mary raised their ten children on biscuits and gravy every morning. I can imagine where Uncle Danny's trailer sat across the road. Now, even the fence post where he let me shoot his gun, is gone.

Eckman Road is only used by coal trucks now, hauling coal from the mine site at the top of the mountain, down the windy road, out of the holler, and out 52 to the interstate. Gravel bigger than my skull paves the road now, something good for the trucks to drive on, not so great for my little Jetta. And I think I saw old Boo's truck coming down from the mountain where he goes to drink a beer sometimes, but I can't be sure.

At the head of the holler, before the road curves up toward the mine, I parked my car. Down past a yellow metal gate is a grove. The road beyond the gate has grown over long ago. And I think this is near to where the yellow house used to be, Grandma Christian's house, where my mom lived for a time with her two older sisters. I never saw the house, but from my mother's stories, I know it was a beautiful and peaceful place.

It's all so dusty now, not fresh anymore. No one's allowed to live here, but I don't see how they could, or why they would want to. But once, it was green, I know it was. I know because I've asked my mother so many times to talk about growing up in the holler. I imagine my great-grandmother there in the clearing. Her mouse grey hair, the color of my mother's roots when she lets it go, is pulled back tightly in a bun, and her patterned polyester dress falls over her knees, leaving a gap above her sagging knee-highs in laced-up black shoes. She picks blackberries with the girls in the late summer, while clothes wash in the wringer on the porch. She takes care of her three granddaughters on $52 a month from the government, dressing them in dresses made of large flour sacks. The girls walk to Sunday night service at the upper church in the brightest, clearest light of a full moon. After *The Lawrence Welk Show*, their grandma takes out her hearing aids, and they laugh because she doesn't realize how loud her whisper is. Kneeling by her bed in the next room, she asks God to keep his hand on her girls. Once in a while, she complains about "the strippin'" that had recently started shaking her house. But she didn't ever go anywhere, except maybe Keystone just a few miles down the main road. She didn't need to. Her world here in the head of the holler was all she needed, with no real society or authorities around to tell her what to do. Just the Lord, and the needs of her girls. These were the rules that guided her days.

My mother left her West Virginia holler when she was 19, four years younger than I am today. After graduating from Northfork High School, she received a full scholarship to West Virginia University in the northern city of Morgantown. Without any knowledge of what a degree would mean to her later in life, and without anyone in Eckman Holler to tell her differently, she turned down the scholarship and took a job in the Welfare Office in Welch, the county seat.

Shortly after her older sister married and moved to the suburbs of Cleveland, my mother followed. "I wanted to be anywhere but that holler," she says any time I ask her about the move. It's a sentiment typical of the area. Any older, wiser person in the coalfields generally advises young people with an ounce of ambition to get out if they ever want to make something of themselves, like old Charles has started saying about Dustin.

Along with this sort of pessimistic realism is what I call holler-nationalism. It's the idea that if you'd rather move to an area with more opportunity, you are some kind of turncoat. I imagine this is what kept anyone from encouraging my mother to take her scholarship to WVU. It's also part of the mindset that made her leave the state altogether.

I have also been put in the "young and ambitious" category – I've taken off into the wild blue yonder with no knowledge of what I was getting myself into, lived with my band out of a pickup truck for several weeks, and generally done things many of my friends would not do. And I want to move to dilapidated, dying Coal Country, USA. What's more, in a way that almost scares me sometimes, and which I could never admit to my coworkers, I know I'm not moving there to change things. At the same time, I cannot move there and stop trying for something more and better and different.

Southern West Virginia is the most beautiful place in my world, not just because of what it can be and the future that I believe in for the land and the people, but because this place is my land and my people. The ground my roots grew from is – and I'm proud to say it – the ground that is the crossfire zone between an oppressive past and a just future. The ground that can be the difference in the future of energy and thus everything else in our country. I do the work I do as an activist, but I believe in the work as a descendant, not just of a coal miner, but of the coal-stuffed hills themselves. I believe there is a spirit in the hills just as big as the coal monster, and even older.

Roots in West Virginia

I don't remember the first time I ever came to West Virginia. I was born and raised in two counties in Northeast Ohio by a coal miner's daughter and a Cleveland machinist. Together they made trips down I-77 to Eckman Holler before my time, before they were even married. Her daddy and mommy were still living then, though I think it safe to say, barely – he in a sanatorium, she in a mental institution. They went often because my Papaw missed my mom so much; he'd once made the trip up to Cleveland but was too sick with black lung and tuberculosis to do it anymore. My sister was there when they went to visit him in the hospital, but I never met him. The trips to the holler were regular family practice, though, and remained so until I was a teenager.

I remember when my sister hit the age when she stopped loving the holler. I guess she became frustrated with all the sausage gravy mornings, big screen TVs in tiny mobile home living rooms, overcrowded beds, smelly water, and pregnant teenage cousins. I'm not sure why, but at 23, I still haven't hit that age. I grew to love my mother's home, that feels more like my home every time I say goodbye, perhaps because I feel it being ripped from my grasp. And my love grows.

Eckman Holler was fun for a strange little girl like me. Staying at Aunt Sally's house, I could jump on the bed, play in the church next door (she had a key), get muddy in my bare feet and lay in the bed with my mom, aunts and sister, laughing until we hurt at nighttime. Sometimes we could hear the rats drag bags through the kitchen at night. Once we heard one running around between the ceiling and the roof, and it fell through a hole and down into the kitchen. If we hadn't been laughing so hard, it probably would've been a little scary.

We had to flush the toilet with a bucket of water at that house, for some reason. The other day, I thought of that as I dumped a basin of sink water into the toilet at my own house. I do it to save water, but I'm pretty sure that for my aunt, it was just the only way to make it flush. And I'm certain Aunt Sally never heard of the eco-friendly concept of "gray water," where you use what would normally go down the drain to do jobs around the house that don't require clean water, like toilet flushing. Really, none of her water was *clean*. All the metals made it orange and stinky, and I'd gag when I had to use it to flush the toilet. Now, in my own home, I do this by choice.

The last time I saw my mom's brother, he was sitting in his big La-Z-Boy watching TV, breathing in pure oxygen from a machine, dying of the same black lung that killed his coal-mining daddy before him. It had been a while since our last visit, and I had just started to play guitar and write some songs. My mother was bragging on me to him. "I wish we'd have visited earlier, Rebekah, we coulda made some beautiful music together," my uncle said to me. Buddy, as he was known to everyone, was an all-star self-taught musician. He could fiddle, play guitar and piano, sing, and pick a banjo like Flatt and Scruggs, but he couldn't read a note of music. A marvel of the mountains, thinning out along with the jobs and coal towns of central Appalachia.

Uncle Buddy died when I was in high school, and I think it was his funeral in Keystone, West Virginia, that got me thinking and resulted in tearful conversations with my mother when we returned to Ohio. I noticed the absence, the hiatus of family visits, that happened to me after Aunt Sally moved out of the holler and into a better life with her cousin in a big town. A period of moping finally resulted in a trip on my own to Eckman Holler. I met up with some cousins who didn't recognize me and my mother's third brother, Danny. Somehow in this visit, I rediscovered old ties to the home of my Lambert family, and the piece of soul that typically accompanies such roots discoveries. I also discovered new ties to an area in dire need of new life.

Betrayal

Sitting on our front porch on Coal River, I'd venture to say that 90percent of the traffic on the road across the river is part of the coal machine. It doesn't all look like it, and maybe less than 50percent of the vehicles are actually hauling coal. But there are also the logging trucks, big 18-wheelers hauling scoops for the giant shovels and draglines, coal company pick-ups, and then many others are going to work or coming home after the whistle blows. The rest, the ones who have nothing to do with coal, are just in the way.

I am in the way, and I know it. Initially, I came to the Coal River Valley to be in the way. I brought it on myself. Lorelei Scarborough, a lifelong resident of the Coal River Valley and community organizer for a local wind project, says "they mine coal where we live." The point of this Mountain State is for her to live, and this coal machine is getting in the way of that. I'm here to get in the way of the companies working, or at least that's how they see it. But they see her just the same way they see me, and she didn't come here to change things like I did. She didn't come here at all because, unlike me, she was always here.

I struggle, or at least I did struggle for a long while, with my desires to spend time in southern West Virginia and even move there after college. Back on that first weekend in 2006, sitting in the living room of our house, I was surrounded by college students, most of them from privileged backgrounds with highly-educated parents.

Along the way, I've met journalists and filmmakers from New York and California, and vegan anarchist activists with perfect ideals about what mountain communities should look like (everything home-made and hand-carved). I've felt almost angry at times, secretly (sometimes openly) criticizing everyone who didn't have working class parents and upbringing, who wasn't a coal miner's granddaughter. Despite my friendships with these people, and the fact that I owed my involvement in the work to people such as them, I found myself often judging their motives because their roots weren't my roots. Who were they to say that things should change here? They won't even eat a home-cooked meal from the neighbor because she used animal products – it's all she has to offer to the people she believes are trying to help make a better world for her and her granddaughters.

But the more time I spent talking with local people, including my West Virginia family, the more I discovered I am one of those outside college activists, despite my West-by-God-Virginia roots. On the flip side, the more time I spent with friends at my Ohio college, the more I realized I am the daughter of a soup beans-eating coal country girl, and that does mean something. I am the product of my mother's decision to flee everything ugly about her home, but I am also raised by all that she learned is true and good in the hardworking coalfield culture that is disappearing, as the hollers themselves become fewer with every permit issued by regulatory agencies like the Department of Environmental Protection. I've been trying to figure out which one I *really* am. I now realize, I am both, but I am neither one exclusively. I am the product of the two together, an outside coalfields activist with her head in academia and her heart in the holler. My mother gave me her values, without the circumstance to go with them.

Four-Wheeling

On one of those Technicolor-vibrant October days in the mountains, one of those days when it's hard to believe that some of the trees aren't being illuminated by something more than the sun, I went four-wheeling with Rory, Matt and a filmmaker named Chad.

At our house, we talk all the time about the slurry pool down the road from our house, the one by Marsh Fork Elementary. But I've never actually seen it. It sits too far away from the road, and it's hard to get up there. No one ever sees many mining operations around the coalfields unless they work for the coal companies. Some places cannot even be reached by a car or truck unless you go through security clearances and gates. These places are the ugliest, strangest looking places in the Southeastern United States. But there are old trails that four-wheelers can handle with no problem, and there are old friends who have lived there long enough to know where all of them lead.

Near the end of our trip, the sun was hovering above the ridge opposite to where we stood at the dead end of our trail, trespassers obscured by the branches. We stopped for a moment to look around at what may some sweet day be the site of a wind farm, the site of 150 everlasting jobs, 440 megawatts of everlasting energy, white spinning promises that a future in coal cannot make.

But a greasy black pool kept budding into my fantasy. The side of the mountain we stood on is the wall of a slurry pool that could someday hold nine billion gallons, more than three times the size of the pool by Marsh Fork Elementary. Now it is thick and still, but if the earthen dam at the end of the pool were to break, that volume of sludge would rush out, killing hundreds of people in Colcord, the holler below us.

A dam like this one failed in 1972 in Buffalo Creek, West Virginia, killing hundreds of people. Another like it broke in Martin County, Kentucky, in 2000. These dams were constructed in the same way, and I wonder what is keeping this one and the one by the elementary school from breaking and flooding over hundreds of unsuspecting people, seeping into their skin, running down their throats, death by toxic asphyxiation. I wonder what the workers at the processing plant on the same site would say. Would they call it "an act of God," which is what the coal companies called the other disasters? How much would the news stations cover it?

Making Sense

I recently attended a community picnic in a Virginia town, organized by a small anti-MTR group my friends are working with. A little less than one hundred people in the town showed up at the park for burgers and a concert, the bigger draw, really. Rich Kirby and two other bands constitutes a large scale musical event for this rather lifeless old coal town, in a county with more coal-fired power plants than any other in the United States and 25percent of its land now flattened by surface mining.

My band was playing soon, and I walked across the park to use the bathroom before it was time to start. A few young boys were hanging around the building, the smooth cement good for their skateboards to roll on. One friendly blonde boy pointed out which was the women's bathroom. I don't remember exactly what was said after that, but it must have had something to do with people coming to the picnic from out of state. I believe he asked where I was from. Whatever the details, his commentary was forthright: *Nobody cares about us, and we don't care about them.* I wanted to argue it, but I had to go.

In truth, however sad his comment, it is indisputable. Had I stayed, all I could have offered in the face of his young cynicism would have been some sappy honesty about caring. It is a sentiment no one, including me, really understands or puts faith in, especially a cynical child.

A song about taking away a mountain features the lyric, "They can't put it back." Like the mountain, I can't make my life be something that it hasn't been. I can't not know about surface mining from an activist-student's perspective, because that is how I learned it. I can't have been raised in West Virginia, because I wasn't. I know that my caring will not save a little boy or his home – maybe nothing will do that, and maybe nothing needs to. I learn that this might be true, every day that I fumble with the pieces of this people, this landscape, trying to help put it back together.

REBEKAH AINSWORTH, Ohio

The Last Unmined Vein

Now it's neither here nor there
to most folks
but then I've never figured myself
to be like many
much less most
I know what they do
no matter what they say
I know how they come
with trucks bigger than ary road
can hold
and drive her through yer yard
and right up on the porch
and park her next to yer rocking chair
and you ain't go a howdy-do
to say about it neither
once you put yer name
to that paper
that's it

Now my daddy and me
we used to dig a little coal
out of that vein across the bottom
Just a pick and shovel
and what could be wheelbarrowed
out of there
was all that was took
and didn't hurt nothing
and kept a fire real good
and that's it
but that ain't what they got in mind
They wanting to make steel in Ohio,
turn on the lights in New York City
and heat houses in Detroit
Shoot – I don't know a soul
in the whole state of Michigan
but that ain't really it

It ain't my business what they do with it
but this farm and everything that's in it
is plenty my concern
and I know how they come
with their mouths full of promises
and leaving with every one
of your fields full of ruts
and the mud sliding down the hillside
right onto your back steps
and there ain't a creek left
what would hold a living thing
and that's it
and the money
just don't mean that much to me
I done seen all I need to see
about where that money goes
and what's got with it
Last thing this county needs
is another new mobile home
with a four-wheel drive truck
parked on a mudbank in front of it
and that's it
and not another thing to show
for where and what your mammy and pappy
and their mammy and pappy
not to mention your own self and family
always had

So when that man in his new suit
and smooth-as-silk talking
came to my door
I didn't even ask him in
Said I wasn't interested
He laughed and said he wasn't selling
Said I didn't figure I was either
and that was it
Of course, I know he'll be back
but probably after I'm dead and gone
and if the children want to be so foolish

as to put an end
to what came long before them
ain't nothing I can do about it then
but I been laying plans
to remind them
of what it's gonna cost them
I done got my marker
and laid out the lines for my grave
right smack in the middle
of that vein
They gonna have to chip out the coal 6 foot by 6
and then put her right back on top of me
and that will be the end of that

LEE HOWARD, Kentucky, Tennessee and Oregon

Originally published in The Last Unmined Vein, © *1980 Lee Howard; used by permission of the Literary Estate of Lee Howard*

My Father's Mountains

None are alike,
all sculpted and planned,
put here on purpose
by my Father's hands.

He grew flowers and trees,
gave animals new birth
forming a breathtaking garden
for the mother of Earth.

The sweet spruce and pine
and heavenly air,
clear my mind of doubt,
and leave me without a care.

I've just returned,
to the mountain I knew.
To find in its place,
an astonishing view

Not a single birch
Or blade of grass near my foot
Just a lifeless plateau,
and cold hard soot.

There's an absence of music,
no melody of nature.
The life's been sucked out,
and exchanged for green paper.

The divine beauty gone,
all evidence stripped away.
Nothing left in its place
but the dim light of the day.

CATHERINE DAWAHARE, *Kentucky*
High School Sophomore

My Mother, Breathing

It's late summer and I'm driving along Highway 23 between Pikeville and Prestonsburg on my way to see my mother. If she sees what I do, it's a changing landscape with a dozen new fast food restaurants and the strangeness of liquor barns in territory that used to call itself dry. I pass signs for places like Waylon and Betsy Lane, the latter the spot where my parents got married over 50 years ago. There used to be no signs for these places some people would call holes in the road, and I do not find the new markers welcome. Nor are the straight walls of granite cut out of the sides of mountains any pleasure to me, even if new roads mean a couple hours less on a 12-hour drive.

Following an experience with an illness that has kept me back in Georgia, where I teach, I haven't been home to see my mother in almost two years. Add to that the fact that I'm an "outlander." I haven't lived in and called the mountains a true home since I was in my early 30s. My shame about all of this makes me unusually alert to the road, the town, and the mountainsides. Everything seems glaringly new to me and I'm relieved when, at last, I come to the outskirts of Prestonsburg. It's a two-lane, the last stretch of Highway 1822, through Lancer and on to the house where my mother has lived for the past 35 years. Here, there are more subtle changes. A huge billboard I've always liked – *Jesus Saves!! Mountain Home Realty!!!* – is yellow from sunlight. The drug rehab and social services center I remember seems bigger, more opulent. A cinder block ex-garage next to my mother's house still calls itself a Pentecostal Holiness Church.

As I step from my car, I stand for awhile, looking up from the road at the house. My mother lives in the small brick house where she's lived for about 40 years, since she and my father divorced. The house is four rooms and a front porch, immediately down the hill from her brother's, my Uncle Roy's house. She used to live in the brick house with my grandparents, both of them now deceased, and they used to love sitting on this porch and watching the world go by.

I notice that a large shrub once overpowering the sidewalk is gone, a stump in its place. The front porch, as I climb the steps, is strewn with chips of dark green paint from the metal chairs Granny and Pa used to love.

During the last three years, my mother has been diagnosed with dementia. *Chronic mental and emotional deterioration.* Any good dictionary gives me this definition. The doctors, when I call them, just say that the condition will get worse and that we can't know how soon. They have given her a cocktail of drugs to keep her more coherent, although when I phone her, she sounds more and more lost.

My mother, on nearly every trip I've ever made home to the mountains since I was 20, has always spent the day pacing, looking out the front door when she thinks she hears a car. Today, she is nowhere in sight.

Most people would say that the mountain towns I grew up in – Paintsville, Hager Hill, Prestonsburg, Allen – have all benefited from development. In Prestonsburg, my main barometer on the growth of those towns, there's now a Super Wal-Mart. There are larger grocers. Bigger and better shopping centers. Clinics. Vocational school additions to the nearby community college. An arts center with country music concerts. Renovated high schools and grade schools. So many doctor's offices I couldn't begin to name them. Fitness centers, Shoe Shows, hair salons, movie rentals, convenience stores, lottery ticket purveyors, even a natural foods store. And my own desire, friends tell me, to summon the past, my imaginary world of an Eastern Kentucky Past, is mere sentimentality.

In that past, I am at my mother's mother's house in Dwale. We are sitting on the front porch in her green metal chairs and she is combing her long hair. Usually, she wears her hair in a single braid she winds three times around her head and then fastens with combs. In my memory day, her hair is down and she is letting me brush it for awhile. She is telling me about the garden below the house, the "maters and taters" we will eat for supper, beets she has canned, ones the color of garnets. She is describing to me, with her strong, blunt hands, how to string beans, make biscuits lighter than air. As she braids her hair again, I take hold of that long, slender rope. I climb up into her lap and hold on, and she takes me, in this memory world, all the places she has loved. Her own mommy's house, up the road just a mile, a place where there is well water so sweet you shiver to think of it. There's a smokehouse, where the boards themselves smell of hams and salt. The side yard, where she wrings clothes through and back in the washer. Life, my memory tells me, is a hard thing, a worked thing, but satisfying and real. Later, we pretend that the porch chairs are cars, ones with stick shifts she lets me move up and back as I tell her, even then, about all the places my life will take me.

On this visit to Prestonsburg, the fact that my mother has a condition is finally completely clear to me. When she comes to the door at my knock, I am shocked, the kind of shock that sends ice up your back. She is wearing green, knee-length polyester pants, ones stained in the crotch, safety-pinned holes in the backs of the legs. Her graying hair is in stick-out-from-her-head knots, and her unbuttoned blouse is fastened in the front with a large safety pin. She is shorter than I remember, bent over at the spine. I can feel a twist at her center as I take hold of her, try to hug her. We have never been close, my mother and me, but today, as I hold her in my arms for a few seconds, I feel how small she has grown, like a little girl.

This visit, I'll stay two days, like I always do, but it's clear that the territory has altered drastically. As I walk through her kitchen into the front room, I can see right away that she is less organized, less tidy. Saying that my mother is less anything related to cleanliness is huge, since she has suffered from OCD throughout my adult life. The tops of the china cabinet and the hutch, I see as we walk through the dining room, are coated with dust. As I take a seat in the vinyl recliner where I always sit, I see lack of order everywhere. A profusion of papers are scattered across the floor near the kitchen chair that is her customary seat, near the front door. Shoved up against the television set is a very low ottoman, and she tells me, right away, that this is where she sits to watch The Weather Channel.

During the 48 hours of our visit, I will become familiar with this weather routine of my mother's, and with other routines and questions. She brushes her teeth at the kitchen sink, spits in a broken handled cup. She sleeps in her clothes and keeps half the bed made up, in case she needs to get up quick. She keeps the curtains in the living room and the bedroom pinned shut, she tells me, so that the boys in the yard outside, the ones she kept from coming in last week, won't come back again. She gave them a good one, she tells me, when I note how the curtain rod is partly off the wall, and the mattress slid off its box springs. And that pillow on the chair in the living room, the chair where her mommy used to sit, before she passed. The pillow is a handmade affair, big squares of brightly colored polyester, and the one square, in the right-hand corner. Doesn't that look, my mother asks me, just like a little girl crying? This pillow and that square, which in no way resembles a child weeping, becomes the only key I can find to what has happened to my mother in the last couple of years, her descent into a kind of madness.

The physical world that is my mother's home ground, the mountains, has to be deteriorating fast. On one website alone, a site found at random with a common enough search engine, I find some 80 coal companies, most of them in or near the Eastern Kentucky mountains my mother calls home. Some of their names are evocative, musical in their own way: Ferro, Phalco; Carbon, Colona, Cobra; Emerald, Diamond; Kiva, Kentucky Star. Onyx. Black Fire. Vision. Slybranch. Ram. If I consider the routes I've taken back home to the mountains over the last 30 years, if I envision the tipples, the vast piles of coal, the car after car on trains moving out, and I multiply that unknown vast quantity by these 80 names, multiply them again, by the hundreds of names of companies from coal country that I don't know, then multiply them again by the years of coal industry time past and the coal industry time ahead of us, the sheer volume is simply, for lack of a better word, overwhelming. In the United States, I read, 100 tons of coal are extracted every two seconds. According to activist and writer Erik Reese, around 70 percent of that coal comes from strip mines, and over the last 20 years, an increasing amount from mountaintop removal mining.

Even more overwhelming are readily available statistics from the U.S. government. A list, ugly and bulleted, slashes its way across this narrative about memory:

- *Coal production in the US in 2004 was 1,151.2 million short tons.*
- *Coal production in the Appalachian Region in 2004 was 389.9 million short tons.*
- *In 2005 Eastern Kentucky mines produced 93.4 million short tons of coal, while Western Kentucky mines produced 26.4 million short tons of coal.*
- *The increases in production in these five mines (Matrix Energy's No. 1; Massey Energy's White Cabin No. 7; Miller Brothers' Trap*

Branch; R & R Mining's Mine No. 30; and James River's Mine
No. 23) totaled 3.7 million short tons.

• *Of the 57 Synfuel Plants in the country, 36 are located in the central*
  Appalachian region, with the majority in Eastern Kentucky and
  Southwestern West Virginia. These 36 plants processed 75.2 million
  short tons of coal in 2005, making up 54percent of the Synfuel
  market.

• *724 miles of streams across the central Appalachian region were*
  buried by valley fills between 1985 and 2001 (many more miles have
  been permitted but not yet buried).

I have, of course, omitted facts about human impact from
this list. Facts about air quality. Facts about valley fill. About
haul roads. Illegally overloaded coal trucks. Flyrock. Enormous
dislodged boulders from removal sites. Blasts strong enough to crack
the walls and foundations of houses. Contaminated water. Toxic
coalfield streams below valley fills. Coal slurry. Selenium. Arsenic.
Mercury. Lead. Copper. Chromium. Nickel. Sediments in headwater
channels. Downstream channel erosion. Impact on aquatic life, fish
spawning and stream productivity. Sludge waste. Watershed damage.
Flooding. Deforestation. Consider this fact alone: without additional
restrictions, a total of 2,200 square miles of Appalachian forests (6.8
percent) would be eliminated by 2012 by large-scale mining operations.
This is an area that would encompass Floyd, Knott, Leslie, Letcher,
Perry and most of Harlan counties in Eastern Kentucky. Without
additional environmental restrictions, mountaintop removal mining
will destroy an additional 600 square miles of land and 1000 miles
of streams in the next decade, according to the Energy Information
Administration.

Most powerful of all is a description of the earth "from a
small, prop plane at Zeb Mountain, Tennessee, [following] the spine
of the Appalachian Mountains up through Kentucky, Virginia and
West Virginia" (Erik Reece, "Moving Mountains," *Grist*, 16 Feb
2006). From that plane, "an unfolding series of staggered green hills
quickly giving way to a wide expanse of gray plateaus pocked with
dark craters and huge black ponds filled with a toxic byproduct called
coal slurry. The desolation stretches like a long scar up the Kentucky-
Virginia line, before eating its way across southern West Virginia."

When I was little my father took me, on some Sunday
afternoons, to a garbage dump on the side of Abbott Mountain, where

he showed me how to shoot a .22. My feet were clad in patent leather shoes and little white anklets. No fastidious child, I knew how to line up hand and eye and shoot straight down into piles of old tires and into the sides of abandoned washing machines. *Go for that one, over there.* My spine tingled with the sound of the ping into metal. Then, the slant of the hill down the valley into a heap of debris was straight and true. My feet crunched on the road side in cinders and ash. And in my memory, too, that earth, littered as it was, is still resonant with its own power.

On this first morning after my drive to Eastern Kentucky, my mother is already up at six o'clock, and I get up too, once I hear the sounds of news and clattering spoons. She's in the living room, sitting on a brown vinyl ottoman inches from the television screen, but when she sees me, she scurries to her feet. She's wearing the same green pants she wore yesterday when I arrived, and she tugs at them in irritation. Her shirt is held together by only one button this morning and I feel sad again that, at bedtime, she refused, no matter what I said, to undress and put on a gown.

I fix her breakfast – a cup of frosted shredded wheat with a cut-up banana on top – and she eats while I drink some instant coffee. She tells me that the weather has been fair of late. Not much rain for this time of year, and a hot spell that lasted, but don't I think its cold in here? I have already observed the plastic box screwed to the wall atop the thermostat; the temperature stays right at 68 degrees that way, without her checking it a hundred times an hour, something my Uncle Roy told me about on the phone before I got here. *It's cold in here*, she says again, the first of the phrases she'll repeat to me a multitude of times. *It's cold in here. Do you take any medication? Where's my insurance card? Do I have Blue Cross Blue Shield? It's cold in here. Do you brush your tongue? Should I turn up that thermostat? It's cold in here.*

In between questions and answers, we sit in the living room and watch The Weather Channel. I am used to visiting my mother and watching Nick at Nite and its reruns of the old family sitcoms she has always loved – Mayberry, *I Love Lucy, Petticoat Junction* – shows in which the world is put right again. This morning we sit and watch the bands of red and orange and green that mean weather, the start of the cycling of seasons in other parts of the country. Used to be, if we watched some map of the country, she'd remember that, for awhile, I lived out west and she'd point with interest at states like New Mexico, Arizona, Utah, wondering if one of those places was where I used to send letters from. Since I'm visiting, she sits in a kitchen chair near the recliner where I'm sitting, rather than on the ottoman and brushes her teeth. She brushes her teeth, she tells me, her mouth full of paste, about a half hour each morning. She wonders whether I floss, brush my tongue. She gestures toward the screen, its panoramic view of states and patterns of rain and drought and unusually early autumn. I wonder if she remembers the shape of Kentucky, the name of the town, the road, where she's now living. *It's cold in here*, she says. *Don't you think?*

These days, the memories both my mother and I have these days of coal country are disconcertingly limited. The house she lives in is one that her parents bought, about 40 years ago, when the new U.S. 23 bought up the whole place where she grew up. Dwale, that community was called, was a few houses, a teeny post office, and a store where my mother and her sisters and I used to walk for cokes and nabs when I was little. I know that if I was able to reach inside her, her heart, her memories, Dwale would be not just a little place that was a neighborhood gone in the wake of a highway. It would be where she was raised. The garden beside the house. Stone pear tree in the bottom. Outhouse and smokehouse and well that drew water that stained our palms like rust. Road up the mountain to her own granny's house and a spring house with water so sweet. The scent of coal dust from the grate in the front room and the black map of lines on her daddy's hands in the evenings when he came home from working the mines. That was, once upon a time, part of her life.

I remember that same grate in the front room and a story about some other little girl who fell face forward into a coal fire. I remember Pa's metal lunch pail, his coveralls streaked with black at the end of a work day. I remember train tracks and Granny picking up what she called "slack" to burn. The distinct sound of a shovel crunching down into a mound of coal. Much later on, I remember coal trucks lumbering by on the highway, and then heaps of coal dumped in the road, a strike, workers with signs. *We need our pay!!!* *Scabs be-wear!!* I remember neighbors, Clifford and Junior and Jerry, men down in their backs or their shoulders or their knees or their lungs, the wait for disability checks, the lethargy of that waiting place, neither miner nor not, no job, sickness become the thing ahead of them, the time that passed and how. My Pa's long petition for black lung benefits. Did he have it or not? My Uncle Dave, my mother's sister's husband, and the stories of his air-conditioned fork-lift up at the strip mines at David. I remember my cousin Greg, the one who shot himself, the way he worked the mines for awhile, then worked on the trains, then fell to not working at all. I remember the place at Dwale being sold off when the highway came. The family came to rest in that little brick house where my mother lives today, alone, with whatever home place resides in the now fragmentary nature of all our memories.

That night, I head to bed as early as possible. The day has been full and I've done all I know to do to help put my mother's world into some order that she can understand. I have answered questions again and again, and I have watched The Weather Channel's cycle of forecasts. We've driven to Save-a-Lot, eaten at the Dairy Cheer, visited her doctor for a blood test. I've bought her new pants at Wal-Mart, helped her change, combed her hair, changed the sheets on a bed that I find full of dry skin shavings from the soles of her feet. By the end of this day, I wish that I were a kinder, more loving person. I wish that I knew how to stop it, this deterioration of memory and mind that my mother is experiencing. This now inevitable journey toward a loss of herself.

When I'm back in my own bed, I find that I can't sleep at all. My room is right next to her room with door ajar in between. I toss, turn, need to pee more than once, and that journey takes me through her room to the only bathroom. I tiptoe past her sleeping shape, the crossed arms over her chest, the light drape of the bedspread almost kicked down onto the cool linoleum. I stop, straighten her covers as well as I am able. The bathroom door is swollen with humidity and I lift it, set it in its track as softly as I can, so that I won't wake her. Later, back under the sheets again I lie there, staring at the ceiling. In the small space of these rooms what I can hear is my own my mother, breathing in fits and starts and, for just a little while, I'm afraid she's not breathing at all.

Breath. Later, to write this essay, I will read about breath. Facts. About the high rate of nausea, diarrhea, vomiting, shortness of breath traced to sedimentation and dissolved minerals drained from mine sites into waterways. I'll read about asthma problems, severe headaches, blisters in mouths, constant runny noses. I'll read about cancers. Liver. Kidney. Spleen failure. Bone damage. I'll read about something mysteriously called "blue baby syndrome." I'll begin, slowly and painfully, the process of educating myself about what is happening via coal and mountaintop removal to the very land and people I have called my homeplace – a place I have left and loved and come back to again, again.

But this night, I have no facts to count to send me to sleep. This night of a visit home to the mother I love with such a mixture of emotions – sadness, wistfulness for the connection we have not had and will no longer have – I lie there, relieved when I hear her again, the shift and turn in her bed. Breathing. After awhile, I summon a connection of images to ease my own descent into sleep. A building. A place called the warm house, where canned goods and potatoes and beets, were stored for the winter. Was it in Dwale? Or in some other memory-town I now need so badly I can taste it. I remember standing beside an opening in the stone floor, the spring water that fed up through that hole keeping the building cool. The shiny, black water, if you stood and stared down into the dark, was smooth and still, almost peaceful.

KAREN SALYER MCELMURRAY, *Georgia*

The Pay is Good

Split blunt the skull
of the mountain.
Lay it open, lay it out.
Gouge out the glistening

black vein which chains
inside the mountains as secret
as the threads
of the maidenhead fern.

Gauge it out sickly yellow
In the throttling dust.
Leave the mountain's guts
To hang shredded like

A bombed out house.
Leave it with a stubble
of broken trees.
Your Tonka toys can do it.
Leave it split. But never

Will your children hear the
First inquiry of the redbird
rippling through the forest
as a flame would, up and down
the beautiful barks of beech.

NOEL SMITH, New York

The Death of Appalachia

I have been on this earth for 27 years, and I can remember 26 of them. During the past quarter-century I've witnessed something that deeply saddens my heart. I was raised by my grandmother until I was 13, and then by my father who turned 68 this past June. I'm very grateful for this because I had the opportunity to see and learn things that many from my generation have not had the opportunity to experience. And it's because of this that I stand before you today as a witness to the death of Appalachia.

Through the short course of my life I've watched a process that started long before any of us were born continue at an almost exponential rate. I've seen the indoctrination of our youth into a culture that places no merit in the traditions of Appalachia. I've watched us, as a people, become separated from the land that sustained us for so many generations. The people of Eastern Kentucky and Appalachia as a whole are becoming urbanized. Not in the physical since, but in the way we view the world and our economy. The economy of Eastern Kentucky's past was one characterized by subsistence farming and community. Much of what we consumed we produced, from the food on the table to the quilt on the bed. The region and the people of Eastern Kentucky have been characterized as poor, and while I don't mean to over-romanticize, this couldn't be further from the truth.

The threat that I see in the urbanization of our youth manifests itself as a disconnection with our natural world. The wealth the people of Appalachia possess is the land. Large urban communities lack the access to land and attached resources that rural communities possess. Urban communities can't sustain themselves in the way that rural communities can, so they are forced to sell their labor and have their lives dictated by the market. The advent of mass media has created a mindset among our youth that places value in an economy that is owned by a handful of people and leaves the individual without a voice. If we have no voice, then we have no power. Our children are taught to fear nature and think of themselves as separated from their ecosystem, separated from the land, and separated from the culture of the region. It is nothing to watch it all be destroyed, because to them it will be worthless and without value.

    Though we can try to free ourselves from the natural world, in the process we bind ourselves to the chains of debt and to the will of those who guide the mechanisms of our economy and profit from our fundamental needs in life. The irony is that we can never free ourselves from nature because we are inexplicably interwoven with the eternal cycles of life and death, of uplift and erosion, of joy and pain. The advantage that our ancestors had, and that we are so quickly losing, are connection to the land and to the fundamentals of what it truly means to be human.

    When I flip through the pages of my Maw's old picture albums and look into the faces of my family long lost to time, I see a humble wisdom. I wonder if – when someday it is the faces of today's youth whose pictures remain as a testament to a hopefully long life – those who look into their eyes will see that same humble wisdom. Or will their lives have been consumed by the tenets of greed? I wonder if their faces will be an epitaph to a culture and a land that can only be studied in books and dreamed by those who strive to be free.

CODY SIMPKINS, Kentucky
College Junior

Afterword

In 1996, when Ellen Davis, a scholar of the Bible at Duke Divinity School, was taken to a mountaintop removal site in Kentucky, she remembered Jeremiah:

> *I have seen the mountains, and here, they are wavering,*
> *and all the hills palpitate.*
> *I have seen, and here, there is no human being,*
> *and all the birds of the heavens have fled.*
> *I have seen, and here, the garden-land is now the wasteland...*

If you take seriously the knowledge that humans are capable of neighborliness and caretaking, are capable of caring well for the earth for the earth's own sake and for the sake of their neighbors now and yet to come, and if you know that according to our greatest teachers this neighborliness is *expected* of us, then you will grieve in knowing that we humans are destroying the earth. You will be offended in knowing that we are doing so with governmental approval and with governmental encouragement. If you are at all a normal human, you will find that hard to swallow. You may find it, in fact, a putrid lump that will gag you somewhat before you can get it down.

And yet to the Kentucky state government, a wholly owned subsidiary of the coal corporations and of any other corporations that bid high enough, earth destruction is a normal economic enterprise. Earth destruction by strip mining has been an officially accepted practice in the Eastern Kentucky coalfields for nearly half a century. In the Knott County Court room on the night of July 15, 1965, confronting, as he had and would, the already catastrophic damage of strip mining that was going to get worse, Harry Caudill spoke of "the gleeful yahoos who are destroying the world, and the mindless oafs who abet them."

Forty-three years later, bad has come to worse, and worse has come to worst; the gleeful yahoos still reign supreme in the coalfields, and the mindless oafs who abet them still hold dominion in Frankfort.

This is not because money talks, as Sen. Mitch McConnell seems to think. It is because money votes, and money buys people who vote. It is because might, with enough money, does not have to worry about right. It is because, in the magnetic field of money, the flags and crosses on certain political lapels turn into price tags.

I must hurry to say that I am not talking about all Kentucky politicians. There has always been in this Capitol a "saving remnant" of women and men who are not for sale. It is because of those people that we, the powerless, have never yielded to despair, but have continued to come here with the hope that at last this government will see the truth and do its duty.

Over the last 40 years, with other powerless people, I have been here many times. We have come, moneyless into the magnetic field of money, trying to stop the mindless destruction of the land and people of our state. We have made our protests and our arguments, presented our facts, appeared before committees, spoken to those willing to speak to us. And virtually always we have failed. The destruction has continued. Nothing has changed.

Newly reminded of our political nonentity, we have gone home to await another chance to try again. Meanwhile the destruction has gone on. When I return from one of these tours of the Capitol, if the Kentucky River is raised and running, I can see the land of our mountain counties flowing past my house. And I know that that river, vital to the future of our state and its economy, is seriously impaired at its headwaters and degraded in all its length by pollutants, and that the most powerful among us simply do not care.

What are we to do? Well, to begin with, there is no "we" that I can confidently speak for. I have been speaking for myself so far, and I will continue to do so.

Human nature, which I fully share, tells me that in the face of great violence it is easy to think of retaliatory violence. I reject that entirely. I do not believe in violence as in any sense a solution to any problem. I am willing also to take the further step into Scripture and say that we should love our enemies – or at least act toward them as if we love them.

The next temptation is to do as our enemies do, to say, "If they do it, so must we." And I have in fact spent some time on the argument, which can be logically made, that Kentucky conservationists ought to start a fund drive and apply for grants in order to *buy* our fair share of the state government. I reject that also. Even a good cause cannot justify dirty politics.

But thinking of that argument, I convinced myself of a proposition that is more difficult: If current governmental practice affords no apparent recourse but to become as corrupt as your opponents, you have got to become more radical.

Kentucky conservationists are not the first people to have to confront their own helplessness before an alien government. Others have done so, and you know some of their names. Mahatma Gandhi and Martin Luther King are two of them; there have been many others. Their solution to the problem of powerlessness is to make of the powerlessness a power.

The name of this solution is non-violent resistance or insistence, including civil disobedience.

If your government will not rise to the level of common decency, if it will not deal fairly, if it will not protect the land and the people, if it will not fully and openly debate the issues, then you have to get in the government's way. You have to forbid it to ignore you. You have to provide it with two new choices: either it must grant you the consideration that it rightfully owes you, or it must expose itself openly as a government not representative of the people but owned by the privileged few.

And here yet another temptation asserts itself. Why not wait until our cause becomes vivid and urgent enough, and our side numerous enough, to vote our opponents out of office? Why not be patient?

My own answer is that while we are being patient, more mountains, forests and streams, more people's homes and lives, will be destroyed in the Appalachian coalfields. Are 400,000 acres of devastated land and 1,200 miles of obliterated streams not enough?

This needs to be stopped. It does not need to be "regulated." As both federal and state governments have amply shown, you cannot regulate an abomination. You have got to stop it.

Speaking for myself still, I will say that I don't like the idea of resorting to non-violent obstruction, and I don't feel very brave about it. It involves more time and trouble that I want to donate; the penalties can be unpleasant, and they can be much worse than that. Furthermore, as I am now out of patience with useless protesting and lobbying, I have no interest in useless civil disobedience. You are not going to catch me making a merely symbolic gesture. But I began my opposition to strip mining on that July night in the Knott County Court room in 1965. I have been patient for 43 years. And there are now enough of us who are concerned – there are enough of us here today – to require our government either to accept its responsibility or, publicly, and to its everlasting disgrace, refuse to do so. Surely the members of this government who represent coal corporations will be impressed by the tenfold increase in our numbers from February 14, 2007. Surely they will notice, more to their dismay, that many of this increase are young people.

If this General Assembly and this administration give notice as usual that they are blind by policy to the ongoing destruction of the land and the people they are sworn to protect – and if you, my friends, all other recourse having failed, are ready to stand in the way of this destruction until it is stopped – then I, too, am ready.

WENDELL BERRY, Kentucky

Speech delivered on the Capitol steps at I LOVE MOUNTAINS DAY in Frankfort, Kentucky, 14 February 2008

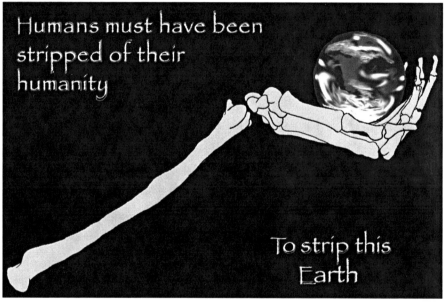

Having a deep appreciation for nature means helping stop its destruction in any way possible.

MACKENZIE KIRCHNER-SMITH, Kentucky
High School Junior

Contributor Biographies

REBECCA AINSWORTH is a senior at Hiram College where she has majored in Political Science and minored in Writing with a focus on nonfiction genres including Literary Journalism, Personal Essay and Memoir. Her work outside school focuses on community organizing around local organic farming, as well as fighting mountaintop removal. After graduating, she plans to work as a full-time volunteer with the Upper Guyandotte Watershed Authority in Mullens, West Virginia, assisting in written media generation and water quality monitoring. Ainsworth loves bonfires in the woods and making music.

SEAN ANGERMEIER is a fifth grade student in Ms. Collins's class at Crestwood Elementary. He resides in Pewee Valley, Kentucky.

WENDELL BERRY, an essayist, novelist and poet, is the author of more than 40 books. He lives in Henry County, Kentucky.

JEFF BIGGERS is the American Book Award-winning author of *The United States of Appalachia* and *In the Sierra Madre*. His next book, *Reckoning at Eagle Creek: The Secret Legacy of Coal in the Heartland*, is forthcoming in the fall of 2009. His website is: www.jeffbiggers.com.

BETH BISSMEYER, of Louisville, Kentucky, is a student Berea College, majoring in English with a minor in Appalachian Studies. She is active with Kentuckians for the Commonwealth and hopes to work for a non-profit after her 2009 graduation.

JESSICA BOGGS, a resident of Whitesburg, Kentucky, is currently a sophomore at Campbellsville University. Her work has previous been published in *The Puck Review*. Boggs's essay "Unnatural Disaster" was written for a coal education scholarship contest in Spring 2007. She is the recipient of the 2009 "MotesBooks Young Activist Award" for her submission published in this anthology.

JULIA "JUDY" BONDS is co-director for Coal River Mountain Watch. She is a coal miner's daughter and granddaughter. She is an Appalachian American, and her family has lived in the Coal River Valley in West Virginia for 10 generations. Bonds has been fighting for social and environmental justice for the Appalachian coalfields since 1998. In 2003 she won the coveted Goldman Environmental Prize. Bonds has worked on safety issues on overweight coal trucks and is on the Governor's Safety Committee for commercial trucks. She was named the "Earthmover Award" winner in *GEO Magazine*, is on *Organic Style Magazine*'s Environmental Power list, and has been featured in *National Geographic*, *Vanity Fair*, *O: The Oprah Magazine* and *People*.

PATRICIA BRAGG began fighting for better mining practices in 1994 when an Arch Coal deep mine dried up her neighbors' wells. A few years later, a mountaintop mine began taking down the mountain behind her home. She and other members of the West Virginia Organizing Project went to the state legislature and won stronger controls on blasting. Then she joined attorney Joe Lovett's first valley fill lawsuit, which was named after her, *Bragg v. Robertson*. During the height of the battle over mountaintop removal, she went to college and earned her bachelor's degree summa cum laude.

IVY BRASHEAR is a Journalism major and Appalachian Studies minor at Eastern Kentucky University, where she is in her senior year. A born-and-bred Appalachian from Viper, Kentucky, Brashear hopes to return to Eastern Kentucky and use her journalism training to fight mountaintop removal.

NEVA BRYAN's poems and short fiction appear in several literary magazines, including *Appalachian Heritage* and *Appalachian Journal*. She has received a dozen writing prizes, including a James Still Award for Poetry. *St. Peter's Monsters*, her debut novel, was published in 2009. Bryan, a resident of Southwest Virginia, was born in Kentucky. She graduated from the University of Virginia and earned her Master of Professional Writing from Chatham University in Pittsburgh.

FRANCES BUERKENS, a Berea College student, is a Spanish and Biology major. Passionate about photography, she completed a summer internship as a resident artist at the Los Amigos Biological Research Station in the Peruvian Amazon.

JOSH BULLARD is a fifth grade student at Crestwood Elementary in Kentucky.

COOPER BURTON, a student at St. Francis High School in Louisville, Kentucky, identifies as a city dweller who "never had a strong connection with nature, but [has] come to understand the condition our Earth is in." He advises breaking free from oppressive frustration when taking a stand against mountaintop removal.

BROOKE CALTON has been published in *Appalachian Heritage, Appalachian Journal, Southern Cultures* and *The Nantahala Review*. A native of western North Carolina, she is a graduate of the University of North Carolina at Chapel Hill and the MFA program at Queens University of Charlotte. Currently she lives in the Piedmont of North Carolina with her husband Matthew Mulhollem and their son Rowan. She goes home to the mountains every chance she gets.

JACK CARTER is 15 years old and attends Pikeville High School, where he is a sophomore. He is currently on the Varsity Academic Team and tests in Arts & Humanities, Language Arts, as well as participating in Quick Recall.

BEN CHANDLER was first elected in a special election in February 2004 (and subsequently re-elected) to represent Kentucky's 6th District in the United States House of Representatives. In January 2007, Chandler was selected by his Democratic colleagues to serve on the coveted House Committee on Appropriations. He lives in Woodford County, Kentucky, with his wife, Jennifer, and their three children.

BRENNAN CLARK is a junior at St. Francis High School, an independent, forward-thinking school in downtown Louisville, Kentucky. He is the co-founder of the school's environmental club and a representative to EcoLouisville, a coalition of high school environmental clubs across Louisville.

LINSEY CLARK attends the fifth grade at Crestwood Elementary. She lives in Oldham County, Kentucky.

SCOTTY WAYNE COX is a 16-year-old sophomore at North Laurel High School in London, Kentucky. He is the nephew, son, grandson and great-grandson of coal miners and grew up not only hearing their stories but also seeing the devastation being done to his homeland. He is an avid reader and a member of the ROTC at his school.

STEPHEN COUCH is a songwriter, multi-instrumentalist and lead singer of The Betweeners, an acoustic band playing a hybrid of American roots music. The band's debut album, *Matador Karma*, garnered them comparisons to The Band and Fairport Convention. Couch based his song "East Kentucky Water" on his childhood in Big Willard, Kentucky.

HAL CROWTHER is a syndicated columnist, essayist and critic whose work appears regularly in the *Oxford American*, *Atlanta Journal-Constitution*, *Independent Weekly* and *Progressive Populist*, among many other publications. In former years, he was a staff writer for *Time* and media editor for *Newsweek*. He was a finalist for the National Magazine Award for Commentary in 2003 and winner of the H.L. Mencken Writing Award from the *Baltimore Sun*. His books include *Unarmed But Dangerous*, *Cathedrals of Kudzu: A Personal Landscape of the South* and *Gather At The River: Notes From The Post-Millennial South*. He lives in Hillsborough, North Carolina, with his wife, the novelist Lee Smith.

CATHERINE DAWAHARE is a sophomore at Pikeville High School. Her loves are math and science. She lives in Pikeville, Kentucky, with her parents.

DAVIS DEJARNETTE is in the fifth grade at Crestwood Elementary in Kentucky.

PAMELA DUNCAN was born in Asheville and grew up in Black Mountain, Swannanoa and Shelby, North Carolina. Her first novel, *Moon Women*, was a Southeastern Booksellers Association (now Southern Independent Booksellers Alliance) Award Finalist, and her second novel, *Plant Life*, won the 2003 Sir Walter Raleigh Award for Fiction. She is the recipient of the 2007 James Still Award for Writing about the Appalachian South, awarded by the Fellowship of Southern Writers. Her third novel, *The Big Beautiful*, was published in March 2007. She lives in Cullowhee, North Carolina, and teaches creative writing at Western Carolina University.

JOYCE DYER is director of the Lindsay-Crane Center for Writing and Literature at Hiram College in Hiram, Ohio, and serves as John S. Kenyon Professor of English. Dyer is the author of three books, *The Awakening: A Novel of Beginnings* (1993),

In a Tangled Wood: An Alzheimer's Journey (1996) and *Gum-Dipped: A Daughter Remembers Rubber Town* (2003), and the editor of *Bloodroot: Reflections on Place by Appalachian Women Writers* (1998). She has published essays in magazines such as *North American Review, cream city review* and *High Plains Literary Review*. Dyer has won numerous awards for her writing, including the 1998 Appalachian Book of the Year Award and the 2009 David B. Saunders Award in Creative Nonfiction. Her new book, *Goosetown*, will be released in the fall of 2009.

BOB EDWARDS, a native of Louisville, Kentucky, is the host of *The Bob Edwards Show* on XM Satellite Radio and Bob Edwards Weekend distributed by PRI on public radio stations. His one-hour documentary about mining in Appalachia, "Exploding Heritage," can be heard at www.bobedwardsradio.com.

BEV FUTRELL was born and raised in Central Texas before moving to Madison County, Kentucky, in 1974. A few years later, she and four other women formed the Reel World String Band. Influenced by Guy and Candie Carawan of the Highlander Center, Jean Ritchie, Si Kahn and Hazel Dickens, they have recorded numerous albums and toured in the United States, Canada and Italy. Futrell has two children and three grandsons, and wants them to value the mountains and mountaineers as much as she does.

LUCY FLOOD grew up on a farm in Kentucky, and is fascinated by people's ties to the land. A graduate of the University of Texas Creative Writing program, she currently is working on a novel that deals in part with mountaintop removal mining.

SARAH FRANCIS, a sophomore at Pikeville High School in Kentucky, enjoys performing in musical productions and is a member of Pikeville's 4-H archery team.

DENISE GIARDINA is the author of *Storming Heaven* and *Saints and Villains*, which won the Boston Book Review Prize. She is an ordained deacon in the Episcopal Church and lives in Charleston, West Virginia.

BRIANNE GOLDBERG is a fifth grade student at Crestwood Elementary in Kentucky.

EARL HAMNER's novels, television and films are deeply rooted in the Appalachian soil. Born in Schuyler, Virginia, in 1923, he lives today in Studio City, California, where he continues to write. On a recent trip to Kentucky he witnessed the assault on our land and his reaction is recorded in this poem.

TOM HANSELL is a documentary filmmaker affiliated with Appalshop, a media arts center located in the heart of the Appalachian coalfields. Hansell's documentary work has been broadcast nationally on public television and screened at international film festivals. He has taught community documentary workshops throughout the United States, in China and in Indonesia. Hansell teaches Appalachian Studies and Documentary Studies at Appalachian State University in Boone, North Carolina. His documentary project, *The Electricity Fairy*, is scheduled for release in 2009.

VICTORIA HENRY is in the fifth grade at Crestwood Elementary in Kentucky.

JANE HICKS is an award-winning poet and quilter from East Tennessee. Her first book, *Blood and Bone Remember: Poems from Appalachia*, was published by the Jesse Stuart Foundation in 2005 and won the Appalachian Writers Association Poetry Book of the Year. Hicks's poetry has appeared in *Wind*, *Now & Then*, *Appalachian Journal*, *Appalachian Heritage* and *Shenandoah*. Her "literary quilts" illustrate the works of playwright Jo Carson and novelists Sharyn McCrumb and Silas House. A retired teacher, she is putting the finishing touches on her first novel, tentatively titled *Daughter of Necessity*.

RON HOUCHIN lives downstream from Pittsburgh on the banks of the Ohio River, across from his hometown of Huntington, West Virginia. His fourth book of poetry, *Birds In The Tops of Winter Trees*, was published by Wind Publications, 2008. A fifth book, *Museum Crows*, is due out in 2009 from Salmon Publishing of Ireland.

CHEYENNE HOUSE attends eighth grade at South Laurel Middle School. Her photographs have appeared in *Kentucky Living* and *Southeast Kentucky Family* magazine, as well as a variety of newspapers. In her spare time, she loves to read and make movies. She lives in Lily, Kentucky, with her family and dogs, Holly Marie and Rufus.

OLIVIA JEAN-LOUISE HOUSE is ten years old and lives in Lily, Kentucky. An avid writer and artist, she is in the Gifted and Talented program at her school and was recently selected for the Duke University Talent Identification Program. She plays piano and autoharp and has two dogs, Rufus and Holly Marie. She went on her first mountaintop removal tour when she was seven.

SILAS HOUSE is a bestselling author of four novels: *Clay's Quilt* (2001), *A Parchment of Leaves* (2003), *The Coal Tattoo* (2005) and *Eli the Good* (2009), as well as two works of nonfiction, *The Hurting Part: Evolution of an American Play* (2008) and *Something's Rising* (2009, with co-author Jason Howard). For his work in the movement against mountaintop removal, House received the 2008 Helen Lewis Community Service Award. He has received many awards, among them Appalachian Book of the Year, Kentucky Novel of the Year and the Award for Special Achievement from the Fellowship of Southern Writers. House lives in Eastern Kentucky and is writer-in-residence at Lincoln Memorial University.

LEE HOWARD (1952-2003) was a Kentucky native whose poems appeared in *Southern Exposure*, *The Washington Review* and other publications. Though not as well-known as the countless writers her work has influenced, Howard was crucial to giving birth to a style of writing in which character-driven narrative, first-person point of view and mountain speech are incorporated into modern Appalachian poetry as essential literary elements. Her only book was *The Last Unmined Vein*, published in 1980. In 2010 MotesBooks will publish *New & Collected: The Works of Lee Howard*, edited by George Ella Lyon. Lee Howard is buried in Clay County, Kentucky.

PATRICIA HUDSON is co-founder of LEAF, the Lindquist Environmental Appalachian Fellowship, a faith-based "creation care" group based in Knoxville, Tennessee. She is an eighth-generation East Tennessean who has spent the past 20 years traveling the Southeast and Mid-Atlantic as a travel writer. Her work has appeared in publications such as *Southern Living, Americana*, and *American Heritage*. She is also co-author of *The Carolinas and the Appalachian States* in the Smithsonian Guide to Historic America series, as well as co-editor of *Listen Here: Women Writing in Appalachia.*

SYDNEY JONES is a fifth grader at Crestwood Elementary in Kentucky.

ASHLEY JUDD is a Golden Globe-nominated actress who has appeared in such films as *De-Lovely, Come Early Morning* and *Double Jeopardy*. She devotes much of her time to social activism as the YouthAIDS Global Ambassador and as a fierce opponent of mountaintop removal mining. Judd lives on a farm in middle Tennessee with her husband and menagerie of animals.

JESSIE LYNNE KELTNER works as a nursing home social worker. She sings and plays autoharp, fiddle and other instruments. Keltner performs with Public Outcry, Gabbard Sisters and the Cosmic Mamaws. She also plays violin in the community orchestra in London, Kentucky.

JUSTIN KENNADY attends the fifth grade at Crestwood Elementary. He loves mountains and is an activist for the Stream Saver Bill. He lives in Oldham County, Kentucky.

ROBERT F. KENNEDY, JR's reputation as a resolute defender of the environment stems from a litany of successful legal actions. He was named one of *Time* magazine's "Heroes for the Planet" for his success helping Riverkeeper lead the fight to restore the Hudson River. The group's achievement helped spawn more than 130 Waterkeeper organizations across the globe. Kennedy serves as Chief Prosecuting Attorney for the Hudson Riverkeeper and President of Waterkeeper Alliance. He is also a Clinical Professor and Supervising Attorney at Pace University School of Law's Environmental Litigation Clinic and is co-host of *Ring of Fire* on Air America Radio. Among Kennedy's published books are the *New York Times'* bestseller *Crimes Against Nature* (2004), *St. Francis of Assisi: A Life of Joy* (2005), *The Riverkeepers* (1997) and *Judge Frank M. Johnson, Jr: A Biography* (1977). His articles have appeared in *The New York Times, The Washington Post, Los Angeles Times, The Wall Street Journal, Newsweek, Rolling Stone, Atlantic Monthly, Esquire, The Nation, Outside Magazine, The Village Voice*, and many other publications.

WALTER KING attends the fourth grade at Third Ward Elementary School in Elkins, West Virginia. He enjoys hiking, camping, fiddling, growing pumpkins, building things and playing soccer.

MACKENZIE KIRCHNER-SMITH is a junior at St. Francis High School in Louisville, Kentucky. She first learned about mountaintop removal through her teacher, Mr. Keith Ashley, in a community service group.

KAITLYN KLABER, a fifth grader at Crestwood School, lives in Crestwood, Kentucky.

KATE LARKEN is an entrepreneur – songwriter, playwright, author, producer, publisher, and former teacher and journalist. Her musical, literary and river influences range far and wide (with the confluence of the Ohio and the Mississippi at her personal epicenter). A native of rural farmlands on what she has coined "the west coast of Kentucky" and later a transplant into the great nation of Appalachia, Kate currently lives on the Ohio River in a big old city with a rich working-class history. She's an energized urban-dweller (and avid voter) who is not at all shy about her country accent and rural roots. In addition to having three books and hundreds of articles and photographs published, she's been playing music and writing songs for going-on 50 years.

ANNA LEIDECKER is nine years old and lives in Berea, Kentucky. She is home-schooled and goes to a writing class, which has sparked her interest in writing. Her hobbies include swimming, archery, art and animals, especially birds and snakes.

PENNY LOEB lives in Loudoun County, Virginia, with her husband and assorted pets, including Jesse and Zeke, rescued from the coalfields. She is a former senior editor at *U.S. News and World Report* and a former investigative reporter for *Newsday*. Her book *Moving Mountains: How One Woman and Her Community Won Justice from Big Coal* was published in 2007. Loeb has received numerous awards for journalism and was a finalist for the Pulitzer Prize in 1988.

DENTON LOVING lives on a farm near the historic Cumberland Gap. A graduate of Lincoln Memorial University, he now works there as a fundraiser and co-directs the Mountain Heritage Literary Festival. He is the winner of the 2007 Gurney Norman Prize for Short Fiction and the 2008 Alabama Writers Conclave Fiction Prize. Loving has been published in *Kudzu, Birmingham Arts Journal, Appalachian Journal, Somnambulist Quarterly* and in the anthologies *Outscape: Writings on Fences and Frontiers, Freckles to Wrinkles, Mountain Mysteries II: The Unexplained* and *Motif: Writing By Ear.*

SYLVIA LYNCH has published three books of non-fiction and her short fiction has appeared in *Kudzu* and *Louisville Review*. She has also been the recipient of the Josefina Nigglie Award for Playwriting from the Appalachian Writers Association, second place in the Scratch Contest for short fiction, Tennessee Mountain Writers Award for Creative Non-Fiction, and the 2008 Gurney Norman Prize for Short Fiction. Her short story, "Milkshake Run," appears in the 2009 MotesBooks anthology, *Motif: Writing by Ear*. Lynch is a high school principal and a lifelong resident of East Tennessee.

GEORGE ELLA LYON is the author of 36 books for children and adults. Recent titles include *My Friend, The Starfinder* (2008) and *Don't You Remember? A Memoir* (2007). Among her earlier books are Appalachian favorites *Come A Tide* and *Mama Is a Miner*. Her best known work is the poetry collection *Where I'm From*. Originally from Harlan County, Lyon now lives in Lexington, Kentucky.

MAURICE MANNING's poems have appeared in the *Southern Review*, the *Virginia Quarterly Review* and the *New Yorker*, and his first collection of poems was awarded the Yale Younger Poets Award. He teaches English at Indiana University. Manning lives in Bloomington, Indiana, and Danville, Kentucky.

GRAHAM MAREMA attends Norris Middle School in Norris, Tennessee. She enjoys writing, acting, singing and taking care of the environment.

BOBBIE ANN MASON, who grew up in West Kentucky, is a novelist and short-story writer. Her story "Shiloh" has been widely anthologized, and her memoir, *Clear Springs*, was a finalist for the Pulitzer Prize. Her novels include *Feather Crowns*, *An Atomic Romance* and *In Country*, which was produced as a feature film. Her most recent book of stories is *Nancy Culpepper*. She is writer-in-residence at the University of Kentucky.

SUE MASSEK is a musician committed to using the music she writes and the songs she sings as tools for social justice. As a member of the Reel World String Band from its beginning in 1977, she has been heavily influenced by her experiences at the Highlander Center. With the band, Massek has toured throughout the United States, Canada and Italy. Though she was born a "flatlander" in Kansas, Massek embraces Kentucky and Appalachia as home. She lives with her partner in Willisburg, Kentucky, on a small farm.

ALEX MASTERSON is a junior at St. Francis High School in Louisville, Kentucky, where he focuses on creative writing. When he moved to Louisville from Pittsburgh, he was affected by the vast difference in air quality and was inspired to explore why Kentucky has such a higher rate of air pollution.

BEVERLY MAY was born and raised on Wilson Creek in Floyd County, Kentucky. In 1962, her family's land was auger-mined against their will as the result of a broadform deed. Two decades later, May worked as an organizer for Kentuckians for the Commonwealth and was a leader in the fight against the broadform deed amendment. Now a family nurse practitioner at a clinic for the uninsured and homeless, she recently built a house on Wilson Creek and each year invariably plants a bigger garden than she can manage. The Miller Brothers Coal Company had big plans for a mountaintop removal site on the mountain above her garden, but things haven't turned out too well for them due to May's leadership. This year, she hopes to add asparagus, grapevines and a few hens.

CODY MCCLANAHAN was raised in the Kentucky foothills of the Appalachian Mountains. She spent her summers camping with her father atop Wildcat Point where they danced around bonfires, beat drums, told ghost stories and brushed their teeth with a single glass of water. She currently resides in Greenville, South Carolina, and has been previously published in the fall 2008 issue of *New Southerner*.

DONNA McCLANAHAN grew up on the banks of the Kentucky River ("where the bluegrass kisses the mountains"). She currently resides at the edge of the Daniel Boone National Forest where she writes both fiction and nonfiction. Her nonfiction has won such awards as the Emma Bell Miles Award, The Wilma Dykeman Award and the Betty Gabehart Prize for Creative Nonfiction. She received the 2008 Sue Ellen Hudson Award for Excellence in Writing for fiction. Her work has appeared in *Kudzu, Now and Then, The Minnetonka Review* and has been anthologized in *Outscapes: Writings on Fences and Frontiers, Blink: Flash Fiction Before You Can Bat an Eye* and *Standing on the Mountain: Voices of Appalachia*.

KAREN SALYER McELMURRAY, who has been a landscaper, a casino employee and a sporting-towel factory worker, is in her current life a writer and a teacher of writing. She is the author of *Surrendered Child: A Birth Mother's Journey*, described by the *Atlanta Journal-Constitution* as "a moving meditation on loss and memory and the rendering of truth and story." The book was the recipient of the AWP Award for Creative Nonfiction and a National Book Critics Circle Notable Book. McElmurray's debut novel, *Strange Birds in the Tree of Heaven*, was winner of the Thomas and Lillie D. Chaffin Award for Appalachian Writing. Her newest novel is *The Motel of the Stars*. She is at work on essays, a new novel about an Eastern Kentucky gas station and diner called The Black Cat, and a memoir about adoption reunion.

JANNA McMAHAN is the author of the bestselling novels *Calling Home* and *The Ocean Inside*. Her short fiction has won numerous awards including the Imaginative Writing Award from the Kentucky Women Writer's Conference, the Harriette Arnow Award from the Appalachian Writers Association, the South Carolina Fiction Project and the Piccolo Spoleto Fiction Open. McMahan's fiction has appeared in journals, magazines and newspapers such as *Wind, Limestone, Yamassee, The Nantahala Review, StorySouth*, and *Alimentum: The Literature of Food*. She has also published many personal essays and articles on visual and literary arts. A native Kentuckian who resides in South Carolina, she writes frequently of Appalachia and its people.

ABBY MILLER is a graduate of St. Francis High School in Louisville, Kentucky, where she was first introduced to mountaintop removal as a sophomore. Her hobbies include activism, watching old movies, listening to experimental music and drinking tea. She was accepted at Sarah Lawrence College, but unfortunately the school didn't meet her expectations and she is back in Louisville. While plans for her future remain unclear, Miller intends to make solving issues of social justice part of her life.

DANIEL MARTIN MOORE is a musician from Cold Spring, Kentucky, whose debut album, *Stray Age*, was released in 2008 and hailed for its understated complexity. Labeled "an artist to watch" by NPR, Moore is currently in the studio recording an album to raise awareness about mountaintop removal mining with fellow Kentuckians Ben Sollee and Jim James.

WILL NELMS is in Ms. Collins's fifth grade class at Crestwood Elementary. He lives in Pewee Valley, Kentucky.

ANN PANCAKE is a native of West Virginia. Her first novel, *Strange As This Weather Has Been*, features a southern West Virginia family devastated by mountaintop removal mining. Based on interviews and real events, the novel was one of *Kirkus Review's* Top Ten Fiction Books of 2007, won the 2007 Weatherford Prize, and was a finalist for the 2008 Orion Book Award. Her collection of short stories, *Given Ground*, won the 2000 Bakeless Award, and she has also received a Whiting Award, an NEA grant, and a Pushcart Prize. She earned her BA in English at West Virginia University and a Ph.D. in English Literature from the University of Washington. Currently, she teaches in the low-residency MFA program at Pacific Lutheran University.

LISA PARKER is a poet, musician and photographer who was born and raised in Fauquier County, Virginia. She received her MFA in Creative Writing from Pennsylvania State University in 1998. Her work has appeared in numerous literary magazines, journals and anthologies such as *Southern Review, Pamassus: Poetry In Review, The Louisville Review* and *Flint Hills Review*, among others. Splitting her time between Virginia and Manhattan, she works in the Defense and Intelligence Sector. Parker admits to "having a thing for dictators."

JANISSE RAY is the author of three books of literary nonfiction: *Ecology of a Cracker Childhood* (1999), *Wild Card Quilt: Taking a Chance on Home* (2003) and *Pinhook: Finding Wholeness in a Fragmented Land* (2005). She has won a Southeastern Booksellers Award, an American Book Award and a Southern Book Critics Circle Award, among others. Ray is on the faculty of Chatham University's low-residency MFA program, and is a Woodrow Wilson Visiting Fellow. She attempts to live a simple, sustainable life on a family farm in southern Georgia with her husband, Raven Waters.

ERIK REECE teaches writing at the University of Kentucky in Lexington. His work appears in *Harper's, Orion* and *The Oxford American*, among other publications. He was the recipient of the Sierra Club's David R. Brower Award, and his *Harper's* story on which *Lost Mountain* is based won the Columbia University School of Journalism's 2005 John B. Oakes Award for Distinguished Environmental Journalism.

MARK REYNOLDS is a fifth grader at Crestwood Elementary in Kentucky and writes against mountaintop removal because the mountains matter to him.

JEAN RITCHIE is a folksinger, songwriter, dulcimer player and author. Known as the "Mother of Folk," she has recorded numerous albums including *None But One*, which was awarded the Rolling Stone Critics Award. Her songs have been covered by artists such as Johnny Cash, June Carter Cash, Judy Collins, Emmylou Harris, Kathy Mattea, Dolly Parton and Linda Ronstadt. Her memoir, *Singing Family of the Cumberlands*, is a beloved piece of Appalachian literature. Born and raised in Viper, Kentucky, Ritchie currently lives in Port Washington, New York, with her husband, noted filmmaker and producer George Pickow.

BRADLEY ROBERTSON is in fifth grade at Crestwood Elementary. He lives in Pewee Valley, Kentucky.

ELLEN ROBERTSON is 16 years old and lives in Blacksburg, Virginia, where she is home-schooled in the 10th grade. She enjoys dancing, reading, math, science and history, and she is a member of the Historic Smithfield Junior Guild.

SARAH KATHERINE "KATIE" SAYLOR is a 14-year-old home school student from Hazel, Kentucky. She lives in the woods and enjoys writing stories, hiking, searching for rocks and taking classical violin lessons.

ANNE SHELBY's books include essays (*Can a Democrat get into Heaven?*), poems (*Appalachian Studies*) and folktales (*The Man Who Lived in a Hollow Tree* and *The Adventures of Molly Whuppie*). A member of Public Outcry, she has written a number of songs about mountaintop removal. She lives near Oneida, Kentucky.

CODY SIMPKINS is a student at Morehead State University majoring in Horticulture with a minor in Appalachian Studies. He is a farmer who utilizes organic production methods and advocates a return to more traditional lifestyles for the people of Appalachia. Simpkins lives in Eastern Kentucky where he was born and raised.

J. MATTHEW SLEETH, M.D., a former emergency room physician, felt like he was straightening deck chairs on the Titanic saving one patient at a time while the whole ship (Earth) was going down. Together with his wife and two teenaged children, he began to bring his lifestyle in line with his values, cutting back on their fossil fuel by two-thirds and electricity use by nine-tenths. Following a new calling, Dr. Sleeth resigned from his position as chief of the medical staff and director of the ER to teach, preach and write about faith and the environment throughout the country. He is currently the executive director of Blessed Earth and noted national speaker and author of *Serve God, Save the Planet* (Zondervan) and *The Gospel According to Earth: Why the Good Book is a Green Book* (fall 2009, HarperOne).

KATHLEEN SMITH is a sophomore at Pikeville High School in Kentucky. She likes to read, write, sing and play sports with her friends.

NOEL SMITH was born and raised in New York City and worked in Eastern Kentucky as a medical social worker on horseback. She also taught second and third grades in Rockland County, New York. Smith's poems have appeared in many journals including *New Letters*, *Shenandoah* and *West Branch*. Her first collection of poetry, *The Well String*, was published by MotesBooks in 2008. An avid conservationist and lover of the outdoors, she is currently working on a new book of poetry.

Ben Sollee's debut album, *Learning To Bend*, was inspired by the stout cat-poles around the lake at his grandfather's farm in Kentucky. His distinctive cello technique, soulful voice and masterful songwriting blend genres from folk to jazz to country. Also a member of the Sparrow Quartet (with Abigail Washburn, Bela Fleck and Casey Driessen), Sollee is currently recording an album to raise awareness about mountaintop removal with fellow Kentuckians Daniel Martin Moore and Jim James.

Erin Stapleton is a ninth generation East Tennessean and a freshman at West High School in Knoxville. She has worked many hours fighting mountaintop removal as a volunteer for the Lindquist Environmental Appalachian Fellowship (LEAF).

Katie Ulrich is in the fifth grade at Crestwood Elementary in Kentucky and cares about Appalachia very deeply.

Neela Vaswani is the author of *You Have Given Me A Country* (forthcoming 2010) and *Where The Long Grass Bends* (2004), a collection of short stories. She is the recipient of a 2006 O. Henry Prize, a 1999 Italo Calvino Prize and is currently Visiting-Writer-in-Residence at Knox College, a position she has previously held at the Whitney Museum in NYC, the Jimenez-Porter House, University of California-Santa Barbara, and other institutions. Her work has been widely anthologized, most recently in Norton's inaugural anthology of multiracial literature. She has a Ph.D. in American Studies from the University of Maryland, teaches fiction in Spalding University's brief-residency MFA in Writing program, and is instructor of Adult Literacy and ESL at the Center for Reading and Writing in New York City. She is founder of the Storylines Project, bringing together Young Adult authors and Adult Literacy/ESL students at the New York Public Library. She works with various activist and educational organizations in India, Kentucky and New York.

Jocelyn White is originally from Smilax, Kentucky. She is currently a senior at Union College in Barbourville, Kentucky, majoring in English Communications and Secondary Education. White plans to become a high school teacher and hopes to instill a love for writing in her students and inspire them to do great things.

Terry Tempest Williams has been called "a citizen writer," a writer who speaks out eloquently on behalf of an ethical stance toward life. She has served time in jail for acts of civil disobedience, testified before Congress on women's health issues, been a guest at the White House and worked as "a barefoot artist" in Rwanda. Williams is the author of *Refuge: An Unnatural History of Family and Place; An Unspoken Hunger: Stories from the Field; Desert Quartet; Leap; Red: Passion and Patience in the Desert* and *The Open Space of Democracy*. Her new book, *Finding Beauty in a Broken World*, was published in 2008 by Pantheon Books. Recipient of the Robert Marshall Award from The Wilderness Society, the Distinguished Achievement Award from the Western American Literature Association and the Wallace Stegner Award given by The Center for the American West, among others, Williams is currently the Annie Clark Tanner Scholar in Environmental Humanities at University of Utah. She divides her time between Castle Valley, Utah, and Moose, Wyoming.

TIFFANY WILLIAMS holds a B.A. in English from Pikeville College and a M.A.T. from East Tennessee State University. She is the recipient of the 2008 Jesse Stuart Prize for Young Adult Fiction and currently teaches English at Pikeville High School in Pikeville, Kentucky. Williams is a native of McRoberts, Kentucky.

MEREDITH SUE WILLIS was raised in Shinnston, West Virginia, where she grew up in the shadow of multiple strip mines. Her father, from Wise County, Virginia, came to West Virginia when his family followed jobs with Consolidation Coal. Her mother's father witnessed the Monongah, West Virginia, mine disaster of 1907. Meredith Sue now lives near New York City, and her 14 books include short stories and novels published by many presses including West Virginia University Press, Scribner's and HarperCollins. She also publishes books on writing, and her book about strategies for starting a novel is due to be published in early 2010.

MARIANNE WORTHINGTON, a native of Knoxville, Tennessee, is a poet and educator living in Williamsburg, Kentucky. Her poetry chapbook, *Larger Bodies Than Mine* (2007), was chosen as the 2007 Appalachian Book of the Year in poetry. She is editor of *Motif: Writing By Ear, An Anthology of Writings About Music* (2009). Worthington is book reviews editor for *Now & Then: The Appalachian Magazine*, associate professor of Communication Arts at University of the Cumberlands and a creative writing instructor for the Kentucky Governor's School for the Arts. Her poems, essays, reviews and feature articles have appeared in over 60 publications and in several anthologies. She received the Berea College Appalachian Music Fellowship for 2009, the Al Smith Fellowship from the Kentucky Arts Council in 2008, an Individual Artist Grant from the Kentucky Foundation for Women in 2007, and the Denny C. Plattner Award for Creative Nonfiction in 2007. She teaches writing workshops in various venues throughout Kentucky and the Southeast.

JACK WRIGHT is an artist whose work is strongly informed by the culture of the Appalachian Mountains. A founding member of Appalshop, a multi-disciplinary arts and education center in Kentucky, he is an actor, documentary filmmaker and musician whose work has appeared on NPR, PBS, June Appal Recordings and in Hollywood films. His articles about Appalachian art and artists have appeared in *Ace Magazine, Independent Spirit, Iron Mountain Review, Appalachian Journal, Old-Time Herald* and other publications. He most recently produced *Music of Coal: Mining Songs From The Appalachian Coalfields*.

Acknowledgments

My heart is full of gratitude for the contributions and support of so many loved ones to this project: my chosen sister, Marcy, and niece, Garrison, who are always right there; Silas House, for his ideas and constant encouragement; Kate Larken for her patience and willingness to return to the drawing board; Neela Vaswani, for her good heart and love of the mountains; Marianne Worthington, for her line breaks and poetic expertise; Jan Goff, for making the trains run on time; Donna Conley Birney, for her sweet spirit and garage; my Public Outcry comrades (Anne, Lynne, George Ella, Silas and Kate), for good songs and stories; my Hindman, Gap House Writers and KFTC families; my aunt and uncle, Bud and Ann Hayden, for their unwavering support; and lastly, my parents, for reading to me as a child and not pitching a fit when I decided to forego law school.

Likewise, I sometimes wonder if I would have become a writer had it not been for the encouragement and support of the following: Josiah Akinyele, Terri Alford, Rich & Emily Bradley, Will Burger, Kimber Colton, Diana Shalom Cubbison, Jennifer Elliott, Amanda Fretz, Garrett Garrison, Leighann Garrison, Patrick Kennedy, Eric Kleiman, Elizabeth Lamont, Mary Jean Gambrel Lang, Rob Lofberg, Alejandro Mongalo, Debbie Moore, Steve Roberts, Sandy Slater, Sandra Stapleton, Caleb & Ashley Stewart, Alanna Swiatkowski and all of the people who paid a quarter for *The Dorton Branch News*.

Mountaintop removal is a treacherous political subject, especially if you represent a coal state. Congressmen Ben Chandler and John Yarmuth are true profiles in courage. I honor them for their steady leadership at the federal level. They'd better watch out, though — I'm convinced that one of the fifth-graders in Angela Collins's class may want their jobs one day. Ms. Collins has educated her students about mountaintop removal in the classroom and beyond, taking them to rallies and to lobby their state legislators at the risk of flak from parents and the administration. I salute her bravery.

Finally, I'm indebted to the generosity of the contributors. Your passion and eloquence inspire me in this fight. I hope you all are as proud of this book as I am.

Not one more mile.

– JKH

About The
EDITOR

JASON HOWARD is a writer, editor and musician from Eastern Kentucky. He is the coauthor of *Something's Rising: Appalachians Fighting Mountaintop Removal* (with Silas House). He is a former senior editor and staff writer for *Equal Justice Magazine*, based in Washington, D.C. His works have appeared in such publications as *Paste, Kentucky Living* and *The Louisville Review*. An accomplished musician, he plays piano, bass and autoharp. Howard graduated from The George Washington University with a degree in Political Communication, an interdisciplinary major of Political Science, Journalism, Communications and Electronic Media.

Printed in the United States
147670LV00003B/4/P